Becoming Your Real Self

*A practical toolkit for managing
life's challenges*

DR EDDIE MURPHY

PENGUIN LIFE

AN IMPRINT OF

PENGUIN BOOKS

PENGUIN LIFE

UK | USA | Canada | Ireland | Australia
India | New Zealand | South Africa

Penguin Life is part of the Penguin Random House group of companies
whose addresses can be found at global.penguinrandomhouse.com.

First published by Penguin Ireland 2015
Published by Penguin Life 2016

003

Copyright © Dr Eddie Murphy, 2015

The moral right of the author has been asserted

Set in 11.88/14.20 pt Garamond MT Std
Typeset by Jouve (UK), Milton Keynes
Printed in Great Britain by Clays Ltd, St Ives plc

A CIP catalogue record for this book is available from the British Library

ISBN: 978-0-241-25773-9

www.greenpenguin.co.uk

MIX
Paper from
responsible sources
FSC
www.fsc.org   FSC® C018179

Penguin Random House is committed to a
sustainable future for our business, our readers
and our planet. This book is made from Forest
Stewardship Council® certified paper.

*To the brave individuals who have come to my
therapy room and workshops*

*This book would not exist without the lessons you have
taught me and the inspiration you have given me*

Contents

PART THREE

Taking on life's challenges

Challenge One. Stress

Challenge Two. Depression

Challenge Three. Anxiety and panic attacks

Challenge Four. Anger

Challenge Five. Self-esteem

Challenge Six. Shyness and social anxiety

Challenge Seven. Emotional eating

PART FOUR

Putting it all together – becoming your real self

Appendix

Introduction

Let me start with an invitation. You are invited on a journey of change, one that will enable you to become your real self – authentic, positive, confident, compassionate and wise. You'll be able to fill your life with positive emotions and positive relationships with yourself, family, friends, and your community. You'll have mental fitness and a sense of health and well-being, not just the absence of ill-health. You'll be in a place where there is meaning and a sense of accomplishment.

Business people ask the question, 'What is the BHAG?' That's the *big hairy audacious goal*. The BHAG of this book – and one I invite you to share – is for you to become your real self. That's the person you always wanted to be: positive and confident, unconcerned about the opinions of others, comfortable in your own skin, at peace.

In life, people sometimes work very hard to present a front that they think is acceptable or that will help them get through. If you put your energy into a front and neglect your real self, a gap will be created between the self that you present to the world and the person you really are inside. That space will become filled with negativity: fear, anger and sadness; or, worse, panic attacks, anxiety, depression and low self-esteem. Inside, the real self is neglected, malnourished and weakened.

Too often people try to numb their emotions and fill the gap with alcohol, overeating, no exercising and hours in front of the TV. Their bodies send signals – aches and pains, stresses and strains. This stress can play havoc with the immune system. Many people go to their GP, seeking some explanation of their distress. The healthcare system duly obliges with diagnoses: stress; depression; anxiety and panic attacks; fibromyalgia; chronic fatigue syndrome/myalgic encephalomyelitis (ME) and post-viral fatigue syndrome; irritable bowel syndrome (IBS).

To be clear, I know these conditions are real and cause people distress, pain and despair. I never think they are made up or 'all in the mind'. Pain is real, be it physical or psychological or both. But with many conditions there are underlying psychological factors. The gap between our front and our real selves can cause stress, which makes these conditions worse. Would you believe that recent research shows that almost 50% of all GP visits have a psychological origin?

GPs struggle with this. They do not have the training, nor are they set up, to engage in in-depth psychological work. Very often the only tools in their armoury are anti-depressant or anti-anxiety medications. Worryingly, there is an increasing use of these medications. While medications have their role, I am not convinced they are the best starting point for taking back control in your life.

Many people who come to see me are lost. They have lost themselves and their path in life. During these lost phases, things like stress, depression, panic attacks, anger and crushing self-esteem become dominant. Since this is the nature of my work, people sometimes wonder whether my head gets wrecked listening to people's problems. It's a common question for people in my business. I always point out that I'm not listening to problems; I'm listening for the solutions – the stepping stones out of the problem.

Of course, I listen – that's the cornerstone of the work – but as I do I am always trying to answer this question: 'What is keeping this problem going?' This question is critical. If you are reading this book to get insight into a problem that you can't shake off, or if you are trying to understand the experiences of someone you care about, or if you're simply looking for greater understanding of how your emotions work, being able to answer this question is the point at which change starts to happen. *What is keeping my problem/challenge/difficulty going right now? What is sustaining it?*

Like many clinical psychologists or counsellors, I regularly work with people's past. However, I believe therapy that focuses solely on the past will never help a person live a life in the present. And you want to live in the present, in the *now* – it is the *now* that you can control.

Understanding the pattern of your thinking and behaviour is central to the process. Particular problem areas have unique thinking and behavioural patterns. These thinking and behavioural patterns keep your problem going, perpetuate fear, sadness, worthlessness and anger.

The good news is that if you are part of the problem, you are also part of the solution. Indeed you are the most important part. I am going to show you the tools to firmly kick these patterns out of your life for good; they will allow you to make changes now, so that you can claim your future.

And once the problem areas have been dealt with, it is possible to grow. It is in this growth phase of nurturing and developing that you will become your real self. Why settle for anything less? It's time now for you to be at the centre of your life. That is where you make choices: about what you think and do, about how you feel, about managing those who limit you and encouraging those who help you to grow. It's time now for you to start living, truly living.

Think complex, talk simple

One of the great things about being a clinical psychologist is that learning works in both directions. One day a client was telling me about how a decisive friend kept herself moving. She had a calendar on the wall and on every day it said THE TIME IS NOW. If there was a discussion about beginning a project, her friend would point to the calendar and say, 'The time is *now!*' For a number of years I'd been thinking about writing a book and yet I'd done nothing about it. Right after meeting this client I got in touch with Penguin.

My background is in nursing. In May 1985 I went to Romford in Essex, where I trained as a general nurse. Apart from almost one year in the US, I spent the next twelve years in England. It was a profound and positive experience, as it's really where I grew up. As a nurse I had many years' experience working in cardiology. Caring in a compassionate way, supporting sick people when they were at their most vulnerable, was a humbling experience. From nursing I stepped into psychology, specializing in health psychology – which explores the psychological impact of physical health conditions such as cancer, diabetes, chronic pain, and heart disease. I then trained as a clinical psychologist.

Psychological science has a lot of great things to offer, but too often its message lacks clarity and is too complex. I always remember the words of my professor in UCD, Alan Carr: 'Psychology is for everyone. We work with children, adults and seniors who are struggling. We need to think complex, talk simple.'

These four words have really stayed with me: *Think complex, talk simple.* For thirty years in healthcare I have always tried to work with people respectfully and empathetically, understanding where they are in their lives and talking plainly about how they could make things better for themselves. That's where I'm coming from in writing this book. My goal is not to overwhelm you with research and complicated jargon, but to distil some key thinking into practical tools that you can use.

I want to take you on a journey. I would like to transport you to my office, where you can slow down, take off the mask and look inside. The work in the therapy room is about shifting people away from an array of negative emotions – fear, sadness, low confidence, stress, anger, low self-esteem – to a place where they are free, authentic, contented, powerful, confident, humble, wise and compassionate. To where they are their real self.

I hope to bring my work in the therapy room to life in this book. Through powerful stories of transformation, you will be able to see how change happens and you will be able to follow the pathways from:

- stress to relaxation;
- depression to hope;
- anxiety to freedom;
- anger to calm;
- low self-esteem to self-worth;
- social anxiety to confidence;
- emotional eating to self-control.

In the therapy room you are not concerned about the opinions or judgements of others. Instead you are forging a life in which you are nourishing yourself, so you are healthier and happier, a life in which you can thrive.

How to use this book

There are no absolute experts here: I bring knowledge of psychology and you bring knowledge of yourself and your world. Combining these two, we can take a shared journey that will lead you to becoming your real self. I'm not going to tell you what to think or how to do something. Instead I'm inviting you to take the opportunity to become your real self. To do that, I'll ask you to consider changing what you *think* and what you *do*. I will ask you to take some risks, and to help you with these risks I will give you the tools you'll need in order to succeed.

You can dip into this book or read right through it. It is full of practical suggestions you can take up immediately. It starts off with some fundamental building blocks about the nature of relationships and the core beliefs that influence us significantly (Part One). This is followed by skills building, where the powerful tools that you will implement throughout the book are explained (Part Two). These techniques are drawn from evidence-based psychology, and are practical and effective; I have used them with thousands of clients, and they are at the centre of this book. If you are grappling with a particular issue – stress, depression, anger, anxiety, low self-esteem, social anxiety or emotional eating – each gets a section to itself in Part Three. Once you've read through the first two parts, you can go straight to whichever issue is concerning you in Part Three. I am confident you will find immediate help for your problem. The area of concern is first explored and then followed by material on how to resolve it effectively.

To assist you in identifying problem areas, I have developed some self-assessment questionnaires (they are in the Appendix). In treatment I often use questionnaires such as these at the beginning, middle and end of treatment to determine movement and change. Something I took away when I did an MBA was 'What gets measured gets done.' You too can use the self-assessment questionnaires to assess your progress. In pointing up improvement in this way, you'll generate momentum and avoid assessing your progress on an impressionistic basis; rather than just being 'grand' or 'doing okay', you'll be dealing with something much more concrete. With the measuring tools, you can actually see the change in the numbers as they fall.

If you're struggling to voice your feelings, or to get things started; if you're scared, or stuck in your head; or if you believe you're invisible – then jump straight in. The time is now! Among other things you will learn how to:

- care for yourself and family members in a smart way;
- make and maintain positive relationships by having healthy boundaries;
- tackle the toxic people in your life;
- understand the cost of the quiet life;
- understand the core beliefs you have about yourself that may be holding you back;
- think more clearly about the merits of using medication for your problem;
- stay on track and overcome obstacles;
- deal with the difficult issue of suicide;
- communicate effectively.

I say the same thing to everyone who comes to see me: 'The session is just one hour. It's the effort you put into the rest of the week that brings about change. Those that make the greatest and quickest progress are those who are committed to working outside of the hour.' I always provide a homework exercise – reading something, completing a task, looking at a movie with a message, writing out thoughts, composing a letter, going online, going for a walk, and so on.

Homework helps us to apply the lessons learned in the therapy room to the real world. I will ask you to complete homework in this book too. Research shows that people who consolidate the work done in the therapy room by doing homework outside it have significantly better, faster and more sustained outcomes than those who don't. Please devote at least one hour a week to putting the ideas offered in this book into practice. The more time you put in, the more likely you are to experience change quickly and positively. That being said, I am confident that even one hour a week will move you towards significant change.

Here and there I suggest that it might be helpful for you to consider getting the help of a counsellor or psychologist. When I first meet an individual, I complete an assessment. I am trying to answer a number of questions, the first being 'What is the problem?' A good assessment is critical. Too many struggling individuals are attending sessions with well-meaning people – clairvoyants, spiritual healers, unqualified 'counsellors' – who claim spurious expertise in psychological difficulties. Here they are getting generic help for generic problem areas, when what they need is targeted intervention for specific problems. But not every qualified therapist will have the right training to use the tools described in this book. In the Appendix, I provide guidelines for finding the right person to work with on your particular problem.

This book is a gift from the thousands of men, women and

children I've seen over my years in practice. I have used actual stories from the therapy room in order to share learning. I have protected people's anonymity by changing details, while maintaining the central learning points. I thank those brave individuals who are journeying towards their real selves.

Becoming your real self allows you to be vibrant, energetic, resilient and positive. When you are your real self – when all your inner strength, knowledge, integrity and courage is brought together, and positive external supports, such as family, friends and community, are harnessed – you are powerful, peaceful and contented; you are authentic, confident and free. I am inviting you now to go for it: take control and take hold of the future you want for yourself.

PART ONE

. . . .

Fundamentals

The two things that influence your life more than anything else are your set of beliefs about yourself and the nature of your relationships with others. Understanding both of these is a crucial part of becoming your real self and living a happier, healthier and more authentic life.

1

Rewriting the story of your life

Humans like patterns. As we go through our daily lives most of us eat the same foods, do the same things, have similar conversations, go to the same places and maintain the same friendships. Effectively we follow patterns. Patterns are the equivalent of shortcuts, which enable us to put less energy into thinking, and humans love taking shortcuts.

Just as we have patterns for day-to-day activities, we also have patterns for our lives in their entirety. These patterns create the stories of our lives. They tell us about our past and potentially about our future. You can view these patterns as life-scripts. And when you open up and unwrap these life-scripts, you will find your core beliefs.

Core beliefs are your internal shortcuts, and they act as the map for your life, playing a role in who we are and the life we lead. Often these core beliefs start in childhood and are influenced by our parents, family history, culture – in effect, the world around us. Our decisions; our thoughts about ourselves, others and the world; what we can achieve and what is beyond our grasp; how we behave and how we react to other people; our successes and our limitations – all of these are influenced by our life-scripts, and these are informed by our core beliefs.

Are your core beliefs telling you that you are strong,

positive and resourceful? Or are your core beliefs, expressed through your inner voice, harsh, punitive and negative?

Core beliefs are well rehearsed and well practised. They have been compared with magnets, in that they seem to attract evidence that confirms their truth and to repel evidence that puts their truth in doubt.

Our core beliefs are resistant to change. And changing them is even harder when you are unaware of the core beliefs that have been shaping your life. So you may find that when you get close to your real self, you start to become uneasy: after all, this is not the script you're accustomed to following. Your old script said what you could not do, what you were not qualified for, what you did not deserve. It made you settle for second and even third best.

Take, for example, the school-leaving exams. I think for many people it can leave a mark, maybe even a wound. This includes me. Despite spending two years in fifth year, I didn't have the maturity to knuckle down and study, and I got a pretty average Leaving Cert. Really average. These results distorted my judgement of my abilities. They laid down a negative script in which I was second rate in terms of intelligence. Even after completing a number of degrees, I was still struggling with questions about the level of my intelligence well into my thirties.

Here's what I know now. Around Leaving Cert. results time there is an over-emphasis on high point scoring. But there are many different pathways to follow. It turns out I was a late bloomer. I eventually figured out that maturity, a capacity for hard work and persistence were the qualities I brought to the table. In addition, the Leaving Cert. does not test for integrity, respect, honesty, passion, humanity, caring, flexibility, critical thinking, problem-solving, emotional intelligence, team-working and communication skills. The academic path is not the path for everyone. Wish I'd known that sooner – I would have spent less time beating myself up!

Negative core beliefs influence our attitudes and behaviours

If you struggle with being authentic, happy and real, the likelihood is that negative core beliefs are at play. In order for you to create your own life-script, it's important for you to delve into your core beliefs.

Why?

Because your core beliefs can either set limits on your life or empower your dreams.

What else?

Because understanding your core beliefs gives you the power to change your life-script. What core beliefs have shaped you? What patterns do you seek? And from what patterns do you seek to escape?

To uncover your core beliefs, imagine a blank T-shirt with the words I AM . . . on it.

Now what words would you use to complete the sentence?

Here are some common core beliefs that emerge frequently in the therapy room that get in the way of people becoming their real self.

Fearful *core beliefs*	Depressive *core beliefs*	Unlovable *core beliefs*	Worthless *core beliefs*	Helpless *core beliefs*
I am ... scared	I am ... sad	I am ... unlovable	I am ... worthless	I am ... needy
I am ... panicky	I am ... alone	I am ... different	I am ... no good	I am ... a failure
I am ... afraid	I am ... depressed	I am ... bound to be abandoned/rejected	I am ... pathetic	I am ... weak
I am ... nervous	I am ... flawed	I am ... defective, so others will not love me	I am ... valueless	I am ... stupid
I am ... unsafe	I am ... weak	I am ... ugly	I am ... unimportant	I am ... fragile
I am ... worried	I am ... incompetent	I am ... bad	I am ... insignificant	I am ... a victim

When our negative core beliefs are active, our world becomes small. Take Emily, who came to see me many years ago. Emily had chronically low self-esteem. Her core beliefs could be summarized as: 'I am unlovable', 'I am worthless', 'I am unimportant'. Her thoughts associated with these beliefs were 'Nobody would want me', 'I have nothing to offer', 'I wish I could disappear'. Emily wanted to be invisible in the world. Her need to be invisible was so strong that she would only go into shops with no cameras because she could not bear for security people to look at her image. She never went for a spa treatment, or for any beauty treatment, because she did not think she deserved it. She did her best to hide in plain sight.

If you suffer from panic or anxiety, your core beliefs may be 'I am scared', 'I am unsafe', 'I am out of control', 'I am helpless'. If these are your beliefs, you will find the world to be a $cary place. In order to keep yourself safe, you will avoid or escape from certain situations, or do things to seek reassurance, for example, go to your GP for check-ups, or frequently check your body for unusual symptoms or sensations.

If you experience recurring depression, your core beliefs may be 'I am sad', 'I am weak', 'I am flawed'. The thoughts associated with these beliefs are 'I can't do that', 'I am no good', 'Nothing can help me, I have had this depression for so long, I've been on medication for the last ten years', 'Life is to be endured, not enjoyed', 'That's all I deserve, I am pathetic'. Your body manifests these negative beliefs as fatigue, exhaustion and low energy. Your corresponding behaviours are a tendency to stay in bed and poor communication with your family and friends.

Silencing the negative voices in your head

Imagine that your inner voice is slowly and insidiously subverting and sabotaging you. Think of it like a bad choir, full of negative voices from your past: parents, relatives, coaches and teachers. When you were a child, you accepted the songs they sang. After all, you were a child and told not to question adults.

This bad choir inside your head – because the singers think they know you well – feels free to comment, chastise, criticize, ridicule and condemn you. The singers sing in harsh, punitive tones. They have developed an expertise in constantly putting you down, in undermining you. For example, 'You don't deserve to be in a relationship, what have you got to offer?', 'I can't believe you've got this far in work; have they not found you out yet?', 'You're a waste of space', 'Who do you think you are, all those airs and graces?', 'Are you stupid or what?', 'You are so ugly, I don't know how you manage to leave the house every day, even make-up can't cover your ugliness'.

At those times when you're vulnerable, you believe what the bad choir is saying. These thoughts and beliefs can damage your confidence in yourself and in others, and adversely influence what you do and how you think.

But now you are an adult. You know that this bad choir lacks knowledge, compassion, wisdom, insight and vision. You've taken more than enough from this bad choir. In your imagination, you can choose to isolate this bad choir on a stage – and then close the curtains on them to drown out the sound. Or you can put them on to a CD player, or select them on your MP3 device or phone, and then turn down the volume or, even better, simply switch them off.

When your inner voice is punitive or critical, pay attention to it. Then say, 'There is that bad choir again – let's close the curtain, I don't need to listen to this.' Actively divert your attention to something else.

This bad choir has been around for a while, and it will take time and practice to learn how to close the curtain and reduce its dishonourable and unworthy songs.

Over time, you will notice this bad choir less and less. Indeed, you will create a new choir: a group of people – including yourself and other supporters in your life, real or imagined – who will be encouraging your real self. Here the tones and words will be positive, coaching, nurturing and compassionate.

As you get used to quieting the negative voices and listening out for the positive ones, you will start to form new core beliefs that are true to your real self. Imagine what it would be like to hold these new core beliefs. What would your life-scripts look like? What would you put on the front of the T-shirt?

Fearless core beliefs	Happy/ Contented core beliefs	Lovable core beliefs	Worthwhile core beliefs	Self-reliant core beliefs
I am ... fearless	I am ... contented	I am ... lovable	I am ... worthwhile	I am ... autonomous
I am ... calm	I am ... happy	I am ... unique	I am ... good	I am ... independent
I am ... brave	I am ... joyful	I am ... attractive	I am ... authentic	I am ... strong
I am ... relaxed	I am ... precious	I am ... great	I am ... valuable	I am ... intelligent
I am ... open to new experiences	I am ... competent	I am ... okay with being okay	I am ... significant	I am ... real
I am ... able to thrive	I am ... able	I am ... cheerful	I am ... emotionally healthy	I am ... someone who sees things through
I am ... safe	I am ... strong	I am ... wonderful	I am ... resilient	I am ... sturdy
I am ...	I am ...	I am ...	I am ...	I am ...

Changing core beliefs: a step-by-step guide

Step 1. Pick a real self core belief

For example, if your old belief is 'I am afraid', go instead for 'I am brave, I try new things'. Don't compromise: 'I am brave sometimes' or 'I am brave when I feel like it' won't do. NO! Now is the time to reach for your real self. Be bold, courageous and confidently pick your new core belief.

Step 2. Take a measure of your beliefs

On a scale between 0 and 100, rate how much you currently believe in the old negative core belief, where 0 is 'I don't believe it at all' and 100 is 'I believe it completely'. Now do the same for the new positive core belief. (This is not a zero-sum exercise, so the two numbers don't need to add up to 100.) For example:

Old belief: 'I am afraid' – 85

New belief: 'I am brave, I try new things' – 25

Step 3. Understanding if a negative core belief is fixed or movable

A fixed negative core belief is one where you believe you are afraid and have never believed anything else, even when you're in a positive mood. The movable negative core belief goes up and down, depending on your levels of stress, resilience, mood, energy and anxiety. When you are vulnerable and down, you believe the negative core belief much more strongly than when your mood is positive and upbeat. If your negative core belief shifts in relation to feelings of stress, resilience, mood, energy and anxiety, you can be fairly certain that the belief is associated with these things rather than being true in itself.

Step 4. Commit to strengthening your new real self core beliefs

A practical way of committing to a change in your life-script is to log your real self core beliefs for four to six months. That will be long enough to identify how your thinking works and gradually to retrain it. You may choose to work on one real self core belief at a time. Buy yourself a nice fancy notebook and sketch out two pages, facing each other, something like this:

Old core belief to be challenged: ....

New real self core belief: ....

Experiences that show that the old core belief is not COMPLETELY true ALL the time: ....

(List as many as you like here – the more the better!)

Real self core belief to be developed: ....

Task: ....

What you expect to happen: ....

What actually happened: ....

Conclusion(s): ....

In the early stages, actively seek evidence that supports your real self core belief. Say, you are trying to challenge the old core belief 'I am afraid' and are instead trying to develop a new real self core belief, 'I am safe'. Take a trip to the supermarket that you used to avoid. Write down what you expect to happen and then what actually happened. It's all black and white information, evidence that your real self core beliefs are just as valid as the beliefs you've had all along. Don't worry if everything doesn't go completely smoothly. Every little step you take is an important part of the exercise.

Step 5. Measure your beliefs again

Be confident that you will see some change. The more tasks you do and the more evidence you collect, the more you'll find pronounced shifts in these beliefs. Whenever you notice a shift, you can be confident you're moving in the right direction: closer to being your real self. Whatever you do, don't give up. Don't become downhearted if the tasks you set yourself take a while to accomplish or if your thinking is slow to shift. You've had these beliefs for quite a while, so it will take some effort and time before they start to shift.

Step 6. Seek support from someone who believes in you

Getting help and support can help you to develop your new real self core beliefs more quickly. Often people see strengths in you that you discount in yourself. Telling someone about the new belief you're trying to strengthen and the old belief you're trying to eradicate can be very helpful.

Step 7. Figure out behaviour patterns that are in keeping with your old core belief

Are you avoiding situations more than previously? Are you escaping from them? Are you using someone else for social camouflage? Are you angrier? Have you stopped going places or doing things – the shops, church or gym, out walking?

Step 8. Create behaviour patterns that strengthen your new real self core beliefs

Think of someone preparing for a race, of the many training sessions that must take place before somebody does their first 10k run. So be sensible and treat yourself like a sympathetic coach: tell yourself that we crawl before we walk, walk before we jog, and jog before we run.

Figure out what you would be doing if you were a coach devising tasks to strengthen your real self core beliefs. What do you need to be doing? Meeting people, getting out, making phone calls, taking on projects, being a leader at work, exercising, reducing your drinking, taking control of your diet, etc.? Now, what is the very first thing that you can do right now? And is there anything stopping you?

Do this for four to six months. As mentioned previously, patterns that you've had for a long time take more than 5 minutes to change.

Your new life-script powered by real self core beliefs

What have Rory McIlroy, Sonia O'Sullivan, Bernard Brogan, Derval O'Rourke, Johnny Sexton, Cora Staunton and Katie Taylor got in common? They all use visualization and goal-setting to achieve their life-scripts. And you too can use goal-setting and visualization.

Now is your chance to build your own personalized life-script. Create a strong vision for your life-script. Most people can say what they don't want in life but find it a struggle to say what they want. Bring clarity and precision to your vision. Focus on these areas:

- relationships and family;
- physical health – health screening, nutrition, fitness and weight management;
- emotional health – stress management, self-esteem;
- spirituality, humanity and community;
- career, work and financial management;
- social life and lifelong learning;
- real self – becoming fearless, happy, contented, authentic, lovable, worthwhile, self-reliant, secure, playful, creative, passionate.

Write down your vision with as much detail as you can, including your aims and goals for each of these areas. This is your life-script. Make your goals SMART:

- **S**pecific;
- **M**easurable;
- **A**chievable;
- **R**ealistic;
- **T**ime limited.

Adjust your new life-script as often as you need to, until it represents a genuine expression of your real self. Write your story in the present tense, as if you are living it now. It's okay to dream big.

You may choose to develop a vision board – which is a collection of pictures, as well as inspirational words and phrases – that represents your real self and your path to achieving this. Your vision board will provide you with focus, inspiration and motivation. You can take a photograph of this on your smartphone and look at it daily. Alternatively you may wish your vision to take the form of some uplifting music, which can be downloaded to your phone or iPod for daily listening.

Now you are shifting your focus towards your real self future and away from what is amiss in your life. Read, listen and visualize your life-script in the morning and at night-time. By concentrating your thoughts on your real self life-script, your core beliefs, inner voice, attitudes and behaviour will be energized towards your goals – and beyond, to your dreams. Your life will become what you have imagined. You will be living with purpose, fully engaged, not just allowing life to happen around you. Choose to be free from fear.

Whenever you start (and there's no time like the present!), plan to make the next year of your life a year of self-determination, one in which you experience positive emotions – love, joy, curiosity and hope. The year when you truly become your real self.

2

Positive relationships – the key to being real

When it comes to being real, there is nothing like the power of positive relationships. Relationships come in all shapes and sizes, and through all sorts of channels – family, friends, romantic partners, colleagues, and so on. Regardless of the relationship type, in this chapter I provide you with a road-map leading to the answer to this question: *Are my relationships helping or hindering my efforts to become my real self?*

Attachment

'Attachment theory' describes one of the most powerful psychological phenomena shaping our day-to-day relation-ships. Attachment theory explains how the foundations of our relationships are formed. Central to this is our first and most powerful relationship – the bond between ourselves and our primary caregiver, generally our mother. This bond is developed in the first years of our life. However, not every-body is lucky enough to have a responsive mother – possibly because of bereavement, personality style or illness.

More recent research has shown us that a child needs one good person in their life from an early age; this can be an aunt, uncle, grandparent or older sibling. This primary caregiver – through sensitivity and responsiveness – provides the child with a secure base for effectively regulating their emotions. The mother–child attachment bond profoundly influences infant brain development, self-esteem, tolerance of stress, and how people react to the responses of others. More recently it has been shown that the attachment style of someone's childhood is linked to forming and maintaining successful relationships in adult life. The attachment style established in early childhood acts as a working model for relationships in adulthood and influences our strengths and shortcomings in relationships.

A number of different attachment styles have been identified. These include *secure attachment*; *insecure avoidant*; *ambivalent attachment*; and *disorganized attachment*. Let's look at these various attachment styles to see if you recognize the same patterns in your own life and in the lives of those closest to you. Once you can identify these patterns, you are on the road to changing them.

Secure attachment

If you are lucky enough to have a secure attachment, your primary caregiver was warm, sensitive, and responsive to your needs and emotions. As a child you felt safe, and the secure attachment enabled you to explore the world; be self-confident and trusting; and deal with stress appropriately. Providing your children with a secure attachment is the greatest gift you can give them. Adults with secure attachments may be flexible, creative, hopeful and optimistic. In adult relationships, you are secure, and in your connection with your romantic partner both of you are able to move freely and to support each other at times of stress. The relationship is open, trusting and balanced, one in which both people feel independent, yet loving towards each other.

Insecure (avoidant) attachment

In these circumstances your primary caregiver was non-responsive and rejected your emotional needs in childhood. Often there may have been a high level of parental stress and anxiety. There was little sensitivity. As a result, you may have been fearful as a child, avoided situations and lacked confidence. In adult life you may be anxious, insecure, critical, blaming, rigid or intolerant; you may avoid closeness or emotional connection.

If you have an insecure (avoidant) attachment style, you may need constant reassurance from your partner. In relationships the insecure individual can be so unsure of their partner's feelings that they become clingy, needy, demanding, jealous or possessive towards their partner. These relationships can be incredibly draining.

Insecure (ambivalent) attachment

In these circumstances the primary caregiver was non-responsive and neglected your emotional needs in childhood. Often there were poor rules, roles and routines. There was little sensitivity. As a result you may have felt anxious and lacked confidence as a child. In adult life, you may be anxious, insecure, controlling, blaming, unpredictable and insensitive to the needs of your partner.

If you have an insecure (ambivalent) attachment style, your adult relationships may tend to be high in drama and rocky at times. You may struggle with fears of abandonment and have difficulty with being intimate. Pull-and-push situations may develop, in which you are clingy when you feel rejected, then ensnared when close.

Disorganized attachment

In these circumstances the primary caregiver ignored or did not see your needs as a child. Often this occurs when the parents have an addiction problem. On occasions the primary caregiver was frightening, controlling or abusive. In adult life you may be chaotic, insensitive, explosive, abusive or too trusting, craving security.

The effects of insecure attachment

Insecure attachments – arising out of neglect, abuse, trauma, maternal depression or addiction, separation from parents or frequent moves from foster home to foster home – can give rise to difficulties in life. And if you have experienced adversity in your early life, you may feel downhearted after reading all this. Please don't. For some people identifying early attachment issues can explain how they feel, act and relate to others. That's good for them and may help them tackle problems in their lives. But it's important to note that having an early attachment problem is an indication only, and that the die is not cast. *You are not necessarily marked for life by early trauma.*

What was not taken into account by early researchers in this area, psychologists such as John Bowlby and Mary Ainsworth, was resilience: people's capacity to bounce back after adversity. The good news is that research shows that people can overcome the biggest traumas. Most people have one good person in their life. Most people have great strengths, resilience and personal resources. It's just that sometimes we fail to see these things when we are struggling.

Forming a relationship with somebody with a secure

attachment style will be a relatively smooth process. Take, for example, this couple. Mary has been married to Brendan for the last thirty years. She described to me how considerate, thoughtful and sensitive he is to her needs. They are both in their late fifties. When they walk on the beach in Kerry, they hold hands and look at the sea and mountains. Both Mary and Brendan have had their challenges: an adult child with autism who lives in a support house with a disability service. They are connected, committed, together and flourishing.

Mary and Brendan came from an environment in which they had a secure attachment style. This was brought into their adult relationship. On the other hand, Ann and John have challenges.

Ann is married to John. They have four children. She said to me, 'He works all the time, he doesn't want to be at home. He doesn't want to be around the children. He does not want to be around me. He is cold. He is calculating and indifferent. There is no warmth. We never hold hands. We never kiss or cuddle. There is no joy. I come from a very warm family: we cuddled, we kissed, we held each other when it was needed. My dad was warm and supportive, he was my biggest cheerleader. I thought after we got married John would relax more, share more and loosen up.'

It can be seen that Ann came from a secure attachment place, but John came from a disorganized attachment background.

In the therapy room we constantly see the impact of attachment styles on adult relationships. Individuals who experience confusing, frightening, or broken emotional communications because of insecure attachment styles may grow into adults who have difficulty understanding their own emotions and the feelings of others.

Once they have an understanding of these attachment styles, it can be useful for people who are forming relationships to look at the attachment styles of prospective partners. It can help to make what's going on with them more understandable. A partner with a secure attachment style is one who is responsive, sensitive and has the ability to understand and empathize. In any relationship, this partner will possess a greater capacity to bounce back from disappointment and misfortune.

Boundaries

Boundaries in relationships are incredibly important in childhood and in adulthood. The key patterns of boundaries in relationships are *distant*, *healthy* and *intrusive*. How we maintain these boundaries is vital to our well-being. Consider your relationship and ask yourself: is it distant, healthy or intrusive?

Distant

When boundaries are too distant, a disconnect is created. Effectively we are two individuals with nothing in common. Conflicts remain unresolved. Distant relationships are cold, unfulfilling and will fail to give you support in becoming your real self.

Distant

Healthy

Healthy relationships have give and take. Space is woven into their togetherness. Power is shared equally. Each individual helps the other to develop, nurture and grow, which in turn allows the relationship to grow. Conflicts are dealt with quickly and ill-feeling does not fester. Healthy relationships are fertile ground for becoming your real self.

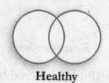

Healthy

Intrusive

Intrusive relationships are characterized by imbalance: one person exerts power over the other. Sometimes this power is overt, and manifests itself through a control of finances or a display of physical strength. Alternatively, power can be exerted covertly, in ways that are subtle yet still destructive. Intrusive relationships do not allow you to become your real self.

Intrusive

So what have you figured out about yourself or about those around you? Regardless of the type of relationship – romantic, work, family or friendship – you need to aim for healthy boundaries and secure attachment, if the connection is to grow and develop. Communication, both verbal and non-verbal, is the glue that holds healthy relationships together. When each party in a relationship is 'tuned in' to the other's emotions, both feel safe and secure. These relationships last longer, are more fulfilling and have higher levels of commitment and trust.

Review your sphere of relationships and ask yourself these questions:

- Do my relationships with my own family help or hinder me in becoming my real self?
- Does my relationship with my partner help or hinder me in becoming my real self?
- Do my relationships with my work colleagues help or hinder me in becoming my real self?
- Do my relationships with my friends help or hinder me in becoming my real self?

Now you have some idea of those people who add to your life. Also, you have an idea of those who undermine your efforts towards becoming your real self. *These are toxic relationships.* In the real world we sometimes need to maintain a connection with these negative people: a boss who is a jerk, an interfering mother-in-law, a boundary-infringing friend — you get the idea. You need a strategy for dealing with these people. If you must retain a toxic relationship, regard it as if it were a dose of toxic medicine: keep the dose to the absolute minimum. Check out Chapter 9 for more advice on this.

Finally, remember that, however much you grow and develop, your power over others is limited! If I received €1 every time I heard 'Why can't he or she change?', I would be able to pay off my Celtic Tiger debts more quickly. The bottom line is: *Don't wait around for people to change*. It is very unlikely that they will.

The point is that *it's up to you to change*. You can't control others. If your behaviour changes, the behaviour of others may follow suit. Your own behaviour is the only thing you can control. And that's a mighty liberating thing to know – that you have the power to change yourself!

PART TWO

. . . .

Tools for change

As a clinical psychologist, I was taught to mix therapy approaches to arrive at a strategy that is unique to each client. Over the years I have used a variety of methods, but there are a few that are so powerful in addressing common emotional and psychological concerns that I return to them again and again. These are truly powerful techniques, easy to take out of the therapy room and bring into day-to-day life – techniques that make all the difference to your success in becoming your real self.

3

Mindfulness – the importance of living in the moment

Our youngest son is called Darragh. At the time of writing, Darragh is four years old; he lives in the moment. He scampers from one thing to another with hardly a thought about what he's been doing or what he's going to do next. All he cares about is what's happening right now. He is happy in himself, in the present. His older brother is Oisín, a wonderful, sensitive boy. Oisín sometimes worries about going to football practice. Normal stuff for a six-year-old. His thinking is in the future, which creates little worries for him. He anticipates things. He has a memory of past anxieties. When he gets to practice – with our encouragement – he loves it. When he lives in the present, his worries dissolve.

Take Jennifer. Jennifer is in her late fifties, and she would tell you herself she's 'out-the-door busy'. She has three adult children: Chloe in Dubai, Dylan in London and the youngest, Aoife, at home. 'I've got to get a dress for the christening, renew my health insurance, pay the property tax, go to the gym, do the laundry when I get home, ring Chloe, drop Dylan to the airport . . .'

Jennifer is very good at 'human doing', but she struggles at 'human being'. Four years ago, Jennifer lost her husband. Perhaps if she stopped for a while, she'd start to think about how much she misses him and the two children, who live so far away. Sometimes 'doing' is easier than 'being'. But

Jennifer isn't quite being her real self by filling her time with busyness. Jennifer will have a richer life and a deeper connection with herself, her children and her friends if she makes space for simply being in the moment.

Does Jennifer remind you of anybody? Is your head full of lists? How do you divide your time between 'doing' and 'being'?

Often in our adult lives we spend too much time in the past and too much time in the future, leaving too little time for the present. The truth is that when you live in the present, rather than regretting the past or worrying about the future, you are more your real self.

Mindfulness is the practice of bringing your awareness and attention into the present moment. Mindfulness takes us from the 'doing' mode, where we are trapped on auto-pilot, into the 'being' mode. When mindful, you work from the standpoint of compassion, curiosity and acceptance towards yourself and your experiences. Mindfulness offers many ways to deepen your awareness, insights that can anchor you in the present and help you to keep things in perspective. It offers tools you can use in your daily life.

While mindfulness is rooted in the meditation and philosophical practices of the East, it has a central role in the twenty-first-century West. Using the techniques pioneered by Dr Jon Kabat-Zinn, I – along with many other psychologists and therapists around the world – have found mindfulness to be incredibly helpful to clients with all kinds of issues – stress, emotional eating, physical illness, anxiety. There is increasing evidence to demonstrate its effectiveness in treating depression and, importantly, in preventing relapse. In addition, mindfulness boosts energy levels and the performance of the immune system, while enhancing people's general emotional well-being. When mindful, you are aware of what you are doing while you are doing it. Mindfulness increases your awareness of your thoughts, feelings and actions. In effect mindfulness is a relationship within yourself, and between you and others.

Like any new skill, it takes effort and commitment to master mindfulness. Yet – and this is going to sound contradictory – despite the techniques and tips described here, mindfulness isn't actually something you do. Rather it is about letting go of doing. It's about simply being as you are. Being your real self – authentic, compassionate and confident. However, the techniques and tips will hopefully bring you to a stage where simply being is as automatic to you as breathing.

Central to mindfulness is the practice of meditation. Meditation is about paying attention to, and focusing on, certain areas, such as your breath, or one of your senses, or your body, or your thoughts, or your emotions.

Mindfulness and meditation take practice. There is no easy way. Some people choose to take 20 minutes out of the day to practise and deepen their mindfulness. Others concentrate on being mindful while cooking, walking, talking to a friend, eating – anything really.

And, like any skill – swimming, riding a bike, dancing, playing golf or baking – the more you do it, the better you become.

Courses are a great way to start. Check out the mindfulness-based stress-reduction (MBSR) courses on my website.

Mindfulness and thoughts

We can't control the thoughts that keep pouring into our minds. Sometimes the stream of thought is like a non-stop, never-ending loop of information and judgements and plans and trivia – a bit like the headlines that run across the bottom of the screens on the 24-hour news channels. But, when you think of it, you are actually aware of your thoughts. Just as you might be aware of a pain in your big toe or an itchy ear. So here's a startling truth:

You are not your thoughts.

Your thoughts are just thoughts. They are not facts. And you are simply an observer of your thoughts.

When truly mindful, you do not attach meaning to thoughts. Nor do you react to them. You just observe them and accept them without judgement. You do not get carried away. And you do not get trapped by negative thinking or swamped by the negative feelings that spring from it.

Because you are not your thoughts.

Often I imagine mindfulness at its most advanced as being like the scene in the movie *The Matrix*, in which the Keanu Reeves character gets to such a powerful level of awareness and being-in-the-moment that he is able to dodge a hail of bullets. In a way these bullets represent the constant barrage of negative thoughts that can afflict you, particularly if you suffer from depression or are in a bad place in your life.

Imagine that you can be aware of these thoughts but not overwhelmed by them. As an observer of your thoughts, you can choose to dismiss them. This is so liberating. It gives you the freedom and space needed to become your real self.

Mindfulness and feelings

Inside a space of compassion and curiosity and increased awareness, you can observe your emotions, in just the same way that you can observe your thoughts. And that leads to another startling realization:

You are not your emotions.

There is a significant difference between you and your emotions, and the practice of mindfulness can help you recognize the difference between the two. You are an observer. In the next few chapters we will look at changing your thinking in such a way as to recalibrate your emotions. Working on your thoughts in this way is a hugely valuable method of dealing with negative emotions. However, in mindfulness you are invited both to acknowledge and to give mindful attention to your feelings, rather than avoiding them or reacting to them. This is a powerful technique that is capable of reducing the strength and intensity of painful emotions. For example, when you experience a strong feeling, such as stress, anger or sadness, try this exercise:

- *Purposefully sense the emotion.* Be aware of the emotion and its effects from a stance of gentle curiosity. Give yourself just enough space to learn from the emotion. Don't run away from it.
- *Feel the emotion.* Open up to the emotion with compassion, kindness and acceptance. Scan your body and notice where this feeling resides within it. Breathe into that part of your body. Allow the feeling to be as it is. Be with the experience. Don't fight it. And don't run away.
- *Be the observer and step back from the feeling.* Notice your awareness of the emotion without becoming the emotion itself. As you observe, notice the space between you and the feeling. You are separate from it. Imagine yourself standing by a riverbank. As you watch the water pass by, you recognize that you are not the river itself. Every so often you may feel as if you are being pulled into the water (feeling), but as soon as you notice you remember

that you are the observer and simply step back from the bank.

- *Breathe.* Bring your attention to your breath. Notice your in-breath and your out-breath. Notice how each one is unique and supports your health and well-being.

Mindful breathing

Breathing is at the heart of mindfulness. It gives you the opportunity to 'tune in' to your body, mind and heart. Try this two-part exercise for 3 minutes.

- First, *sit up straight.*
- *Awareness. Reflect on the following questions.* What emotions am I aware of at the moment? Where am I feeling these emotions? Scan your body. What sensations are you aware of at this moment? Just accept them. What thoughts are you aware of? You are an observer of your thoughts.
- *Breathing. Bring your attention to your breathing.* Notice your in-breath and your out-breath. You don't need to change your breathing; just become mindful of it.
  If your mind is wandering, gently guide your attention back to your breath.
  Be grateful and appreciate your breathing.

Mindful walking

Advanced technology has created robots that walk. However, I have never seen a robot that moves with the fluidity, agility and grace of a woman or a man.

Have a go at mindful walking. It's an excellent way of staying in the moment and of letting go of your anxieties and worries. Try going to the garden, park, forest, river walk, lake or seaside. Become aware of your breath. Notice how many steps you take on your in-breath during this time. Let's say it's four steps. Repeat in your mind: 'In . . . in . . . in . . . in.' And on your out-breath, if it's, say, three steps, repeat: 'Out . . . out . . . out.' This helps you to become aware of your breathing.

Don't try to control your breathing. Just go along with what happens naturally. When you see something beautiful – such as a flower or ducklings on the water or children playing – stop and look at the scene. Notice that life exists in the present moment.

Mindful eating

You eat your breakfast running out the door. You have your lunch in the car or by the computer. You have your dinner in front of the TV. You eat because you are upset.

Sound familiar? Mindless eating leads to overeating and results in unhealthy choices about what you eat and how you eat.

Mindful eating is about slowing down. Look, feel, smell, chew, concentrate on the taste of the food and the speed at which you are eating. Before eating your next mouthful, lay down your knife and fork and pause for a few seconds. Pay attention to the here and now.

Mindful loving kindness

Mindfulness is about being compassionate and loving to ourselves. Find a place where you feel secure, safe and warm. Notice your in-breath and your out-breath. Allow phrases to come from your heart about the things that you deserve, for example: 'May I have compassion', 'May I be healthy', 'May I be accepting', 'May I be happy', 'May I be of sound body and mind', 'May I thrive'. Repeat the phrases over and over again, until they permeate your being. Allow your heartfelt expression to generate loving kindness towards yourself. If this doesn't happen, don't worry: your intentions are more important than the feelings.

Now you can bring your mind to someone you care about. Picture that person and then with your good intention say: 'May you have compassion', 'May you be healthy', 'May you be accepting', 'May you be happy', 'May you be of sound body and mind', 'May you thrive'. This can be a very healing exercise. Allow yourself to practise it slowly, and with compassion.

Of course there are people in your life towards whom you don't feel particularly loving or kindly. Perhaps they've hurt you and you find it hard to get past that. Realistically you're not going to feel very forgiving towards people you think have done you wrong.

If you do feel like this, may I reframe the situation for you? I often reflect on this thought and I share it with clients: forgiving and letting go is not something we do for others; it is something we do for ourselves in order to get well and to move on with our lives. Holding on to anger is a toxic habit.

But forgiveness may take time. Being compassionate with yourself will allow forgiveness to come in. Remember that repeating over and over the story of the pain someone caused you or the wrong they did you only serves to hurt you more. Become an observer and try to let go of that particular story.

Gratitude

The old advice to 'count your blessings' is well founded. Gratitude is a powerful emotion, and studies have shown it to be very strongly linked to our well-being. It's also crucial to mindfulness, since, by definition, when you are grateful you are mindful: you are thinking about what's good in your life right now, not about what you didn't get or don't yet have or will never have. When grateful, we are mindful, because we are open to possibilities, positivity and optimism.

Imagine being grateful as similar to the process of developing a muscle: the more you use it, the stronger it becomes. To strengthen your gratitude-muscle, try this:

- Before going to sleep, think about three good things that you are grateful for today. This is a lovely exercise to do with children.
- Say thank you regularly and genuinely.
- Do something to say thanks: a handwritten card, make someone a cuppa, mow the grass.
- Be grateful for small things: friendships, nature, flowers, fresh air, water . . .
- Now think of something you are not so grateful for – for example, having to go to work. Take 2 minutes to write down all the positive things about your job. You might include the salary, the friendships, the routine, the holidays it pays for, etc. Overcome your natural resistance to your attitude towards work.

Commit to doing this each day for a week, focusing on a different area of your life every time. Eventually you will become grateful for a wide variety of things. Indeed, some people find it so enriching to keep a record of what they're grateful for that they permanently make it a part of their daily routine. Flexing your gratitude-muscle might well be one of the nicest and most rewarding things you can do on your way to becoming your real self!

4

CBT – the importance of managing your thinking

The idea that our emotions are created in our own heads, rather than by anything that happens to us, is not a new one. Yet you would be surprised by the number of people who have not figured this out. Nearly 2,000 years ago, the Greek philosopher Epictetus said, 'People are disturbed not by events, but by the views they take of them.' This idea – that our responses to events are what make up our feelings – is a really helpful way of understanding our emotions, because it allows us to take charge of them.

Here's an example. Helen is in town shopping and happens to spot her good friend Anne coming towards her up the street. Only yesterday Helen and Anne had had coffee and parted on good terms. Helen calls out and waves to Anne, but Anne does not respond and then goes into a shop. Helen's reaction is as follows.

She thinks: 'Why couldn't she stop for a quick chat? I must have upset her. She was definitely ignoring me. Maybe she doesn't like me any more. I haven't been in great form lately. People probably find me hard going. Sure, who would want to hang out with me? Anne is right.'

She feels sad and rejected and a bit teary. She suddenly finds that she's really tired and not up to finishing her errands. She heads back to her car, because she's afraid she's going to burst into tears. She keeps her head down, hoping she won't run into anyone she knows. The shopping bag she's carrying feels like it weighs a tonne. She is supposed to see another friend, Sean, that evening, but texts him to cancel. Later he phones her at home, but she doesn't answer the phone.

What is interesting here is that Anne's failure to respond to Helen's greeting (the situation) has set off a sequence of thoughts that has brought down her mood, sapped her energy, affected her body language and dictated her behaviour for the rest of the day. All because she *thinks* Anne has snubbed her.

Imagine now the same situation and Helen interpreting Anne's action entirely differently.

'Anne must have been daydreaming. Or maybe she was thinking about her mam, since she's only out of hospital. Come to think of it, that was the chemist's she went into. She's probably picking up a prescription for her mam. I must pop in to catch up with her.'

In this instance Helen feels concern for Anne. She's energized and purposeful as she walks up the street. When she catches up with Anne in the pharmacy, Anne laughs and says that yes, she was miles away, and she's glad Helen spotted her. She confirms that her mother is making a good recovery. Anne's good mood rubs off on Helen, and they decide to continue their chat over a cup of coffee.

In the case of the first scenario, Helen's friendship with Anne might have been permanently damaged if she had persisted with that line of thinking. But in the case of the second scenario, their relationship was enhanced.

The point of the story of Helen and Anne is to demonstrate that how we think about a situation influences our feelings, our body and our behaviour. This is at the core of the powerful techniques of cognitive behavioural therapy

(CBT), which I'm going to discuss in this chapter and the following two.

What is CBT?

At the heart of CBT is the idea that our thinking (i.e., our cognitive activity) influences what we do and how we feel. Our thinking is the lens through which we view our world, in order to decide if the proverbial glass is half full or half empty. The choice you make – whether it is optimistic or pessimistic – depends on the way you construe the information in your mind.

If you could take a snapshot of the thoughts of people who continually experience the big three negative emotions of sadness, anxiety or anger, here's what you would find.

- *People who experience sadness.* Their lenses actively filter in negativity from their past, present and future. Think about it: do you know someone who experiences sadness, low mood or depression? You may notice that they tell a lot of negative stories, and that there's a downbeat feeling about them.
- *People who experience anxiety or fear.* Their lenses actively filter in threats generally associated with the future. No doubt you are familiar with someone who experiences fear, panic attacks and anxiety. Here the person works on the assumption that 'If something bad happens, I can't cope . . . I can't escape . . .'
- *People who experience anger.* Their lenses actively filter in the injustice that they see around them. 'It's unfair! Why did my dad leave money to him? After all, I did all the caring . . .'

In summary, this is how we may react to the big negative emotions of our lives:

- stress, worry;
- sadness, loss, low mood, depression;
- fear, anxiety, panic attacks;
- anger, jealousy, envy;
- low confidence, shyness, social anxiety;
- low self-esteem, compulsive overeating, guilt, shame.

I will explore all of these in more detail in later chapters. But the key positive thing to note is that extensive research supports the use of CBT for many of these emotional and psychological problems.

And here's the thing: the tools of CBT are so powerful that they can be used in any area of your life. You don't need to be experiencing major emotional or psychological issues to make use of CBT. Its techniques can be implemented throughout your life to improve your well-being and bring you closer to your real self. It is practical, efficient and invaluable in helping to get you to a better place. When you can change your thoughts, you can change your world.

You are the boss of your feelings!

In the therapy room, people say, 'He made me feel bad', 'She made me angry', 'My boss makes me nervous'. But what really makes us feel the way we do is our response to a particular event, the way we choose to think about it.

When you are your real self, you are independent, self-reliant and accountable. And that means you are also accountable for your feelings. So once you've decided to work on changing your feelings, you need to know that no one makes you feel bad. More importantly, you can become contented and fulfilled by changing the beliefs that cause stress, fear, anger and sadness.

A fun, shorthand way of thinking about the CBT model, one that I use with clients, is to envisage each element – each situation, or thought, or feeling, or behaviour or physical response – as a hat they've put on to consider the problem that's on their mind. (Putting on a metaphorical hat helps some people to focus on just one question to the exclusion of others. If you find you don't need to put on a hat, don't feel you have to!)

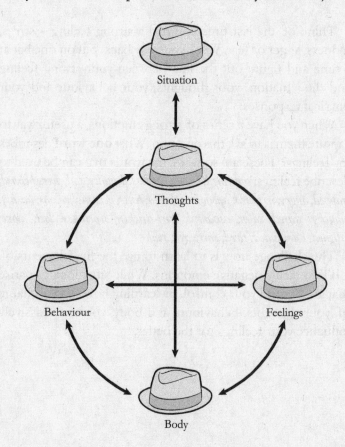

- *The situation hat* represents the 'who, what, when, where, why' elements. It's the particular environment that gives rise to particular thoughts.
- *The thoughts hat* represents the internal chatter that goes on in our heads.
- *The feelings hat* represents our emotions or moods, how we feel.
- *The behaviour hat* represents our actions, what we do.
- *The body hat* represents how our body reacts.

Think of the last time you had a strong feeling – stress, sadness, anger or fear. Work your way back: put on one hat at a time and figure out the link between your strong feeling and the situation, your thoughts, your behaviour and your physical responses.

When you have a series of strong emotions, a useful way to capture them is to ask this question. What **one word** describes my feelings? These are some of the words that can be used to describe feelings: *contented; happy; depressed; guilty; sad; overwhelmed; trapped; angry; irritated; anxious; relaxed; tense; nervous; jealous; uneasy; panicky; scared; calm; ashamed; grief-stricken; worthless; lost; alone; fatigued; humiliated; tired; energized; real.*

The challenge now is to learn to use the five elements of CBT to tackle negative emotions. While situations can arise that are beyond your control, by learning how to take charge of your thoughts, behaviours and body, you can massively influence your feelings for the better.

5

Exterminate those ANTs!

Here is something psychology now knows for definite: specific thinking patterns are present when we are feeling bad. The techniques of CBT can tackle those patterns and change them. Our moods are maintained by continuous *automatic negative thoughts* (ANTs); these make up the internal voice in our head. And boy, do those ANTs take up a lot of headspace.

CBT looks at what sustains emotions such as unhappiness, sadness, fear and low confidence in the here and now. People sometimes think that CBT is just about replacing these ANTs with positive thoughts. But that is too simplistic. The secret is to identify the ANTs, understand them and change them to thoughts that are more realistic and balanced. It's about understanding the pattern of these ANTs and the core belief message that they reveal. Only then can negative core beliefs be tackled.

Imagine that these ANTs are similar to the software code that's used on all the websites we visit. Automatic and continuously running, it allows the likes of Facebook or Google or Amazon to function without our being aware of it. With negative feelings, it's as if there's a fault or bug in the software code of our thinking. I refer to this as *crooked thinking*. Crucially, crooked thinking maintains and amplifies negative feelings.

Here are the fourteen most common types of crooked thinking that lead to bad feelings. As you read through, ask yourself: *Which of these is contributing to my problems?* Most people readily fall into one or more of these habitual patterns of thinking. Once you have identified, and named, the biases in your thinking, you are halfway to defeating your bad mood:

1. *Black and white thinking.* Switching from one extreme to another. 'If I can't get this right, I might as well give up altogether', 'If you can say that, our relationship means nothing at all', 'One mistake ruined the whole thing', 'One false move, and the business will crumble'.

2. *Catastrophizing.* Predicting the worst outcome. If something goes wrong, it will be a disaster. Every twinge is a sign of serious illness, every frown a sign of rejection. 'If I make a mistake, I will lose my job', 'I'll lose control completely', 'My heart is beating so fast I could die'.

3. *Generalizing.* Assuming that because something happened once, it will always happen. 'You always forget to do the things I ask', 'I never seem to say the right thing', 'Politicians always tell lies', 'We always do things your way', 'I'm such a fool. I always blow it at the last minute'.

4. *Exaggerating.* Giving negative events more importance than they really deserve, and positive events less importance. 'I'll never get over it', 'Any fool should be able to pass a driving test', 'I can't bear it', 'The way I look, nobody could take me seriously', 'People never enjoy being with me because I'm too shy'.

5. *Discounting the positive.* Rejecting the good things as if they did not count (or using a negative filter). 'She only said that to make me feel better', 'I could never have done that on my own', 'It's just that I was lucky', 'I happened to be in the right place at the right time', 'What, this old thing? I bought it at a garage sale'.

6. *Mind-reading.* Believing that you know what others are thinking. 'She knows I've made a mess of this', 'They all thought I was stupid', 'He doesn't like me', 'You only say that because you want to get at me', 'They only asked me because they couldn't find anyone else'.

7. *Predicting the future, or fortune-telling.* 'Everything is bound to go wrong', 'I won't be able to cope on my own', 'I couldn't face it if something dreadful happened', 'The interview went so badly I know they won't give me the job', 'It's no use, I'll never get it right', 'I'll never be able to do that sort of thing'.

8. *Taking things personally.* 'They didn't ask me because they don't like me', 'You're criticizing me' (when someone asks you to do something differently), 'That waiter just ignores me', 'If they don't get here, it's because I gave them such bad directions'.

9. *Taking the blame.* Taking responsibility when the fault is not yours. 'It's all my fault', 'Sorry', 'They'd be happier if I'd been a better mother', 'If only I'd done more for *x*', 'He failed the test because I was so nasty to him last night'.

10. *Emotional reasoning.* Mistaking feelings for facts. 'I'm so worried, I know something is going to go

wrong', 'I'm sure they've had an accident', 'I love her so much she's bound to respond', 'I don't care what you say, I just feel the way I do'.

11. *Name-calling.* 'I'm an idiot', 'You're completely heartless', 'Anybody who could do that must be brain dead', 'I'm stupid', 'I'm bad'.

12. *Scaremongering.* 'Maybe she's really ill', 'What if the car breaks down?', 'Suppose they can't do anything about it?', 'People do suddenly drop dead – you read about it in the papers', 'Perhaps I'll fail', 'I couldn't cope'.

13. *Wishful thinking.* Supposing things would be better if they were different. 'If only I were younger . . . thinner . . . smarter . . . not the way I am'.

14. *'Should' statements.* You tell yourself that things *should* be the way you hoped or expected them to be. Similar offenders are 'must', 'ought' and 'have to'. 'Should' statements that are directed against yourself lead to guilt and frustration; 'should' statements that are directed against other people or the world in general lead to anger and frustration: 'He shouldn't be so stubborn and argumentative.' Many people try to motivate themselves with 'should' and 'shouldn't' statements, as if they were delinquents who had to be punished before they could be expected to do anything: 'I shouldn't eat that doughnut.' This usually doesn't work, because saying 'should' and 'must' makes you feel rebellious, and you get the urge to do just the opposite.

Strategies to overcome ANTs

1. Capture the ANTs and squash them

When you have a strong feeling, identify the feeling and capture the underlying thought that is amplifying it. Search to see if you are engaged in any crooked thinking. Try this series of twenty powerful questions to squash your ANTs. If possible, learn them by heart so that they become second nature to you.

1. Do I need to stop to take a deep breath?
2. What type of crooked thinking am I engaged in? Am I mistaking thoughts for facts? Am I assuming that I know what others are thinking? Am I trying to predict the future?
3. If my best friend told me they'd had this thought, what advice would I give them?
4. If my best friend knew that I'd had this thought, what would they say to me? How might they suggest that my thoughts were not 100% accurate?
5. When I am not feeling this way, would I think about this situation differently and, if so, why?
6. Am I wearing 'fear glasses' or 'dark glasses'? What would the more realistic picture be, if I were not filtering out the positives?
7. What evidence is there this thought is true? What other ways might I think about this situation?
8. The words in my mind: are they fact or opinion?
9. Where is my focus – on the past or on the future? How do I get directly into the moment?

10. If it's not about black or white, how do I surf the grey?
11. What might someone else make of this situation?
12. Is my reaction disproportionate to the situation?
13. How important will this situation be in six months' time; in one year's time; in two years' time?
14. When I felt this way before, what did I think about or do that enabled me to feel better?
15. What is the most helpful thing that I can do in this situation?
16. Am I discounting small things that could contradict my thoughts?
17. Am I blaming myself for something over which I do not have complete control?
18. Are there any resources and strengths in me that I am ignoring or that I might use?
19. What are all of my choices in this situation?
20. What consequences might result from my behaviour? Will this action bring me closer to, or further away from, my real self?

2. Move away from the problem

In therapy, I often invite a client to hold a book one inch from their nose. Then I ask them to move it to an arm's length away. It's a simple exercise to get them thinking about perspective. When the book is right in front of their nose, they cannot see anything but the book. But when they hold it out in front of them, they can see the book and everything else as well. Yet the book hasn't changed – just the way they're holding it.

We need a way to see the bigger picture. When you put a

problem – metaphorically – at arm's length from you, it's not as overwhelming. Indeed, imagine being up in a hot-air balloon. That would certainly allow you to see the bigger picture.

To help gain perspective on your problem, try asking these questions.

1. How might somebody outside of the situation see it?
2. What are the different points of view?
3. Are there things on which we can agree as well as disagree?
4. What is the wisest path for me?
5. Can I engage in some mindful practice (Chapter 3)?
6. Can I attach the thoughts that are associated with the strong feelings to some passing clouds and let them go?
7. If I were a coach, what advice would I give to my friend if they were in the same situation?
8. How can I make my coaching advice more compassionate and confident?
9. Can I hold on, focus on what I can control – that is my breathing – and review the situation?
10. Putting on my behaviour hat – is there anything I can do now?
11. Putting on my body hat – is there anything I can do now?

Gaining perspective helps us to reduce negative emotions and gives us more wisdom and confidence.

3. Put your ANTs in the dock

I am a big fan of legal dramas such as *Columbo*, *Law & Order* and *The Good Wife*, particularly when it comes to the courtroom. Now I am going to invite you to take your ANTs to court. To assist in the preparation of the case, you will need a thoughts record. This is one of the most useful tools in CBT for challenging automatic negative thoughts, for arriving at more realistic thoughts and for diffusing strong emotion.

To draw up your thoughts record – essentially the full 'hearing' of the case against your ANTs – you need to get a sheet of paper or a page in your notebook and divide it into eight columns. Now fill it out like this:

Column 1: Situation/trigger
- What happened?
- Who, where, when, what?

Column 2: Emotional and physical responses
- What is the emotion in one word? Rate it from 0 to 100.
- Scan your body. Where do you feel the emotion?

Column 3: Crooked thoughts
- What thoughts are going through your mind?
- Did your thoughts take the form of images or of activated memories?
- Write down the 'hot' thought, i.e., the one that goes to the heart of your feelings.
- What is the worst thing about these thoughts?
- What is the worst thing that could happen?
- If these thoughts were true, what would they say about you?

Column 4: The case for the prosecution
- Evidence that supports the thoughts – what facts support the truthfulness of these thoughts?

Column 5: The case for the defence
- Evidence against the unhelpful thoughts – what evidence indicates that these thoughts are not completely true?
- Go back and ask yourself the twenty powerful questions to squash your ANTs.

Column 6: The judgement
- Alternative, balanced and more realistic thoughts, taking into account the evidence for and against the thoughts.
- For example, what would the view be from the hot-air balloon?
- What advice would you give to your friend if they had these thoughts?

Column 7: Emotional and physical responses at the end of the hearing
- What is the emotion in one word? Rate it from 0 to 100.
- Scan your body. Where do you feel the emotion?

Column 8: Good behaviour
- The recommendation of the court: what can you do that will help you in this situation in the future?
- Are there strategies that you can work on in the areas of assertiveness, mindfulness, deep breathing, etc.? (I will discuss these strategies in later chapters.)

Here's how a thoughts record might look with the first few columns filled in:

Thoughts Record

Situation or trigger	Emotional and physical responses – rate intensity of feeling 0–100	Crooked thoughts, images or memories	The prosecution – evidence that supports the thoughts	The defence – evidence against the thoughts	The judgement – balanced and more realistic thoughts	Emotional and physical responses – rate intensity of feeling again 0–100	Recommendation of the court
My boss asked me to rewrite the report	*Anger (65) Fear (75)*	*He's a bully My job is on the line*					

The more thoughts records you do the better. Most people complete their thoughts records by getting out a page and writing everything down after experiencing a strong emotion. So it's useful to have multiple blank copies of your thoughts records to hand. Keep them in your handbag or pocket, or keep electronic versions on your iPad or smartphone. After a period of consistent use, you won't need to write anything down – you will be able to complete the thoughts records in your mind.

Some of the biggest gains I've seen in therapy were when people adopted this particular strategy and incorporated it into daily life. As soon as they feel upset, they are able to complete thoughts records in their minds in order to diffuse dominant negative emotions.

4. Simply disengage from your negative thoughts

This is about being mindful, which was covered in Chapter 3. Remember, your thoughts are not facts. It may help to view them as passing 'streams of words', or as the different scenes you might see if you were sitting on a train. Your challenge is to observe, rather than to engage with, these thoughts, images or memories.

Use the mindful breathing techniques. Initially you will be distracted, as this is a new skill. Don't get downhearted: remember the more practice you do, the better you will become at using the skills.

5. Tell yourself just how great you are!

Underlying negative thoughts are our core beliefs. Thoughts arising from negative core beliefs can be counteracted by repeating real self positive affirmations and simply letting them 'sit'. I encourage you to choose some and repeat them daily. Then, after a week or so, choose a few more. It's okay if you don't entirely believe them right now. But, as you get closer to your real self, you'll find that the following will resonate with you.

- I am able.
- I am authentic.
- I believe in myself.
- I am strong.
- I am brave.
- I try new things.
- I'm okay being okay.
- I have many good qualities: I am kind, compassionate, caring, funny, considerate, thoughtful, open-minded, easy-going, hard-working, positive, motivated, creative, friendly, flexible, dependable, etc.
- I am smart.
- I am a good and worthwhile person.

- I am a person of value.
- I am a resilient person.
- I have strengths and resources.
- I like myself.
- People like me.
- I am in control of my life.
- I make wise decisions.
- My life has meaning and purpose.
- I am aware of the choices I make.
- I love the person I have become.
- There is space in my life for love.
- I care about others.
- I have determination.
- I am a good helper.
- I am a good listener.
- I am a positive person.
- I am calm.
- I will speak compassionately to myself and others.
- I am healthy.
- I am open to the joy, beauty and harmony of nature.
- I am open to new people and new opportunities that will grow my real self.
- I enjoy growing and developing.
- I love and respect myself.
- I am real.
- I am my real self.

Sometimes we Irish find it hard to do affirmations. It is a part of self-expression that has been squashed over time by powerful others. Despite the Irish saying '*Mol an óige agus tioc-faidh sí*' ('Praise the young and they will bloom'), certainly for those of us who are middle aged and older, praise is not something we commonly heard from authority figures when we were growing up. It did not seem to be part of the philosophy of the majority of the religious who ran our schools. Finding fault was considered the most effective way to form our characters.

So, to do this exercise effectively, I would like you to Think American. That is: don't be afraid to talk yourself up. It's not about showing off; it's just about saying what you are and what you aspire to be.

6

The active side of CBT

Many times in life you know the right thing to do, but you struggle to do it. We are great at giving advice, though we sometimes fail to follow it through. Why? Because life is made up of actions, not words, and actions take more effort. What really helps you to do things is the 'B' (behavioural) part of CBT. This too often gets ignored, because talking (the 'C' – cognitive – aspect of CBT) can be so fascinating. After all, you may be realizing things about yourself for the very first time and that can feel like a result in itself. But, for the therapy fully to be effective, it's necessary for you to focus on your behaviour as well. When it comes to doing things, rather than putting them off, you need tools that work. So, because actions speak louder than words, here are some key strategies that will really help to improve your life, particularly if you have an issue you are finding it hard to resolve. These are the best tools for getting you from knowing what to do to doing it.

Don't wait till you feel like doing something – just do it!

There is one fundamental finding from over 125 years of psychological science: you can act your way into a feeling, but you cannot feel your way into an act.

This means that you can wait and wait for the feeling that you want to do something, but it may never come. Let's say you are waiting to feel like going for a walk or like making that phone call that you have been putting off. The problem is that the feeling may never come – which means that you don't go for a walk or make that phone call. You don't get any of the benefits of the action – fresh air, potential company, being in touch with nature, release of natural endorphins or the resolution of some conflict. Essentially, if you wait around until you feel like doing something, your problems may become more and more entrenched.

However, if you perform the action, even when you don't want to, the positive feelings will come. How many times have you gone on a night out or to the gym when you didn't want to? When you reflect back, you will find more positives than negatives. So, if there is something you need to do – a phone call, a conversation, exercise – don't wait for the feeling, just do it. Don't over-analyse things. The bottom line is: actions create possibilities.

Get up and go

Behavioural activation means increasing your activity levels in order to shift your motivation and mood. Indeed, behavioural activation has been shown to tackle mild to moderate depression on its own. If you are having difficulties with motivation and have lost interest in the things you used to do, you may fall into a vicious cycle in which you do less and less. The idea of getting you up and going is to:

- make you feel better about yourself;
- increase your motivation;

- give you more energy and a healthy appetite;
- help you to think more clearly;
- provide opportunities for pleasurable activities and being with people;
- help you to have achievements, no matter how small;
- shift your thinking to more encouraging thoughts: 'Today I . . .'

In order to get yourself activated, it can be useful to keep a 'Get up and go' log that includes the following steps:

- *Step 1.* At the beginning of the week, plan out a small number of activities for each day that will bring you pleasure, help you to connect with people and give you a sense of achievement.
- *Step 2.* Write down the day on which you aim to achieve them as well as the specific time at which they will take place. Plan one hour a day at first and gradually increase your activity level over a number of weeks.
- *Step 3.* Choose activities that are important to you. Balance pleasurable activities with less enjoyable ones. Build in some rest periods.
- *Step 4.* Set achievable activities. Aim to walk for 10 minutes on each of three days. Mow a section of the garden rather than mowing and weeding the whole garden.
- *Step 5.* Praise yourself on your achievements and give yourself rewards, no matter how small you think they may be.
- *Step 6.* Keep taking small steps. You are aiming to build success, not failure.
- *Step 7.* Maintain your get up and go log so that you can monitor your overall progress.

- *Step 8.* At the end of the week, reflect on your get up and go log. Ask yourself: what went well? What could have been done differently? If something didn't happen, was that because of factors beyond your control? Or did you set too high a target? Did you learn anything? What might you say to a friend who had failed to achieve the same activity?

The golden rule is that if you have scheduled an activity, do it for a first 5 minutes, even if you don't feel like it, and then make a decision on whether to stop. On completing each activity, score your feeling of achievement and pleasure using the following scales:

- *Achievement (A): the sense of achievement you feel.* Score this between 0 and 100, where 0 is 'no sense of achievement' and 100 means 'complete sense of achievement'.
- *Pleasure (P): the amount of pleasure you feel.* Again, score this between 0 and 100, where 0 is 'no sense of pleasure whatsoever' and 100 means 'completely enjoyed doing that'.

Here is a sample log in which someone has completed their activities for Monday and plotted out a few things for the rest of the week:

	Mon.	Tues.	Wed.	Thurs.	Fri.	Sat.	Sun.
10–11	Read paper A = 30 P = 20					Go for swim A = P =	
11–12			Drop in dry cleaning A = P =				
12–1							
1–2		Lunch with Aunt Mary A = P =		Book NCT A = P =			Lunch with Dad A = P =
2–3	Ring Tom A = 45 P = 30				Ring Joan A = P =		
3–4							
4–5							
5–6		Paint front door A = P =					
6–7	Walk 30 min. A = 60 P = 70		Walk 30 min. A = P =		Walk 30 min. A = P =		
7–8							
8–9				Choir practice A = P =		Pizza with the girls A = P =	Make soup to freeze A = P =

You've got to move it

There is significant evidence to support the role of physical exercise in tackling negative states. Three or four 30-minute sessions of sustained physical activity – walking, jogging, running, cycling or swimming – release endorphins, our natural happy or anti-depressant hormones.

I've met many people who have successfully used this strategy on its own to tackle anxiety and depression. On the one hand I applaud and cheer on these efforts. Yet, on the other, I have concerns if the person is using only one strategy. What happens if they are unable to train due to illness or injury? Physical exercise is a critical behavioural strategy; however, you need more than one arrow for your bow. The more strategies you have to tackle negative emotions, the better.

Facing your fears

The most common behaviour associated with fear is avoidance. But avoidance will always keep your problems going. If you imagine your fear to be like a muscle, avoidance exercises your fear-muscle and makes it stronger. Taking avoidance out of your life weakens this muscle, until it no longer has a grip on you.

Avoidance has a number of close cousins: reassurance seeking, safety behaviours, escaping, compulsions and checking behaviours. All these give you a short-term fix in reducing your anxiety. And all of these are fear-muscle enhancers. This short-term fix is like a powerful drug in that it gives temporary relief, causing people to resort to it again and again rather than facing their fears.

What you need are new thinking, breathing and behavioural tools that help you to banish distressing fear and anxiety from your life. Research evidence demonstrates that graded exposure is an essential tool in tackling fears, panic and anxiety. Exposure therapy breaks the vicious cycle that only makes your fear stronger. I know this, I promise you. I have used the tools of graded exposure over many years in many different situations to help individuals overcome phobias: dogs and spiders, fear of flying, many forms of anxiety, agoraphobia, panic attacks, social anxiety.

Here's the thing: when you *face* your fear (of people, places or things) and *remain in* the situation, your fear/anxiety will fall. And here's another law of psychology: the more often you do this, the faster your anxiety will reduce.

The reality is that because you have not stayed in the feared situation, you have not learned that a reduction in anxiety will eventually result. More importantly, the more often you do the opposite of what keeps your fear-muscle strong, the weaker it will become and you will be in control of your life.

There are three aspects to graded exposure: it's gradual (step by step); it's prolonged (a single hour per day); and it's done regularly (one to three times a day). In later chapters – on fear, anxiety, panic attacks and social anxiety – I will discuss graded exposure approaches specific to those issues. But here I'm going to outline the key steps you can use to work on your fears.

Step 1. Measure your anxiety

Write a list of all the things that make you anxious or that you try to avoid or to escape from. Include situations that you think will cause you to panic or that you will confront only if using a 'safety behaviour' (e.g., being with someone else). Rate the level of anxiety from 0 to 100, where 100 is the most anxious you have ever felt and 0 is the most relaxed you have ever felt.

In order to make this more concrete, I'm going to use the example of Sharon. Sharon is thirty-four and the mother of two young children, aged four and six. She has agoraphobia and fear dominates her life. She gets panic attacks and is frightened to go out, in case she loses control. Before Sharon had her children, she was independent and fun-loving, but now her life has gone small.

Sharon's list	Predicted anxiety
Travelling on a plane	95
Travelling on a train	60
Taking on responsibilities	80
Minding other people's children	75
Taking a long walk in the woods	70
Visiting my mother	35
Going on a bus	65
Going to a local shop	45
Taking the children to school	40
Going to the cinema	55
Going to church	50
Going to a busy shopping centre	80

Step 2. Build a ladder of freedom and success

Once you have completed this list, rearrange the items into your own unique ladder of freedom and success, with the most anxiety-provoking item at the top and the least anxiety-provoking item at the bottom. This is Sharon's.

Travelling on a plane
Going to a busy shopping centre
Taking on responsibilities
Minding other people's children
Taking a long walk in the woods
Going on a bus
Travelling on a train
Going to the cinema
Going to church
Going to a local shop
Taking the children to school
Visiting my mother

Step 3. Take the first steps on your ladder of freedom and success

Now that you have completed your list from high to low, start by confronting the first item as soon as possible.

- Expect your anxiety to rise when you face your fear. This is normal.
- Breathe deeply. Breathe in through your open mouth for 5 seconds. Bring your breath right down into your stomach if you can. Hold for 5 seconds. Slowly release your breath through your mouth for 5 seconds (see the last section in this chapter for a little more information on abdominal breathing).
- Tell yourself that you are facing your fear, that you no longer accept fear as part of your life, that you are going to weaken this fear-muscle by facing your fears, that you are brave and you are going to live a life free of fear.
- Expect your anxiety to fall the longer you stay in the situation.
- Score your anxiety from 0 to 100 during the task.
- Stay in the situation until your anxiety reduces by at least half. For example, if your anxiety rises to 50 during an exposure task, you should remain in the situation until it reduces to 25 or (preferably) less. The amount of time this takes will probably vary from task to task. It may take anywhere from 30 to 45 minutes, but commonly happens more quickly.
- Remind yourself that the symptoms you are experiencing are the result of the 'fight/flight/freeze' adrenaline hormone that is being released. Remind yourself that your abdominal breathing exercise will reduce the adrenaline flow and give you control.

- Remind yourself that, even though you may feel unpleasant, there is no danger, and these feelings will gradually pass if you remain in the situation.
- Tell yourself: 'I can do this. I deserve a life free from fear, and I will have that life.'

Step 4. Repeat – and keep repeating!

Now that you have completed the exposure task once, the next step is to do it again. Repetition is the key. Confronting your fears over and over again weakens your fear-muscle and strengthens your muscles of success and control. You will find that each time you confront an item on your list, it will become easier. Ideally, you need to confront your fears daily. The bottom line is that the more frequently you expose yourself to an item on your ladder, the more quickly you will overcome your fear of it.

Step 5. Move up the ladder

Now that you have overcome the first rung of your ladder, you need to follow the same steps as you mount higher. With frequent practice and exposure, your confidence will grow.

You only need focus on the particular rung that you are on at that moment. Don't get overwhelmed by what's at the top of the ladder. You are doing this step by step.

If you are struggling on a particular task, build in an extra step. For example, you might try to do a task with a trusted friend in the first instance. I have often done therapy with clients – sitting in cars, buses, bars, football stadia, going to the airport, getting on planes, walking through towns – when someone believed they were going to have a panic attack as they confronted their fears. Afterwards, I asked the person to do the task themselves. And they did!

In Step 3, I mentioned deep breathing. That's because your body is a big ally when it comes to dealing with negative emotions. Taking control by teaching your body to slow down, calm down and relax is key.

Abdominal, or deep, breathing is the first and most important body strategy. It is a powerful antidote to panic, counteracts the 'fight/flight/freeze' response, puts you in control and centres you.

Start by putting one hand on your stomach. Put the other hand on your chest. Breathe deeply from the abdomen through an open mouth for 5 seconds; hold for 5 seconds; and breathe out, again through the open mouth, for 5 seconds. When you breathe in, your stomach should rise and your chest should move very little. Most people struggle to get their breaths down to the abdomen, so this takes practice. Repeat for 10 minutes.

Having a relaxation tool in your back pocket can help you to tackle stress, anxiety, worry, panic and fears. There are all kinds of helpful techniques that you can find online or in your local gym – everything from tai chi to yoga to mindful meditation to progressive muscle relaxation. I talk about some of these in Chapter 7. There really is something for everyone. And the more you practise it, the more likely it is to be there for you when you really need it.

PART THREE

· ·

Taking on life's challenges

Life presents us with an array of positive and negative emotions. When things are going well, we ride the wave of positive emotion and feel energized and motivated. But when we experience stress, loss, sadness, anger, fear, worry, low confidence or low self-esteem, we can struggle to see beyond them; we can feel stuck in a place where there is no movement, no light, no joy. Your problems may seem to have no solutions, but there are proven techniques to solve even the toughest challenges. This part of the book is all about giving you the means to get your life moving again. You can use these powerful tools immediately, so jump in!

CHALLENGE ONE

Stress

7

The high cost of chronic stress – and how to manage it

You might be surprised to learn that we all need a bit of stress to get out of bed in the morning. It helps us to perform under pressure and motivates us to do our best. We need stress for creativity, learning and our very survival. However, throw some high-stress events – such as relationship difficulties, illness, bereavement, unemployment – into life's mix and we can end up with seriously unbalanced amounts of it. It's a bit like being in your car with your foot fully down on the accelerator without being in gear. What is the cost to your physical and emotional health? How long can you last like that? How does this prevent you from becoming your real self?

Too often people try to cope with stress in ways that make the problem worse. It's easy to turn to drink to unwind at the end of the day, fill up on rubbishy comfort food, space out in front of a screen of your choice, or use drink or drugs (prescribed or not) to relax. When it comes to tackling any emotional difficulty, I truly believe that the more information you possess about that difficulty, the closer you are to overcoming it – and it's the same for controlling stress. So let's ask some key questions.

What is stress – and when does it become toxic?

Stress is a feeling that we get when struggling to cope with the pressures of life. When under stress (real or imagined) our body responds by producing two powerful hormones: adrenaline and cortisol. The body doesn't distinguish between physical and psychological threats. So whether it's having an argument with a friend or being late for an important appointment, your body reacts almost as strongly as if you were facing a life or death situation. These hormones are the body's alarm call or emergency response. The heart pounds faster, muscles tighten, blood pressure rises, breath quickens and senses become sharper. This protective response, as I've mentioned earlier, is often called the 'fight/flight/freeze' response. It can work in your favour – if you are in an interview, for example, it can sharpen your senses and make you rise to the challenge.

When the stress response and the attendant hormone presence are persistent, chronic and long term, the situation is toxic. Stress then starts to cause harm to our health, mood, productivity, relationships and quality of life. Extensive exposure to stress can lead to serious health problems. Chronic stress impacts on nearly every system in your body. It can cause high blood pressure, suppress the immune system, increase the life risk of heart attack, stroke and cancer, contribute to infertility and leave you more vulnerable to anxiety and depression. It can also cause ulcers, migraines and insomnia. There's nothing good to say about chronic stress!

Where does my stress come from and what keeps it going?

It's important to figure out where your stress is coming from. For some, stress can be associated with factors outside of their control, e.g., illness in the family, bereavement, divorce. On the other hand, stress may also come from how we think (poor self-esteem, pessimism, chronic worry, etc.), what we do or how we react to people, situations or places. This is the kind of stress that is within your control!

How many times have you avoided situations that need to be tackled – asserting yourself to family, boss, co-workers, friends, husband, wife, partner and children? How many times have you said 'Okay, I'll do it' when you really want to say no? Have you put off a visit to the GP about a health worry because you can't be bothered/don't want to know? The health worry won't go away, you know.

Too often we allow stress to creep up on us, and many of us get so used to it that it becomes our 'normal'. It can be hard to identify which bit of our 'normal' – the way we feel physically or the way we think about things – is actually a response to stress rather than a part of our real self. Many people experience physical symptoms that signal the onset of stress. For example, when I'm stressed my shoulder muscles tense up. This is my body signal that something is wrong and I need to address things. It means I've taken on too much or that I need to have a difficult conversation with someone.

Tackling stress

You need strategies to tackle stress, but if you don't put real work and commitment into each one, they won't work. We will go through four key approaches here: changing the situation, changing how you think about the situation, increasing your coping strategies, building resilience.

Approach 1. Changing the situation

Completely changing your situation can be either the weakest or the strongest of solutions. Let's consider David, who moved from Germany to Ireland eight years ago. He described his situation to me: 'I was unhappy in Germany, I was working all the time. I had little fun in my life, my relationships were unfulfilling, I was disillusioned and stressed out. I thought a move to Ireland would be the thing, Irish people seem to have a better understanding of how to balance work and play.'

Now David sees himself as stressed, frustrated and irritated, working long days with a long commute. Same stress, different country. Changing countries without changing 'thinking and doing' responses is a weak strategy. For David, his old style – lack of flexibility, poor assertiveness and a dominant work ethic – caught up with him.

On the other hand, Michelle shows us how this approach can work. She had been living with chronic stress for fifteen years, because she had been married to an abusive man. She was constantly on high alert, trying to assess his mood and worrying that he might harm the children. She felt lonely and isolated, and found it difficult to make sense of what was happening. Her shame prevented her from talking to close family and friends about what was happening to her. She needed to change the situation.

Michelle came to see me, and together we developed a strategy – her 'real self strategy' – which involved the following steps:

- Understand the situation and what keeps the situation going.
- Start to take control step by step.
- Develop a safety plan and an exit plan.
- Build up a network of support – connect with a women's refuge.
- Use CBT thought tools to tackle negative emotions – fear, stress, sadness.
- Use mindfulness and breathing tools to reduce stress.
- Picture my future as a strong woman, with my children and on my own.
- Speak to myself with compassion and wisdom rather than beating myself up for the choices I made.
- Focus on my strengths, resilience and resources.
- Exit the situation.
- Do not return to the situation.
- Live my life as my real self.

After about five months of preparation and planning, Michelle left. Three years later, although struggling as a lone parent with three children, she is confident, pursuing her dreams, energized, contented and relaxed. For Michelle, changing the situation was the best solution, because she was *ready to change everything*.

Approach 2. Changing how you think about the situation

Although this strategy takes the most work, it is the most rewarding one. When you change your thoughts, you change your world. It is rooted in the ideas of mindfulness and cognitive behavioural therapy that I described in Part Two. Changing how you think (cognition) and what you do (behaviour) will help you to reduce stress significantly.

Here is a story that shows how approaching how you think about a situation can have a powerful impact. Robert and Kathleen, a garda and a nurse, were suffering the triple whammy of mortgages taken out at the height of the boom, dependant children and long commutes to work. They were trying to cope with a mountain of stress that was threatening their well-being and relationship. When they first came to me, they looked totally worn out:

'We thought we were securing our future,' Kathleen said. 'We didn't have children yet, but we were planning to, so we thought we would try to organize something for their educational needs and our retirement. I had a house which I sold and made a few quid. We put it straight back into deposits. The rents were going up, the values were going up, the bank manager was supportive, and we decided to invest. We ended up with two properties in Longford. Imagine two! I got caught up in it, Robert did as well. Now, it's like a ball and chain. We have three kids now – they're three, four and six. We are in negative equity. The rents don't cover the two mortgages. Our wages have shrunk by 20%. We are stuck in an extremely small house, and we're driving each other nuts and always arguing. We haven't had a night out in the past year.'

Robert jumped in: 'I can't think straight. My concentration is fecked, I go to bed at night, turn my back to Kathleen and lie awake trying to think of a way out of this hellhole. I blame myself. We've been thinking of going to Australia, but my mother is sick and Dad is frail. Kathleen says she would be heartbroken – her sister is her best friend and she loves her nieces and nephews.'

We were able to apply various CBT and other helpful techniques to Kathleen and Robert's situation. The challenge was for Robert and Kathleen to apply these tools to their high stress and to reduce it.

Putting on the CBT behaviour hat. Actions create new feelings. Instead of being in the frozen stress response, as they had been in the past, Robert and Kathleen decided to get some advice from the advocacy group New Beginnings. They armed themselves with information. They developed a plan, and with some professional support they put this plan into place.

Putting on the CBT thoughts hat. New ways of thinking gave Kathleen and Robert new perspectives on the problem and started to shift their stress. They were able to take a long-term view of this debt. They did not have to eat the elephant all in one bite; instead, they were going to eat it bite by bite.

Putting on the CBT body hat. Robert and Kathleen looked at the impact of the stress on their bodies over the past two years. This included an increased number of visits to the GP by Kathleen for irritable bowel syndrome and a health scare for Robert, which was initially thought to be a heart problem but turned out to be a one-off panic attack. Both committed to improving their physical health as a way of tackling the physical impact of stress.

Mindfulness. The future was a place of great fear and apprehension. Kathleen learned to be in the present: to accept that currently they could only control what they could control. Robert got the idea but struggled to put it into practice.

On top of everything, there was a blame game going on between Kathleen and Robert that was contributing to their stress. Kathleen was blaming Robert for their situation. But both had signed off on the loans, and the debt was equally shared. They accepted that each had had good intentions when it came to securing their family's future, but that circumstances had gone against them. Underlying Kathleen's resentment was a desire to reduce her working hours so that she could spend more time with her children, and her belief that this was impossible because of their financial situation. So, instead of saying this openly, she took out her frustration on Robert. When they discussed this directly and examined the numbers calmly, they discovered there was scope for Kathleen to reduce her working hours by 25% because Robert could get overtime. They agreed to do this, and it brought them both great relief. They also started to discuss their financial situation and the stress they had been under with their families. The result was that they gained additional supports, both emotional and financial.

You can see that no one thing shifted the stress. Rather, it was displaced by a number of different strategies. What was most important was that they were now focused on working together as a couple. This strengthening of the relationship was what Robert and Kathleen said was the most significant element in the reduction of their stress. But be aware that it's not a happy-ever-after story: life is not like that. But things are a lot better than they were, and Robert and Kathleen can see light at the end of the tunnel.

Approach 3. Increasing your coping strategies

Unfortunately, there are some stressful situations, such as bereavement, chronic illness, cancer or chronic pain, that are not going anywhere soon. These are situations that we need to learn to live with. Rather than sinking under the weight of worry, you need to work on coping strategies.

It's only when you look after yourself that you can be available to others. It's not selfish to look after yourself; it makes perfect sense. To build a stronger you, you must seek to promote healthy changes in your lifestyle. Here are just a few coping pointers to consider.

- Ease off the alcohol. It will interfere with your mood, affect the quality of your sleep and only add fuel to emotions such as low mood, anger and anxiety. There is a strong link between alcohol and panic attacks of which many people are unaware. So ease off the drink.
- Avoid excessive caffeine intake, sedatives or other drugs, and cigarettes – none of these will aid your coping strategies.
- Build up your physical health and strength.
- Nourish your body with nutritious food.
- Get a good night's sleep.
- Go for a good walk, swim, dance or cycle.
- Build a consistent routine to give you structure.
- Work on your surroundings: tidy spaces promote calmness.

- Develop and maintain positive relationships with your family.
- Be open and talk to your trusted friends about your difficulties.

Chronic stress drains your energy levels. Increasing your coping strategies recharges your battery and acts as a protector against the harmful aspects of stress. Once you think about it, you'll see that there is an amazing array of things that you can do – for free and without too much effort – that will build up your strength and protect you against the worst aspects of stress. Look at them as psychological vitamins. I've come up with an A to Z here, but you can add your own. Please select at least five from the list below every day. Psychological vitamins can be taken liberally!

A **Acceptance.** Accept that change is a part of living. Accepting circumstances that cannot be changed can help you to focus on circumstances that you can alter.

Action. Do what you are avoiding. Avoiding situations keeps stress going.

Appreciation. Appreciate yourself, family, friends, health, sight, hearing, mind, nature, pets, laughter, music, love.

Ask. Ask for help and support.

Assertiveness. Learn to ask for what you want in a confident way; learn to say no.

Awareness. Become aware of your body signals. Becoming aware is about bringing your attention to what you are doing at any given moment in the present. When we are unaware and mindless, we are disconnected from ourselves, family and friends.

B   **Belief.** Believe you can do it, believe you deserve it – don't let your beliefs limit you.

Blessings. Count your blessings, not your problems.

C   **Care.** Remember each day to do something that involves caring for yourself.

Commitment. Make a personal commitment to yourself for a healthier future. Write down specifically what this healthier journey means to you and your loved ones. Sign the bottom of the paper. In effect, you have made a binding contract with yourself and with your loved ones.

Connect. Connect with family, friends and your community.

Courage. Use your courage to get over your fear and avoidance behaviours. Courage is like a muscle: the more you use it, the stronger it gets.

Curiosity. Remain curious and keep learning. Look for opportunities for self-discovery. People often learn something about themselves and may find that they have grown in some respect as a result of their struggles. Many people who have experienced tragedies and hardship have reported better relationships, a greater sense of strength (even while feeling vulnerable), an increased sense of self-worth, a more developed spirituality and a heightened appreciation of life.

D   **Deal with it, delegate it or dump it.**

Determination. This is about keeping going, even when times get tough. If you slip, it's okay: refocus by doing one simple step to put you back on your pathway.

Dream. If you can dream it, you can do it. Dream it, believe it, achieve it.

E   **Encourage.** Become your own best coach – encourage and support all your efforts by building hope and confidence.

Exercise. Walk, swim, jog, cycle, run, play tennis, dance, play football, play golf.

F   **Fairness.** Do what is right and have a sense of justice. Remember what it feels like when something is unfair to you.

Faith. The power of faith can offer help, support and sustenance during times of need.

Forgiveness. Not something we do for others, but something we do for ourselves to get well and to move on.

Future. Visualize your future as full of hope, courage and authenticity – a future in which you are your real self.

G   **Goals.** Move towards your goals. Develop some realistic ones. Do something regularly – even if it seems like something small – that enables you to move towards your goals. Instead of focusing on tasks that seem unachievable, ask yourself, 'What's one thing I know I can accomplish today that helps me to move in the direction I want to go?'

Gratitude. There is always something to be thankful for. Learn to practise gratitude. When you become grateful for small pleasures, your outlook changes and opportunities emerge in many areas of your life.

H   **Hope.** Maintain a hopeful outlook. An optimistic outlook enables you to expect that good things will happen in your life. Try visualizing what you want, rather than worrying about what you fear.

Humanity. Be good to others.

Humility. Humility is a strength. It is a form of self-respect to admit mistakes and to make amends for them.

Humour. Laughter is the best medicine.

I **Imperfection.** It's okay, it's real, to be imperfect. Don't seek perfection. Don't let perfection become the enemy of the good. Most people who are perfect are unhappy.

Integrity. Choose your thoughts and actions based on your values – and choose wisely.

J **Justice.** Be fair to others.

K **Kindness.** No act of kindness is wasted; as Mark Twain said, 'Kindness is a language which the dead can hear and the blind can see.'

L **Leadership.** Show leadership in the different areas of your life: physical, social, emotional, spiritual, learning, home and love.

Learn. Never stop learning, because there are always lessons in life. Start a new course. Try something out of your comfort zone. Learn to dance.

Love. Love is patient, love is kind, love always protects, love always trusts, love never ends.

M **Meaning.** Find meaning beyond the material world.

Meditate. Quiet the mind and the soul will speak. Invest time and learn to meditate – it's a great stress buster.

Mindfulness. Breathe, savour the moment.

N **Nutrition.** Take care of your body – it's the only place you live in.

O **Openness.** Be open and travel light. Live an open life and allow in new opportunities.

P **Passion.** Passion is energy. Feel the power that comes from your passions. Go and find new passions.

Persistence. Stick at it, even when you don't want to. Dreams happen when your actions are greater than your excuses.

Perspective. Keep things in perspective. Even when facing very painful events, try to consider the stressful situation in a broader context and keep a long-term perspective. Avoid blowing the event out of proportion.

Play. Go out and play. The body heals with play and the mind heals with laughter.

Pleasure. Healthier lifestyles require pleasure. List the pleasures in all aspects of your life – people, the sea, Dingle, music, movies, studying, singing, walking, swimming, dancing, gardening, talking, pets, etc. Are you getting enough pleasure in your life? Go on a pleasure diet. Enjoy these activities, and when it comes to food don't eat or drink anything that drains your pleasure.

Pray. Prayer soothes the soul and eases the mind. Happy are those who have prayer.

Q **Quality.** The happiness of your life is linked to the quality of your thoughts.

Quiet. Take time to be quiet. You will find it interesting to see what emerges.

R **Real.** No more putting energy into false fronts. Put your energies into being authentic, contented, grounded, happy and real.

Relationships. Grow, nurture and sustain your relationships.

Relaxation. Learn the skills of relaxation. Take time out. Relaxation is the opposite of tension. Sometimes you need to take a moment, stop, relax, breathe, and focus on something that is beautiful.

S **Self-control.** With self-discipline you can achieve almost anything.
Social. Remember we are social animals: get out there and enjoy connecting.
Spirituality. Find a space in your life for something bigger than you.

T **Talk.** Talk it over. Confiding in someone you trust and who will listen and be supportive is a great way of reducing stress and worry.
Time. Learn to take time out for yourself.

U **Unconditional.** There are no measurements in the unconditional. Give freely, love freely.

V **View.** Nurture a positive view of yourself. Developing confidence in your ability to solve problems and trusting your instincts helps to build resilience.
Volunteer. Give and you will receive.

W **Water.** Drink two litres a day.
Wisdom. Ask yourself: what are the important things in my life? Build your answer to this question with wisdom and courage.

X **XXX.** Sex is a great stress buster – with yourself or others!

Y **Yoga.** Learn yoga, one of the best relaxation exercises.

Z **Zzzzz ...** Sleep and rest are essential stress busters.

Approach 4. Building resilience

Sometimes letting go of the 'illusion of control', of how things 'should be', and meeting difficult circumstances with resilience, is an approach that can help us to tackle stress. Resilience can be described as our ability to bounce back from adversity. Being resilient means being flexible, adapting to new situations quickly and thriving in an atmosphere of constant change.

While the previous three approaches – changing the situation, changing how you think about the situation and increasing your coping strategies – are techniques to practise *in the face* of stress, building resilience is something you do *in advance* of potential stress. It's simply a good thing to do for better mental health. It will help you to prevent self-generated stress and will be hugely beneficial if you are confronting either foreseen or unforeseen events that may cause you major stress.

Developing resilience is a personal journey. People do not react in the same way to the same stressful life events. An approach to building resilience that works for one person may not work for another. Imagine that resilience is like a muscle – here are some strategies to strengthen it.

Be optimistic. Can you imagine wearing glasses that actively select optimism? Just as a person has physical fitness, so too there is mental fitness. How often do you train your brain!

Give back. Do you have the energy and the heart to help others? There are lots of opportunities for volunteering. Check www.volunteer.ie, where you will find opportunities to volunteer in areas that may interest you – from social justice to animal charities.

Be spiritual. Faith, prayer and spirituality play an incredible role in some people's emotional life. There is massive research to show that all of these act as important stress buffers. Many of us have latent beliefs that could be activated. This can afford you another avenue for growth and exploration.

Live a life with meaning and passion. Sometimes we need to move beyond our own personal world. Individualism only leads to alienation and narrow interests. Get beyond yourself: find meaning and passions and fill your life with them. I think of Penny, a woman who experienced depression. Having lost many family members through cancer, she wanted to raise money for hospice services. She has swum, walked, run, climbed mountains and had her hair shaved. Her life is full of meaning and passion, and her depression is now at bay.

Laugh at yourself. How much can you laugh at yourself? Laughing at yourself when you do something foolish can release negative emotions. Humour can help to pull many through the most horrendous traumas.

Find role models. We all need wise people in our lives – people we can look up to and from whom we can get advice. Real people who are their real selves. Can you think of anyone? Look around – they are often closer than you think! Sometimes you can also pick 'parts' of people to emulate – someone's assertiveness, another's sensitivity, another's capacity to slow down and take in the big picture.

Get out of your comfort zone. We need to challenge and to stretch ourselves; otherwise our world only gets smaller. I know people who have had a lifetime full of money and yet won't spend any on themselves – generous, thoughtful people who won't go on a holiday, who number their successful days by how little they have spent, who won't go out for a meal. Why? You only live once.

Adopt new approaches to challenges and setbacks. Rather than seeing setbacks as failure, or challenges as stressful, ask your-self these questions. What is the best thing I can do here? What options have I got? Is there anything I can learn from the situation? When you adopt the stance of a learner, your questions promote acceptance and empower your undertak-ing of new actions.

Nurture friendships and relationships. Having a network of friends or family provides us with social support that is incredibly important for both happy occasions and challen-ging times. It is true a problem shared is a problem halved. It breaks down the isolation, opens up new opportunities and lets us know that we are not alone.

Take control. Nobody is responsible for your life except you. Take control. By believing that you have some control, your confidence will shift in the right direction. This means taking control of all parts of your life, particularly your phys-ical and emotional health. Tackle things straight on. Don't procrastinate. Don't ignore or wish away your problems. Just do things today. When we shift the stuff that occupies our mind, we are more at ease and can more easily move on to new demands.

The importance of relaxation

Now that you've learned the four approaches to tackling stress, we need to talk about a very important stress buster that may seem obvious but is easier said than done! Relax-ation is the opposite of stress. It is that state when low tension and a sense of calmness prevail. There are different types of relaxation techniques; your challenge is to find the one that works best for you. Remember relaxation is not crashing out on the couch or sleeping – it's an *active* process in which the body learns to relax and be calm. Like any skill, it takes practice, at least 15 minutes a day. Here are some techniques.

Abdominal deep breathing. This was described in Part Two. But it bears repeating, because it's such a useful technique, one of the most powerful tools available to calm the fight/flight/freeze – i.e., stress – response. Start by putting one hand on your stomach (which rises) and the other on your chest (which will move very little). Most people struggle to get their breaths down to the abdomen; that's why it takes practice. Breathe deeply from the abdomen through an open mouth for 5 seconds, hold for 5 seconds; and breathe out, again through the open mouth, for 5 seconds. Repeat for 10 minutes.

Progressive muscle relaxation. Progressive muscle relaxation (PMR) involves the tensing and relaxing of different muscle groups in the body. PMR allows you to tune into your body's tension and relaxation states. You need to consult with your doctor if you have a history of muscle or back problems before practising PMR. There are lots of online PMR exercises, including some on my website.

Body scan. A body scan is similar to PMR, but instead of tensing and relaxing muscles, you simply focus on the sensations in each part of your body. Awareness is not judging your body and all its aches, pains and tensions, but simply noticing and bringing your attention to your body with awareness to release any stress, tension or illness. There are many variations of body scan meditation involving specific breathing techniques and points of focus. Again, you will find a lot of resources online, including on my website.

Yoga. Yoga combines deep breathing with both moving and stationary poses. You can do it at any age. Its usefulness in reducing anxiety and stress has been well demonstrated. The upside of yoga is that it also improves flexibility, strength, balance and stamina. From the stress point of view, yoga strengthens your relaxation response, the opposite of being stressed.

Tai chi. Some men struggle to get their heads around going to yoga. If so, tai chi is a good alternative. Tai chi improves general and psychological health. It consists of a series of slow, flowing body movements, involving concentration, relaxation and the conscious circulation of vital energy throughout the body. It calms the mind, conditions the body and reduces stress. It's a form of movement meditation with the focus on breathing and keeping your attention in the present moment.

Mindfulness. As previously discussed, mindfulness means being present in the moment, and not in the past. It can be applied to activities such as walking, exercising, eating or meditation.

Visualization. This relaxation technique involves leaving your stress and worries behind and going on a journey of discovery, where you will let go of anxiety and tension. People choose different places to go when they visualize: a safe place, such as their grandmother's kitchen; the couch at home; a lake; the beach; or somewhere in the imagination, such as a tropical island or a snow-capped mountain. Think about a place where you feel relaxed and secure. What do you see? What do you smell? What do you hear? What do you feel?

How you react to stress may influence the relaxation technique that works best for you.

How you react to stress	Relaxation technique
If you get angry, agitated or have muscle tension, go for →	relaxation that calms you down: meditation, deep breathing or visualization
If on the surface you seem calm, but underneath you're struggling, go for →	relaxation such as yoga or mindfulness, walking
If you have low mood and you become withdrawn or depressed, go for →	relaxation that involves movement, such as walking, gardening or tai chi
If you need time by yourself, go for →	relaxation that provides peace and quiet: meditation or PMR
If you need the company of people, go for →	relaxation in a class setting: guided mindfulness

Now that you have learned various relaxation techniques, the trick is to build them into your daily life. Consider getting up 10 to 15 minutes earlier to start. There will be ups and downs. That's okay: it's to be expected. Be compassionate with yourself.

8

Coping with stress when you're a carer

One of the greatest sources of stress in many people's lives is taking on caring responsibilities beyond the routine caring that many of us do either as parents or as adult children. For most of us, raising our children and helping out our parents as they get older is part of the cycle of life, and though sometimes these responsibilities present tough challenges, we have signed up for them and willingly accept them. The demands these roles make are somewhat balanced by the pleasures we get out of the relationships.

However, when your caring responsibilities go beyond the routine, and become the one and only issue around which you and your family live your lives, you can be tipped into a hugely stressful situation. Let's say a member of your family has special needs of some sort. Or an elderly parent or relative has a long-term degenerative condition and you are the one with the responsibility for supporting them and providing ongoing care. Or a partner or adult child has an emotional or mental health crisis. These are all common situations where compassion and decency – or simply familial expectation or a sense of obligation – demand that many of us commit to being carers.

Lauren is sixty years old, married, with three adult children. She looks after her husband, Ross, who has MS. One son, Pat (twenty-five), lives at home and has mental health issues. Her daughter Susan is twenty-four and lives and works in Australia. Her other son, Roy, is thirty and is married but having difficulties in his marriage.

'I can't sleep, because I am constantly anxious and worried all the time. I feel like a failure as a mother and a wife. I get up in the morning and look after my husband. I get him dressed, washed and cleaned, and I make his breakfast. Then I make sure he has taken all his medication. I bring him downstairs to watch TV for the day.

'I constantly worry about my children, even though they are adults and have lives of their own. My son Pat suffers with depression and panic attacks, and spends a lot of time in his room. I check in on him every morning and worry that he doesn't take his medication. To be honest, I'm also checking to see if he is alive and has not killed himself. And when he goes out, I also worry, thinking up horrible worst-case scenarios. I worry a lot about Susan and how she's getting on in Australia; I miss her terribly. She was a great support to me.

'I have no one to talk to. My GP has prescribed sleeping tablets, but they make me feel exhausted every morning when I get up. I used to go to bingo every Friday night, the only enjoyment I had in my life, but I've had to give it up, as I don't have the energy to go.'

Lauren is one of many unpaid, unsupported carers. Caring is damned hard work, and often there is little recognition or reward. Trying to mind someone with sustained care needs without adequate support takes a massive toll.

All of the techniques in the last chapter are important here. Changing how you think about a situation and improving your coping strategies will be helpful with circumstances that cannot be changed. For instance, Avril was the only one of her four sisters left at home on the farm with her father, because she did not have a partner or children. Her father was suffering from advanced Alzheimer's. The unspoken deal was: 'If you mind Dad, you get the farm when he dies.' This 'deal' was suffocating Avril. She was experiencing chronic stress, and her mood was slipping down fast into depression and anxiety. Nobody in the family seemed to notice her stress, and by assuming the 'martyr' role she was not doing herself any favours.

Avril and I worked together using CBT techniques on the basis that if she could change her thinking about her situation (cognition) and what she did within it (behaviour), her stress would be significantly reduced. And it was.

Avril called a family meeting, suggesting that a rota should be drawn up so that care could be shared among them all. The family agreed a workable rota. Each member of the family would contribute €50 per week for the additional costs associated with their father's care. Avril addressed the inheritance issue straight on. She said she had no desire to live an isolated existence on the farm. So they all agreed that the costs and burdens of care would be more equitably shared among them, with the proceeds from the sale of the property also shared on a more equitable basis after their father passed on. This new situation provided Avril with the funds she needed to buy in some respite care and to take well-earned weekend breaks with her walking group. Caring was still hard. But the prospect of burn-out had receded, and neither Avril nor her sisters felt any sense of resentment.

The new situation also enabled Avril to become more emotionally available to her father. Prior to this, she was bitter and resentful. Relationships in the family were no longer strained; Avril's default model – 'If I don't ask, I won't have to deal with a refusal' – changed to one that was much more supportive.

Smart caring for yourself when caring for someone with emotional or mental health difficulties

Supporting somebody with emotional or mental health difficulties is enormously challenging. Even though low mood, depression, stress and anxiety are invisible, they have the power to overwhelm not only the sufferers but also those closest to them. For the carer, it can be exasperating, tiring, irritating, annoying . . . If you are a carer in such a situation, it may be frustrating to be told that your actions may in fact be contributing to your loved one's problems and causing you incredible stress. In order to mind both yourself and your loved one, you need to use the tools of smart caring.

Get support for yourself. In order to look after somebody else, you need to be able to look after yourself. This means eating well, sleeping, exercising and getting support. You're not betraying your loved one by turning to others for support. Look around you and get support from family and friends, or join a support group. It's okay if you decide to see a counsellor to get professional support. Sometimes this can help you to get perspective and allow you to set healthy boundaries.

Accept that you can't 'fix' somebody else's mental health difficulties. Many times we want to be a rescuer, but mental health difficulties are a problem that cannot be fixed for someone else. It's not up to you. You are not to blame for this difficulty. You are not responsible for your loved one's unhappiness or happiness. Ultimately, recovery is a choice for that individual.

Don't be an enabler. Enabling is often linked to the area of alcohol addiction. Some examples of enabling an alcoholic: you make it okay for them to drink; you avoid saying that drinking is the real source of their problem; and you may tolerate their treating you badly. Similarly, there are times when, as a carer, we enable out of love and concern, making excuses for our loved ones with mental health difficulties or taking responsibility for their actions in order to protect them. But often the problem is sustained by our enabling of it. People enable because confronting a problem may often produce an unpredictable or uncomfortable outcome.

Don't do something just for a 'quiet life'. How many times do you suppress your own wants and feelings just to have a quiet life? I believe that the cost of this is the slow suffocation of your real self. If you cannot express yourself, you are channelling your power, energy and vitality into something that is negative. Most often the outcome in these situations, if you do not change your behaviour early, is that you will become emotionally or physically sick.

Valerie has OCD. She fears being contaminated by germs. She has a particularly rigid cleaning routine. Bill, in order to keep the peace, completely follows her rigid routine. Bill has developed a stress ulcer. He minimizes his situation.

'It's not so bad. I know it's been like this for ten years, but she has begun new medication. I think things will get better. I'm now doing more and more tasks, in addition to working – shopping, visiting family, etc. I keep making excuses about why she can't go anywhere. I'm finding it harder and harder to confront her: I just want a quiet life. Yet, inside, I am burning up with anger. If I spill something, I have to get out bleach and wipe clean the area. I can't stand it when she becomes angry with me.'

You may be reluctant to speak truthfully to a depressed person in your life. However, communication will help the relationship in the long run. If you suppress what you need to say and suffer in silence, your resentment will only build. Be honest and sensitive. I will talk more about the high cost of a quiet life in the next chapter.

Don't take on someone else's responsibilities. In every family there is somebody who puts their arms out and takes responsibility for everything. Are you this person? Do you take on responsibilities that are not yours? How does this make you feel? Does this empower you or does this overwhelm you? It's the same when it comes to mental health difficulties. This is a really hard message. But you cannot live somebody else's life. Their choices about how to manage their mental health difficulties are their choices. Your duty to the person is to support them and encourage them to tackle their problems. If they choose not to do so, it isn't up to you to resolve this for them. I know this is hard, particularly for parents caring for their children. Parents face a dilemma, especially when they have concerns about suicide. Sometimes they are afraid to convey firm adult messages, because they fear they may trigger self-harm or worse. As hard as this may sound, at times the best thing you can do is to deliver a firm adult message in a supportive context.

Have healthy boundaries. When you are supporting somebody with mental health difficulties, you need to tread a fine line between not taking on the problem yourself and creating so much distance that the person feels as if they are coping on their own. Honest conversations, in which you express your feelings rather than suppress them, are key to maintaining healthy boundaries. If you find this a struggle, you need to develop your assertiveness skills (see Chapter

19). Assertiveness is a win-win for both parties. If healthy boundaries are not developed and maintained, open tension or suppressed stress will be the result.

It's important to set clear limits of what you are willing and able to do. You are not your loved one's doctor or therapist, so don't take on that responsibility. This is important, because your health will suffer if you let your life be controlled by your loved one's depression. It's impossible to be on the clock 24 hours every day. The cost of this is a life of sadness and misery.

Smart caring for a person with anxiety

Sharing your life with somebody with anxiety (that can be someone who suffers from generalized anxiety or is prone to panic attacks or has OCD) can be incredibly draining. Individuals with anxiety have particular behavioural patterns that can exhaust those closest to them. One of the most common of these is reassurance seeking. However, the more reassurance you give, the more the person wants. If you stop giving reassurance, the person will seek it from other people.

For someone who suffers from anxiety, reassurance only increases it. The best thing you can do for someone with this issue is to let them know that you are not going to play this game, as doing so only adds to their anxiety.

The other key characteristic of those with anxiety disorders is avoidance. So the thing you must do is to support them when they face up to the things they fear. If you want to help your loved one to reduce their anxiety, do not complete tasks for them that they are avoiding. You may think you're helping, but doing so only strengthens their anxiety.

Smart caring for a person with depression

Depression drains a person's energy, motivation and hope. Unfortunately your depressed loved one can't just 'snap out of it'; believe me, if they could, they would.

It's important to realize that the symptoms of depression are not personal. More often than not, anger and agitation are features of depression in men. Unfortunately, when lashing out, men do it to those closest to them. Remember this is the depression being expressed, not your loved one's true feelings. Depression is a condition that disconnects people from their loved ones on an emotional level.

If you are concerned about somebody in the early stages of depression, try to encourage them to seek help. This can be very challenging, because of the stigma associated with mental health difficulties. Nudging and encouraging them to get professional help is the right thing to do. It might be useful to suggest a general check-up with the GP. You may wish to offer to accompany your loved one. In advance of this appointment, you may want to encourage the person to make a list of their symptoms to discuss with the doctor. Mention your observations. For example, 'You seem to be worse in the morning' or 'I've noticed that you are waking up around 5 a.m. and struggling to get back to sleep'.

The importance of active listening

'On the dark days when I cannot get out of the bed, my partner Gerry comes up in the afternoon and helps me to walk down the stairs; he helps me face the day. I can talk to him about my fear, loneliness and sadness.'

Depression sufferer Sally encapsulates the idea that, when it comes to support, providing a sympathetic listening ear is extremely helpful.

When I talk about listening, I mean actively listening. This can be a tough ask, because you have probably heard what has been said many times before. The challenge when listening to your loved one is to avoid thinking for or against them. Try not to direct the conversation, give advice prematurely, tell them how they should feel, problem solve for them or offer advice on what to do. Rather, support your loved one by compassionate listening, so that they can come up with their own solutions. Helpful questions/things to say can promote the right environment for compassionate listening. For example:

- 'I've noticed that you've been down over the last while – I'm just wondering how you're doing?'
- 'I've been concerned about you lately. How are things?'
- 'When did you begin to feel like this?'
- 'How best can I support you right now?'
- 'Have you thought about getting help?'
- 'I'm here for you. You are not alone.'
- 'I may not understand exactly how you feel, but I care about you and I want to help you.'
- 'You're important to me; your life is important to me – you have many strengths.'
- 'It's hard to understand this now, but the way you are feeling will change.'
- 'Tell me what I can do to help you right now.'

It can be very hard to listen to a loved one without wanting to jump in with your own thoughts or advice. Really try to resist doing so. In particular *don't* say things like this to your depressed friend/family member:

- 'We all go through times like this.'
- 'All you have to do is think positively.'
- 'I can't do anything about the situation – I don't understand depression.'
- 'It's all in your head.'
- 'Snap out of it!'
- 'You ought to be better by now.'

It's a hard place to be. Caregivers suffer more stress-related illnesses than others of the same age. My take-home message for you is that you need to look after yourself first. There are things that you can't control, and your challenge is to accept this. I have no doubt you can think of situations where you have been offered help and replied, 'It's okay, I'm fine', when in your heart you knew that this was not the case. Now, if you find yourself in a situation where you need help and support, and somebody offers, say yes.

Somewhere in the caring cycle you need to be able to step out. You need to be able to give yourself a break. Seek support, so that you can get out of the house. Try to focus on the things over which you have control. Somehow, don't allow caregiving to become your sole purpose in life; make sure the other areas of your life aren't neglected. Family, friends, support groups and professional therapists all have a role to play.

9

The cost of the quiet life and dealing with toxic people

In the previous chapter, I mentioned how important it is for carers to avoid doing anything just for a quiet life. But that applies to all of us. We probably all have areas in our lives where facing up to someone would be tricky, and we simply try to tell ourselves it's not such a big deal. But, whatever it is, it is a big deal, and sooner or later it will take its toll in stress.

Ask yourself the following questions. How often do you give in to:

- a sister or brother wanting to arrange a family event at short notice without consultation?
- a teenage son or daughter who persists in badgering you for phone credit?
- a husband who insists on going out to watch all the premiership matches at the weekend and European cup matches during the week?
- a domineering friend?
- a peer at work whose idea is no better than yours, but with whom it's just easier to go along?
- an in-law who interferes with decisions about your family life?

In the therapy room, issues such as these come up time and again. When individuals discuss their stress, it's the wish for a quiet life that emerges as the key problem.

Let's take Emma. Emma is sixty years old, married with two adult children; she doesn't work outside of the home and she cares for her own mother. Her husband, Mike, works outside of the home.

'Adam and Michael are in their early thirties. They have good jobs. Adam works in the civil service on €30,000 a year, and Michael is a trained accountant. Their lives are full of football training, drinking, watching sports and going out at weekends. In they come after training, and the gear-bags are thrown on the ground. It's like they think the laundry fairy comes and picks it up, washes and dries the kit. Take last Sunday. I spent 2 hours preparing dinner – a leg of lamb, gravy, roast potatoes, mashed potatoes, peas and carrots – all wolfed down in less than 10 minutes. Not even a thank you. Then out the door to the pub for the afternoon to watch Manchester United.

'And they don't put up any money. Mike's wage pays for everything. And everything is going up – electricity and gas – and now there's the property tax and water charges coming.

'At times I blow a fuse and there's a change for a week or so, and then it all reverts to normal. I have hinted that they are big boys now and that they should be thinking about getting their own place. Mike says they are "only lads". That's okay for him. It's me doing all the work. I look forward to when they go on holiday, as it's a holiday for me, except for when they come back and hand me all their wash-ing! They still ask me to buy their clothes. They just take me for granted, and I feel like a gobshite. Imagine rearing two sons like that.

'Even when they were young I gave in to them all the time. I found it easier just to do the things that were needed, even at the stage when they should have been getting a bit more independent and doing things for themselves. I'm kicking myself now that I didn't do things different. I was just after a quiet life.'

Doing things for a quiet life is a barrier between you and your real self. I see it as similar to a transaction. What I mean by this is that when you settle for a quiet life, you are giving away self-esteem, confidence, your own voice, power, control and autonomy. It leads to frustration, disappointment and anger. Most often this anger is suppressed. This is unhealthy and, as I said in the previous chapter, if it's not dealt with the stress will take the form of physical ailments or emotional distress.

Changing your behaviour to change the situation

The quiet life is too often kept going by avoiding conversations that you need to have. The sooner you have these conversations, the better. Don't hang around waiting for the other person to change. It just doesn't happen. You need to change. It's only when you change that others do so.

A useful way of thinking about this is to use an idea about how our personalities are structured, pioneered by the psychiatrist Eric Berne. When we interact with one another, we assume a role in one of the three ego states: parent/adult/child. When roles and ego states correspond between two people in an interaction, it will be a well-balanced, healthy interaction.

Parent-to-parent roles. This is when two adults in parental roles are working as a team, agreeing the rules, roles and boundaries of family life with their young children. (Though this is hard to do when your parenting partner continues in the child role!)

Adult-to-adult roles. This is a healthy relationship characterized by both individuals expressing their needs, wants and desires. There is give and take. Conflicts are resolved without the use of power, control or coercion. Both parties are assertive and aim for a win-win.

Child-to-child roles. Children's roles for children are about living in a warm, secure and positive environment. Adults can also be in the child mode, and this can be healthy when it is fun, creative, playful and mutual. It is not healthy when adults take on the child role to avoid responsibility.

However, when there is a lack of equivalence in the roles played in a relationship, problems arise. This is what has happened in Emma's situation, which is characterized by her pursuit of a quiet life.

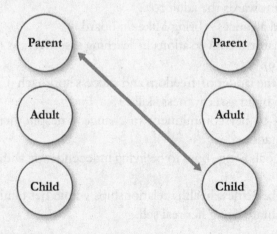

Emma was in parent mode and her two sons were in child mode. All three needed to be in adult-to-adult roles. Sometimes parents and their adult children get locked into this kind of unbalanced relationship out of habit. After all, it has existed for many years. At other times a parent may choose to stay in the parent role in order to feel needed or wanted.

Emma had reached the point of anger. She begrudgingly continued the tasks associated with the parental role, while her adult children took on no responsibilities and behaved like heedless children. Adam and Michael had poor life skills because they had never been forced to develop any.

If Emma wanted to move away from the high price she was paying for the quiet life, she had to start having adult-to-adult conversations. The key to resolving the situation was for Emma to shift roles, become an adult in the relationship and wait for her sons to follow suit. This was easier said than done, because everyone had been playing their roles for such a long time. These were the steps Emma needed to take.

- Understand the situation.
- Shift towards the adult role.
- Build alliances – bring Mike on board.
- Transform conversations by learning assertiveness (Chapter 19).
- Use the ladder of freedom and success approach (Chapter 6) to build assertiveness skills.
- Stick to her commitment to change – despite her sons' resistance.
- Set goals – e.g., boys to be living independently within one year.
- Celebrate new healthy relationships within her family.
- Celebrate being her real self.

Emma developed a thorough understanding of this dynamic and the role that she was playing in maintaining the situation. By bringing Mike on board, she ensured that the parental line would not be broken, as had happened before. Transforming conversations by being assertive was a new skill for Emma. Here is her ladder of freedom and success.

Tell Adam and Michael that she wants them out of the house within a year
Ask the boys for a contribution towards the household funds
Tell the boys she is no longer going to do their laundry
Speak to Mrs Brown next door about the problem with the boundary wall
Ask Mike to stop smoking in the kitchen and to smoke in the garden
Ask a stranger for change on the bus
Return an item of clothing

Emma started to build her assertiveness skills outside of the home; when she felt confident, she moved on to making requests inside the home. When she met resistance from Mike or the boys, she used the 'stuck-record technique' – she simply continued to repeat her request clearly and calmly.

Life changed for Adam and Michael. Indeed, life changed for Emma. Within about four months, Emma had made her specific request: that she wanted the boys to leave home within one year. She was giving them a year, so that they could get some money together for their future. But here's what happened. As soon as Emma stopped doing the boys' laundry, they took on this responsibility immediately – although on occasions they went to a commercial laundry and bulk washed. Money was contributed to the household. Bills were shared. Emma and Mike were able to go on a decent holiday to Lanzarote, and they managed a few weekends away too. Adam had gone within nine months, Michael at the end of the year.

The family dynamic shifted to a healthier space. Emma came to realize that she and Mike avoided certain conversations for the sake of a quiet life. She said this was one of the things that attracted them to each other.

Emma's influence rubbed off on Mike. Moving from a parent-to-parent to an adult-to-adult situation created a new growth in their relationship. Emma said, 'This is something I wish I had known all my life. I think this is why I never worked outside the home. I never had the confidence.' Emma decided to go back into adult education. She completed her Honours Leaving Certificate English. She got a B+.

Toxic people and how to handle them

Of course, sometimes the reason you seek a quiet life is because you are dealing with someone who exhausts you. It's a matter of self-preservation. It's as if your balloon just deflates when you see them. If you allow them, they can block you from your goal of becoming your real self. These are toxic people, and you need a special set of skills for dealing with them.

Keep in mind the relationships in your life as we look at some stereotypical toxic people.

The blamer never takes on personal responsibilities. Everything bad that happens is always somebody else's fault. This person is unable to see their role in the situation.

The moaner sees the world in a negative light. When you meet with them, all you hear are negative stories. It's like a tornado, and you can get sucked into the vortex.

The critic feels good by beating down others. The critic engages in gossip, judgement, criticism and undermining you, sometimes overtly, more often covertly.

The bully takes all the power and control and uses them to obtain their desires and wants to the detriment of others.

The pessimist is the doom and gloom merchant who sees only negativity in the past, present and future.

The drama king or queen overreacts with excess emotion, such as crying or anger about the smallest things. Then they try to blame you!

The trouble-maker is a stirrer who winds people up in a group situation. They put information into the melting pot that would best be kept discreet or confidential.

The preferred strategy is to keep toxic people out of your life, but life's not always that straightforward. Unfortunately, in the real world, we are often stuck with these people. For example, they may be part of your family or social network.

A toxic person is just like a poison. The only way you can handle such a person is by using your own tools, or 'antidotes', to keep that poison from getting inside you and damaging you. Here are some tools you can try.

- Reduce the dose by keeping your contact conversations to the minimum.
- Be adult in the conversation. Hold that ground. Ensure healthy boundaries. Be assertive.
- Demonstrate no interest in gossip or 'negative talk'.
- Keep your conversations on topic.
- Never create expectations about things that you can't deliver.
- Use 'problem-free talk'. When you are with a toxic person, do not criticize or highlight any negativity. This will only lead to a downward spiral. Stick to problem-free talk, neutral topics such as the weather, things that went well, TV programmes, travel or sports. When the toxic person goes 'negative', try prepared lines such as 'There is so much negativity in the world; I prefer conversations around positive things', then switch the subject to problem-free talk. If that doesn't work, it's time to go. No audience equals no toxicity. Toxic people learn over time to adapt their conversations.
- Remind yourself that your life is better off without toxic people. There are other friendships that will bring you positivity.

Of course, sometimes the toxic person in your life can be somebody very close to you, and it's not possible to shut them down or to avoid them. You may even end up caring for a parent who was the main toxic person in your life. I've come across many such situations. I am thinking about Siobhan, a remarkable woman who came to see me with panic attacks. Siobhan made great progress but still felt trapped. What emerged was that Siobhan was caring for her elderly mother. In Siobhan's early life there had been little love and warmth, few hugs. Siobhan told me she felt obligated to care for her mother – whom she loved but had never really liked. Siobhan was a wonderful, talented, humorous, kind, open and intelligent person. I wish she could have heard those words from her mother.

If you're wondering whether your parent might be toxic, ask yourself these questions.

- Did your parent tell you that you were bad or worthless?
- Did they call you insulting names or intentionally embarrass you in public, perhaps in front of random shopkeepers, your friends, your friends' parents?
- Did they constantly criticize you, or tell you that you would never amount to anything?
- Did your parent frequently use physical force to discipline you?
- Were you frightened of your parent?

Imagine answering yes to any of these questions and actually having to care for that same parent in their old age. Often the adult child of a toxic parent will continue to seek recognition from that parent. More often than not they won't receive it. The crunch point arrives when the parent becomes older and the adult child is expected to provide care for a parent who never cared for them. Usually it's daughters who end up in this situation. More often sons seem to avoid such caring responsibilities.

The cost of this type of caring is high. Providing care for someone, after a lifetime of being at the mercy of their bad temper, narrow-mindedness and angry outbursts, creates an untenable situation for the (now adult) child.

A parent's toxicity scars you so badly. In adulthood you may feel inadequate, unloved and worthless. Your challenge is to build your self-confidence, inner strength and emotional independence.

Strategies for coping with a toxic parent

Be unpredictable. Frequently people don't phone or call in to their toxic parent for long periods of time. Generally a feeling of guilt then builds up. Thoughts such as 'Oh, God, I'd better ring her, I just can't face it, she is so negative, yet I haven't rung her in over four days . . . Oh, I will ring her tomorrow.' The strategy here is to ring or pop in for very short periods at unpredictable intervals. For example, don't get caught into ringing, say, every Tuesday night at 9 o'clock. Ringing at random times allows you to control the situation.

Let's take Ruth, whose parent is toxic. She likes watching the news. Her mother would ring most evenings during the news after *Coronation Street*. It used to drive Ruth mad. Now Ruth rings her mum during *Coronation Street*. The conversations are short. The toxic dose is limited. And her mum doesn't ring back during the news.

Don't feel guilty about these feelings of delaying phone calls or visits – such thoughts are to be expected, because toxic parents are so very different from normal parents.

Be detached. Use the strategy of 'detaching'. Detaching is where you set boundaries to protect yourself. You will need to give up the notion of controlling your parents' behaviour. You will also need to take responsibility for your own behaviour and stop allowing them to control yours. It's hard. It takes practice. Detaching means that you affirm that you love the person, but will no longer tolerate being treated with meanness or disrespect.

Bring in support. Set clear boundaries, call in reinforcements and carry through by letting others take over the caregiving role when you need respite. Prioritize your health and well-being. Develop a care plan with family members, drawing up rotas so that everyone takes a turn and everyone gets a break. Engage external carers to provide in-home and out-of-home respite.

What if I am that toxic person?

Now that you have thought about your current relationships, have you figured out who gives you energy and who is toxic in your life? It's time to deal with this by booting those toxic people out of your life or by minimizing their impact. Turning your life into a toxic-free zone means you can nurture your real self.

But perhaps you've received a fright – maybe you have read this and realized that some of *your* behaviours are toxic. If so, it's likely that your role models failed to teach you properly about healthy boundaries in relationships. This pattern will hold you back. Healthy people are not attracted to negative energy or behaviour. If your behaviours are toxic, you cannot be as decent and as mature a person as you have it in you to be. However, by working on yourself and using the tools in this book, you can change and become your real self.

CHALLENGE TWO

Depression

10

Understanding grief and depression

Both grief and depression have a common characteristic: a deep sense of loss. They also share many of the same symptoms. The key distinction between the two is that, while grief can be profound and life-altering, it is part of the normal life cycle; and, though it may not seem like it in the immediate aftermath of a loss, most of us are equipped to get through grief and out to the other side. Depression, on the other hand, may have no obvious 'cause', and it can be chronic and recurring. A depressed person may need to do a lot of ongoing work, and perhaps want to use medication, to deal with the symptoms and to live as fulfilling a life as possible.

A good assessment is essential to distinguish between grief and clinical depression. The inner world of the bereaved person differs significantly from that of someone experiencing depression, and sometimes GPs are too quick to medicate normal sadness, loss and grief. The grieving individual experiences a mixture of emotions: some painful but also some positive ones. People experiencing grief feel that someday they may get back to their 'old self'. Thoughts of suicide are rare, but the grieving person may fantasize about reuniting with their lost loved one. This is normal. The grieving person maintains their self-esteem and their connections with families and friends. Finally, the bereaved person has the ability to be consoled.

Everyone experiences loss and grieves differently. Grief is an emotional response to loss and is a personal journey of the heart. A person can grieve a loved animal as much as a loved family member: it's all about the relationship. Grief can be triggered by a breakup, retirement, loss of health, loss of a family home, a miscarriage and the end of a dream. The point is not to judge someone's grief response but rather to support the person who has suffered the loss.

Of course, traumatic and sudden deaths, such as death by violence, by suicide or the death of a child, are particularly difficult to deal with. These create the profoundest of intense, painful grief. Suicide is like a tsunami hitting a family and adds complexity to the grieving process.

Grief can be physically painful. Some people carry stress and tension in their back and shoulders. For others, there is a void or a profound emptiness that is unique to them. From the outside, people who are grieving seem okay; they put up a brave face and carry on. For many, that's what they need to do, to prove to themselves that they are not cracking up.

In the grip of grief, people have complex emotions. Sometimes they hold on to the pain, because they are afraid that if they let it go, they would be letting go of their loved one. Individuals choose different ways of coping with their loss. Sometimes these different pathways can lead nowhere, and someone becomes stuck with grief. That's when they might choose to see someone like me. In the therapy room, a person gets the opportunity to set aside the brave face and to come to terms with their loss. From the outset, let me tell you there are no experts on grieving.

There is lots of writing on grief. I have seen most of the lessons borne out in the therapy room: ignoring your pain will make it worse in the long run; it is okay to feel vulnerable, sad, frightened and lonely; there is no timeframe for grieving; you don't need to protect your family by putting on a brave face – showing your true feelings can help them and you. The only way to get through grief is to go all the way in and through to the other side. This can be a very scary thought for the survivor. Find someone to support you.

Grief can remain unresolved when there is an intense longing and yearning for the deceased; when there are intrusive thoughts or images of the loved one long after they have gone; when things that remind the person of their loved one are avoided; and when there is extreme anger or bitterness over the loss.

If you (or someone you know) experienced a loss more than two years ago, you may need some help if you are still struggling with blame; avoiding the grieving process; avoiding talking about the loss; preserving the loved one's room; experiencing grief feelings that seem as raw as they did in the early days; or suffering flashbacks or nightmares.

The sadness of losing someone you love never goes away completely, but it need not be the core of your existence; it shouldn't stop you from picking yourself up and living your life. What would your loved one want? If you could imagine them sitting in the chair opposite you, what would they say to you? I have no doubt that they would be compassionate, that they would want you to reconnect with the world and live again. They would want you to be your real self. Don't be afraid of letting go of the grief; you will always have the memories of your loved one.

Examining the label 'depression'

When I first meet individuals struggling with mental health difficulties, I try to explore what their sense of the problem is. I am always amazed how quickly people label themselves as depressed. Maybe that's unfair, as I think about depression in a clinical context and not in layman's terms. But it's important to challenge the labels we give ourselves. These labels have the power to keep your problem going. Labelling yourself as 'depressed' is a bit like seeing your state of mind as an express train between Dublin and Cork on a track with just two stations – 'Not Depressed' and 'Depressed' – and no stops in between.

If you think about depression in this way, it's a one-way ticket to hopelessness, despair and pain. You start to live the belief 'I am depressed'; it becomes a self-fulfilling prophecy. You adapt the things you think, feel and do to fit the label you've given yourself – which makes you feel even more hopeless and desperate. You end up thinking in all or nothing terms: 'I am no good', 'Nobody loves me', 'Life is totally crap', 'Nothing matters'. Next, you may start to do things you've not done before: staying in bed, not returning phone calls, zoning out rather than tuning in.

Depression does exist; for some people it is a terminus. But your state of mind doesn't have to be on an express route to depression. The journey can be reversed; or you can take a branch line to a totally different place. Instead of going from Dublin to Cork you could stop at Kildare or Thurles; or you could transfer trains at Portarlington or Limerick Junction and go to Galway or Tralee; or you could hop back on the train to Dublin. Lots of options. No inevitable terminus.

So, before saying that you're depressed, you need to identify your emotions appropriately. For example, Judy is
fifty-four years old and was referred to me by her GP with
depression. Though she diligently took her anti-depressants,
the GP thought Judy needed further intervention. Her husband had terminal cancer, and she was distraught. Tom was
the love of her life. They had met as teenagers and got
together against the wishes of both sets of parents to chart
their course in life. They had two children. They had little
money at the start but lots of love. She recalled how, in
the summer, they would borrow a neighbour's mobile home
and go to Tramore for a week. She described supper on
holidays – a loaf of fresh-sliced pan, some ham and chips
from the local chipper. They would sit on the beach, looking
at the waves, sipping bottles of Club Orange. Now she
looked at the chemotherapy line and Tom's steroid-bloated
body; and when she considered the one-year prognosis she
felt devastated.

Was what Judy was feeling depression? In fairness it could
have been, but it needed closer assessment. And it turned
out that Judy's mood was down, but she was not depressed.
She was grieving. In the literature it's called anticipatory
grief – the grief we experience that is associated with a future
loss. This sort of grieving is profound. Judy was trying to
come to terms with the loss of Tom, the loss of her future
life with Tom, the loss of their shared plans and dreams.

So, again I say, let's not medicalize normal sadness. When
we learn to label our emotions more accurately, we enable
ourselves to get off the train with only one destination. Judy
needed a space in which to express her profound sadness,
grief, hopelessness, despair and loss. Judy needed to process
these feelings. Taking a pill to change her brain chemistry

was not the answer for her. She needed to feel the pain of this loss in order to get through it. Scary. But with support Judy made this journey.

So what is depression?

The inner world of a person experiencing clinical depression is characterized by sadness, hopelessness and despair. The depressed person sees the world through a lens that turns the past, present and future into a negative. There are few moments of positivity, and the person can feel as if they are in a black hole with no way of getting out. They may even think about suicide as a solution.

Everyone experiences sadness during their lives. It's part of the human condition. So it is important to distinguish between this sadness and depression. Many health professionals are too quick to label sadness – and reactions to major life events such as redundancy, bereavement or marital breakdown – as depression. But if you are finding it difficult to escape from a low mood and sad feeling after two or more weeks, it is best to seek intervention. A good first port of call is your GP.

You can estimate if you are currently depressed by completing the depression self-test questionnaire in the Appendix. You can also use the self-test questionnaire to track your progress as you use some of the tools and techniques shared in these chapters. Remember the self-test is just a guide and does not constitute a diagnosis or a healthcare recommendation. You should always undergo a thorough clinical assessment by your GP or a qualified mental health expert, with a view to an appropriate diagnosis and treatment.

There are four common depressions that doctors and

psychologists deal with routinely: clinical depression (mostly simply called 'depression'); adjustment reaction; bipolar disorder (formerly called 'manic depression'); and post-natal depression.

Clinical depression and adjustment reaction

Clinical depression impacts on your feelings, thoughts, body and actions. It robs you of the potential to become your real self. You may feel sad, pessimistic, hopeless, self-hating, weak, doubtful, guilty, shameful, angry, irritable, anxious, bleak, cold, isolated, unable to experience pleasure and physically in pain.

Your thoughts when depressed may include: 'I am disappointed in myself', 'My future is hopeless and will only get worse', 'I am a failure', 'It's my fault I am like this', 'I'm useless', 'I'm not interested in anything', 'I'm stupid', 'I can't even make a simple decision', 'I feel worthless'. You may have a sense of being punished. You may feel suicidal. Depression affects your actions: you may find yourself crying, avoiding people or withdrawing from them, procrastinating, shouting and arguing, pacing or staying in bed.

Depression affects your body. You may have very low energy. Your sleeping pattern may be disturbed – sleeping most of the day or waking up 1–2 hours early and not being able to get back to sleep. You may feel restless, wound-up and agitated. You may experience changes in your appetite – from no interest in food to cravings. You may have concentration difficulties and lose interest in sex.

Depression can be long-lasting or recurrent, substantially impairing a person's ability to function at work, school or in many aspects of daily life.

An adjustment reaction is similar to clinical depression, but it arises in response to a particular stressful life event; clinical depression emerges in the absence of a defined life event. Take someone who recently had a mastectomy or whose house was flooded or who was made redundant. They may have all the symptoms of clinical depression with some features of anxiety, but technically what they are going through is an adjustment reaction. Generally the depression lifts as the person processes their new situation and adapts to it.

Examples of stressors that can trigger an adjustment reaction include:

- the breakup of a relationship or marriage;
- losing a job;
- death of a loved one;
- developing a serious illness;
- a disaster situation (fire or flood);
- being a victim of crime;
- being involved in an accident.

Adjustment reactions are different from post-traumatic stress disorder, where flashbacks, nightmares, avoidance and hyper-vigilance are present. Symptoms generally begin within three months of the event and may resolve after around six months. I have included this type of depression diagnosis, so that you are aware of it – knowledge is power. The treatment for adjustment reaction is the same as for the other types of depression, with a focus on processing the life event.

Depression doesn't have to be around for months for a diagnosis to be made, so if you have had symptoms like those described above for two weeks or more, it's time to seek advice from your GP. You are not alone: clinical depression is one of the most significant public health problems.

Bipolar disorder

The word 'disorder' crops up everywhere in the diagnosis of mental health difficulties, but I am not a big fan of the word. It's about focusing on the negative, and I prefer to look at people's strengths and to seek out solutions. So I will refer to bipolar disorder simply as 'bipolar'.

Bipolar is a type of depression where typically both manic and depressive episodes are separated by periods of normal mood. During manic episodes, symptoms can include:

- euphoria;
- inflated self-esteem;
- poor judgement;
- rapid speech;
- racing thoughts;
- aggressive behaviour;
- agitation or irritation;
- increased physical activity;
- risky behaviours;
- spending sprees or unwise financial choices;
- increased drive to perform or achieve goals;
- increased sex drive;
- decreased need for sleep;
- being easily distracted;
- careless or dangerous use of drugs or alcohol;
- frequent absences from work or school;
- delusions or a break from reality (psychosis);
- poor performance at work or school.

The signs and symptoms of the depressive phase of bipolar are the same as those for clinical depression, described above.

Bipolar is a serious mental health problem. If you have bipolar, it requires your continuous attention. Unmanaged mood extremes of bipolar are very disruptive to your life and the life of your loved ones. Often people with bipolar are on mood stabilizer medications such as lithium. For some, staying on medication is a struggle, as they enjoy the feelings of euphoria and being more productive that are characteristic of the manic phase. To feel like this again, they come off their medication. However, usually these feelings are short lived and the inevitable crash leaves people with additional legal, financial or relationship difficulties.

Bipolar is one of those conditions where medication is very helpful, and I encourage people with bipolar to stay on their medication. Nevertheless, CBT can play a significant role in relapse prevention and not enough people with bipolar are having appropriate psychological treatment.

Both clinical depression and bipolar can be caused by biological, genetic and environmental factors, and these will be different for everyone. Major life events such as bereavement, unemployment, illness, new baby, separation and divorce may trigger a depression, but such life events in themselves do not cause depression or bipolar. With depression, aspects of our personality that can play a role include: how resilient we are; how we deal with life challenges; how able we are to express our feelings. If we either suppress our feelings or allow them to dominate our lives, low mood and depression may follow. But with bipolar presentation, biological and genetic factors are more likely to make a more significant contribution to its development.

Post-natal depression

Happily for most women, childbirth is an amazingly positive experience. But for some, their feelings post-birth are characterized by depression, panic attacks, distressing thoughts about harming the child and traumatic memories associated with the birth. I believe the medical profession underestimates the emotional impact on a woman in childbirth when things switch from 'Everything is going well' to 'Oh my God, everything is going wrong', and suddenly the baby is in distress or an emergency C-section needs to be performed.

Post-natal depression (PND) is an umbrella term used to cover feelings of significant depression, anxiety and trauma after having had a baby. My experience is that too many women suffer unnecessarily in silence.

While we really don't know the exact cause of PND, factors associated with it include:

- *Birth experience.* A traumatic/difficult birth experience or a premature or unwell baby is sometimes reported by those who develop post-natal depression.
- *Biological factors.* Hormonal imbalances.
- *Impact of caring for a vulnerable child.* The stress of looking after a baby and of having sleep disrupted may also help to bring on the illness in susceptible people.
- *Life events.* Recent bereavements or a serious illness. In addition, women who are isolated from their families or without a supportive partner can be more likely to suffer depression after birth.
- *Previous history of depression.*

Most mums with PND need to be heard, believed and understood. A mum experiencing PND can be irritable towards her other children and occasionally her baby, but mostly towards her partner, who may well wonder what on earth is wrong. Jean recalled:

'I had a lovely pregnancy. Following a very hard birth, I lost a lot of blood. I was scared. I thought I would never have another baby. My baby was taken to the Special Care Baby Unit (SCBU). All turned out fine, or so it seemed. I felt totally miserable, but I did not want anybody to know. After coming home, I fell into a routine. The baby was fed and cleaned, but somewhere in there I was lost. I wanted somebody to tell me what was wrong with me, but at the same time how could I tell anybody that I couldn't cope? Why did I not want this baby? I continued to feel this way for months. My partner knew that something was wrong, but didn't know what to do, and so I felt totally alone.'

Fatigue plays a huge role in PND. Babies are demanding and sleep is in short supply. PND can rob the mother of the confidence needed to deal with the child, and interfering, as opposed to supportive, family members can perpetuate the feeling of being unable to cope. Anxiety is common and often it takes the form of being afraid to be alone with the baby. On many occasions mums have very scary thoughts that revolve around hurting the baby in some way.

When a mum responds with anxiety to these thoughts, it is a clear sign that they love their infant very much and would never harm their baby. Some mothers with PND feel detached from the infant, so drained that they ask themselves: 'Will I ever have any energy again?' 'Why am I feeling so awful and unusual?' 'Am I going mad?' The answer is no!

Early intervention is the key. Don't bottle things up. Talk to somebody about how you feel and seek professional help. Support, possible medications and therapy will help end your PND.

Often mothers believe they have done long-lasting damage to their child. This is untrue. Children are very resilient and adaptable.

Why you can't 'just snap out of it'

Depression is a thief. It disconnects you from yourself and from your loved ones. It zaps the life out of you. It's not possible to just snap out of it. Indeed, most people with depression would trade it for a broken leg, even cancer. This is Alan's experience.

'At least a broken leg is visible; my depression is invisible. Cancer has a treatment pathway; in depression the treatment pathway is unknown. I'm in pain. It's a deep internal pain; some days I want to curl up and sleep and not get up. In work if I had a broken leg, I could get time off. I can't ask for time off with my depression, she wouldn't understand. A broken leg is nothing to the pain of depression, believe me, I've broken my leg playing football. You find out your true friends with depression, as most disappear when they find out that I have been in a psychiatric hospital. Not that I could go into hospital in my local area. I just couldn't face that. For me depression is a failure of my personality; it shows that I'm weak. To think I have to take tablets every day to make myself feel okay.'

When I hear Alan talk, I hear the pain of his depression, and how depression is seeping into his thinking, his body and his actions.

However, this is a message of hope: you can stop depression in its tracks. In the next chapter, I will share with you how the evidence-based tools of CBT and mindfulness can be very effective in transforming depression and helping you to reclaim your life. You will find that the terminus of depression isn't an inevitable one, and that the course of that train journey can be changed. While the beginning is always the hardest, once you tell yourself that there is hope, anything is possible.

11

Transforming depression into hope

The most critical question you can ask yourself in understanding your depression is: what's keeping the problem going? Invariably, the answer can be a mix of family history or life events. In depression, the individual projects negativity on to the past, present and future. Automatic negative thoughts – ANTs – are fuelled by hopelessness, pessimism and self-loathing, to name but a few states of mind. The good news is that proactive CBT has been shown by multiple research studies to be an incredibly powerful treatment for depression; and mindfulness is very effective in relapse prevention.

Let's look at CBT in action in a case of chronic clinical depression. George is forty-eight. He is married to Patricia and they have three children, aged five, seven and ten. George had a successful courier business up until 2009. He worked hard with his wife to build up the business. But it began to go downhill after the economic crash in 2008.

'Like many small businesses, I was owed a lot of money and had massive debts. I had to declare myself bankrupt. The ultimate humiliation was when the debt collectors came to my door. They took away my car and a van that I used for business.

'At one time nothing could stop me. I was respected.

Now I'm nothing. I can't even provide for my family. I'm a failure.

'My mood started to change quickly after the business went. I was angry all the time. I was angry with my children, who I love dearly. I was angry with Patricia, who has always been there for me. I lost all enjoyment in things and became depressed.

'Feeling depressed is many things for me. I can't sleep or eat or function normally. I feel tired and I get awful headaches and can't concentrate. On bad days I just feel numb.

'I have struggled with this now for the past six years. I have been taking medication for five years, but I don't feel much different.

'Most of the people around me are unaware of the debts or my depression. It's very hard to be open about the depression. Some of my friends know that I've been "unwell" over the past year, but they don't know why. Only a few people know that I have depression and fewer still know the extent to which I struggle with it.

'To be honest, I see my depression as a sign of weakness, and I don't want people to know I have it. I worry that they'll think I'm a bit pathetic or being self-indulgent. I don't want them pitying me or treating me different.

'I know Patricia is worried about me, because she sees me down, not going out, not having fun with the children; and as for our sex life, it's non-existent.

'I'm at the stage now where I don't want to get up in the morning. I dread seeing the postman walking around, as I wonder what bills or warning letters are coming. I feel life is not worth living because I have let down everyone. I'm just hanging on.'

George was referred to me by his GP, who was concerned that even with medication he wasn't pulling out of his depression. His inability to communicate was a huge worry for his wife and it affected his young family. George himself was extremely worried about what his state of mind was doing to his wife and particularly to his children, but he lacked the tools to tackle his serious depression on his own. George said he felt hopeless.

As a clinician I am very interested in hopelessness. Hopelessness about the present and the future is a strong predictor of suicidal thoughts. Along with hopelessness come feelings of helplessness, worthlessness and despair. If these moods are pervasive, I will look at the underlying thoughts that are driving them, which become an early target for therapy. Fostering hope is critical. Hope creates new energies, rekindles dreams, ends despair and reconnects you with yourself and your loved ones. Depression sees the world as dark, dreary and miserable; hope imbues the world with a sense of light and lightness, positivity, confidence, possibility and change. With hope, you have a new lens on the world.

Hope is fostered through actions and goals. Small exercise goals – say, walking, swimming or cycling for 20 minutes every day – all raise hope. Challenging someone's pervasive thinking raises hope. By connecting with someone with depression and by helping them to think differently and act differently, you will be well on the way to raising hope and banishing depression.

The route to recovery for George was for the two of us to work on finding the right blend of CBT and mindfulness techniques – customized for him – that would finally start to shift his thinking and allow him to feel hope again.

Taking on depression using CBT

Recall the five CBT hats from Chapter 4. Wearing the **feelings** hat, someone who is sad, in a low mood or depressed might identify with many of these: hurt; negativity; hopelessness; helplessness; despair; anger; agitation; fear; stress; tension; exhaustion; vulnerability; resentment; emptiness; unhappiness; frustration; fatigue; restlessness; worthlessness; guilt; shame; pain; a wish to be dead.

Reading the feelings of depression may feel like an oppressive weight that is squeezing the life out of you. Such feelings can squash your real self. No wonder someone with depression is in deep internal pain. No wonder George was feeling hopeless.

In order to transform these negative emotions, you need to utilize every strategy that you possess while wearing the other CBT hats. That is what George worked on in therapy.

Remember that some people believe that their feelings are determined by external events and situations. CBT, however, holds that what really makes us feel and respond the way we do is not the situation itself but how we think about the situation. Wearing his **thoughts** hat, George had to assess all the thinking errors that were keeping his depression going. He, like many people with depression, was prone to black and white thinking, overgeneralization, discounting the positives, taking the blame, name-calling and 'should' statements. This underlying negative inner voice is equivalent to the garden being full of tall weeds. It was very difficult for the light to enter with this sort of pervasive thinking. By becoming aware of his crooked thinking errors, George was creating space to allow in the light.

Here are some of the thinking patterns that George identified.

- *Mood: worthlessness.* This feeling is driven by the thoughts: 'Now I'm nothing', 'I'm a failure'. Thinking errors: name-calling, overgeneralization, black and white thinking.
- *Mood: hopelessness.* This feeling is driven by the thoughts: 'I can't even provide for my family', 'I have struggled with [depression and anxiety] for the past six years. I have been taking medication for five years, but I don't feel much different', 'I feel life is not worth living, because I have let down everyone'. Thinking errors: overgeneralization, black and white thinking, discounting the positives.
- *Mood: shame.* This feeling is driven by the thoughts: 'I worry that [people] will think I'm a bit pathetic or being self-indulgent'. Thinking errors: mind-reading and name-calling.
- *Mood: weakness.* This feeling is driven by the thoughts: 'I see my depression as a sign of weakness', 'I don't want people to know I have it', 'I don't want them pitying me'. Thinking errors: mind-reading, name-calling, overgeneralization, black and white thinking, discounting the positives.

George is engaging in extreme thinking, which serves only to amplify his negative moods. If you are doing this exercise, after you have identified the negative thoughts that you want to work on, apply the twenty powerful questions to squash your ANTs (Chapter 5). Here's how George put his moods of worthlessness and hopelessness into context by using just one of these questions.

If my best friend told me they'd had this thought, what advice would I give them? George's response: 'Your life cannot be defined

by the failure of your business. You have a strong relationship with your wife and a great relationship with your
children. You have struggled but you have also shown great
courage undergoing that struggle. I would suggest that you
might be more compassionate with yourself and not beat
yourself up. It's like you seeing the world and selecting only
the negativity, but there are other more balanced ways of
looking at things. This is your depression talking. You have
started night classes and you are learning new skills. Your
focus is on the past, but you now need to focus on the present. You have the support of your family and friends. You
are a good friend. You are valuable. You are blaming yourself
for an economic crash that ensnared a lot of people. I think
you are ignoring many of your resources and strengths,
including your ability to cope with adversity and your capacity for humour.'

As you can see, when George challenged his own thinking, the picture looked a lot less bleak than previously. That's
what happens when you challenge your thoughts: you are
creating room for more balanced, realistic thinking.

Having applied the twenty questions to his ANTs, George
also used the techniques of keeping a thoughts record and
taking his thoughts to court (Chapter 5).

Column 1: Situation/trigger
- What happened? *Postman came with letters.*

Column 2: Emotional and physical responses
- What is the emotion in one word? *Dread.* Rate it from 0
to 100. *70.*
- Scan your body. Where do you feel the emotion? *In my
stomach.*

Column 3: Crooked thoughts

- What thoughts are going through my mind? *I wonder what bills or warning letters are coming in the post . . . the postman knows I am not working. One day I was driving the big car – now look at me, with no car. He is working. I bet he's looking down at me and saying serves him right, he got too big for his boots.*

Column 4: The case for the prosecution

- Evidence that supports the thoughts – what facts support the truthfulness of these thoughts? *I am unemployed. I am bankrupt.*

Column 5: The case for the defence

- Evidence against the unhelpful thoughts – what evidence indicates that these thoughts are not completely true? *I am over the bankruptcy and I have not had warning letters for the last six months. I am engaged in mind-reading – how do I know what the postman is thinking? When I meet him, he is very courteous and pleasant. I am embroiled in opinions and not engaged in facts. I have met him many times over the last number of years and he has always been genuine.*

Column 6: The judgement

- Alternative, balanced and more realistic thoughts, taking into account the evidence for and against the thoughts. *It's true I am unemployed and bankrupt. It's natural that I would be afraid of letters coming to my door, given my previous experiences. However, I have got on top of this situation. I have my family and my friends. I am looking at ways of moving out of the situation. I am learning to be flexible. I'm learning to be more compassionate with myself. Many people lost their businesses in the downturn. It doesn't define me.*

Column 7: Emotional and physical responses at the end of the hearing

- What is the emotion in one word? *Dread.* Rate it from 0 to 100. *25.*

Column 8: Recommendations from the court
- Practise identifying crooked thinking patterns so they can be spotted in 'real time', i.e., when the events are happening. *By doing this I won't have to go through prolonged levels of distress.*

Within a few months George became comfortable with these techniques. His mood gradually started to lift. Hope replaced hopelessness. He became more connected with himself, his wife and his children. His energy levels increased and that allowed him to engage in some exercise. He developed a better perspective on his situation and subsequently more compassion towards himself. He reviewed his skill set and decided to do some training to increase the number of his options. Following this, he picked up some part-time work and recently became fully employed. He thrives on the structure and routine of work. He says, 'I would not run a company again. I prefer to collect a wage and let someone else do all the worrying.' George is no longer depressed. He is focused on keeping well by being more mindful, by watching for ANTs and tackling them, and by being more flexible and compassionate in his thinking. He no longer defines success by income or status but by how well he is. He is determined to stay well for himself and his family.

Resetting your core beliefs

When tackling your thinking in depression, it's important to see how it links to your core beliefs. In Chapter 1, I talked about the importance of core beliefs. Often these relate to childhood experiences. For some people, though not all, who experience depression, their early childhood may be characterized by emotional loss and sadness. Sometimes this loss is tangible – say, the death of a parent; for others the loss is more subtle: the non-availability of love, growing up in a cold or harsh environment. In these circumstances something is missing, but this goes unrecognized, because the state of loss becomes the child's norm. It's only as adults that we can grasp that the absence of love, warmth and nurturance in our childhoods was detrimental to our well-being.

Uncovering the connection between your pattern of thinking and your core beliefs involves examining the 'rules' laid down by powerful adults in your childhood home or in school. You learned certain lessons about how to negotiate the world, and these lessons may be carefully bound up with how you connected emotionally to the significant figures in your early life. You followed certain rules to obtain approval and love, rather than face the disapproval of your parents/caregivers. Here are some of the rules you may have learned, together with the core beliefs that followed in their wake.

- I must be strong at all times/boys don't cry, love, show emotion. *I am strong. If I don't live up to that rule, I must be weak.*
- To be good enough/accepted, I must be perfect. *I am perfect. If I don't live up to that rule, I must be inferior or I must be inadequate.*
- I don't know what love or warmth means. *I am sad. I am confused.*
- The world is unsafe. *I am unsafe.*
- I must please everyone for them to love me. *If I don't live up to that rule, I must be unlovable.*

The bottom line is that core beliefs of sadness, unlovability, inadequacy and inferiority affect your ability to be your real self. These beliefs are not you. You were young when they were laid down. Now you are a mature adult and can bring new thinking and wisdom to these beliefs. You can change them. They may have helped you when you were a child, but they are not effective now and they limit your life. I am inviting you to an exciting new place where you can be your real self. To do this, review the material about changing old core beliefs in Chapter 1 and commit to strengthening your new real self core beliefs. Use the real self core belief log.

Old core belief to be challenged: ....

New real self core belief: ....

Experiences that show that the old core belief is not COMPLETELY true ALL the time: ....

(List as many as you like here – the more the better!)

Real self core belief to be developed: ....

Task: ....

What you expect to happen: ....

What actually happened: ....

Conclusion(s): ....

If you have negative core beliefs, it is helpful to develop real self positive affirmations that chime with you. Choose some and repeat them daily. It's okay if you don't entirely believe them just now. But, as you heal and grow your real self, positive affirmations will resonate. Here are some I have taken from the more complete list in Chapter 5.

- I am authentic.
- I believe in myself.
- I'm okay being okay.
- I have many good qualities: I am kind, compassionate, caring, funny, considerate, thoughtful, open-minded, easy-going, hard-working, positive, motivated, creative, friendly, flexible, dependable, etc.
- I am a person of value.
- I am a resilient person.
- I like myself.
- People like me.
- My life has meaning and purpose.
- I will speak compassionately to myself and others.
- I am my real self.

Wouldn't you love your children, nieces or nephews, or friends to be able to say this about themselves? So why not you?

Resetting your core beliefs is hard but exciting work. At times when you are vulnerable you may go back to your negative core belief. Stay the course. This type of core belief work is down towards the middle and end of therapy, when someone has a sound grasp of the other thinking tools of CBT.

Obstacles to progress in tackling depression

Guilt and shame are very complex and stubborn emotions to shift in depression. Both are highly toxic. Their roots are in childhood events: exposure to alcoholism, being given too much responsibility at a young age, constant criticism, being blamed for other people's problems, rejection, family rupture or trauma, abuse, bereavement or illness. They are linked to negative core beliefs: 'I am bad, defective or unlovable', 'I am responsible (even though I don't have control)', 'My feelings are wrong', 'I don't do enough', 'I have to be perfect', 'I have to keep other people happy'. You will need to work hard on your real self core beliefs log to shift some of these.

As for feeling guilty, you need to examine what you feel guilty about, in order to move on. In life we all make mistakes. At times good people do wrong things. When this happens, take responsibility for your portion of the problem and express regret. Try to learn from your mistakes, so that in future situations you act differently. Don't take on responsibilities that are not yours.

Rumination can also be pervasive in depression. This involves thinking over and over about self, mood and negative events, with particular emphasis on the causes and consequences rather than on solutions. While some rumination is normal, excessive rumination is a slippery slope to more distress and depression. And once you're over the edge it's hard to pull yourself back; rumination is a style of thinking that keeps depression going.

Examples of rumination questions include 'why' questions: 'Why did it end up like this?', 'Why am I in this situation?', 'What if it never ends?', 'What did I do to deserve this?' At the end of the day, rumination is unproductive; it increases ANTs, makes you more self-critical and can worsen your situation. It's the equivalent of throwing petrol on a fire. If you notice that you are ruminating, ask yourself what you can usefully do right now about your situation. And if there is something, do it! If not, redirect your focus and energy to more productive activities.

Notice if there is a particular time of day at which you ruminate and try to switch activities or environments. Be mindful and view rumination as a fish hook that you want to avoid. If you need to explore certain issues, talk them out with someone rather than getting stuck in that repetitive loop in your head; or write them down. Physical activities push out rumination.

Counselling and therapy

Counselling and therapy can help you to work through the roots of your depression, helping you to understand why you feel a certain way, what triggers your depression, and what you can do to stay healthy. Though the terms are used interchangeably, a helpful way to see counselling and therapy is as part of the same continuum: counselling is often short-term support that addresses the immediate emotional crisis, whereas therapy is longer term and addresses both the immediate crisis and underlying factors unique to the individual. In practice there is little difference between them.

Your counselling or therapy needs to be active. There should be a confiding relationship between you and your counsellor or therapist, a sense of hope, an exchange of information, an opportunity to vent emotions, an opportunity to acquire insight, a sense that you are working together with the necessary tools for managing and banishing depression from your life. Therapy or counselling is not an end in itself and should not go on indefinitely. Instead it's about getting results so you can get on with your life. And a word of caution: some therapists say they use CBT. Before you commit to a course of therapy or counselling, it's worth asking how much CBT training the therapist or counsellor has had, whether they are enthusiastic about its principles and the extent to which they use it in their practice. (See the Appendix for guidance on how to find the best therapist for you.)

To access therapy or counselling in your area, use the HSE National Counselling Service on 1800 234 110 (10 a.m.– 4 p.m.). Details on www.hse.ie.

Using mindfulness in treating depression and to prevent relapse

Remember mindfulness is the practice of bringing your awareness and attention into the present moment with compassion. The word 'compassion' is so important. In depression your internal critic works overtime to beat you up. It's like someone with a whip inside your head: 'You must do this, you should do that.' *Whip, whip, whip.* But it is when you are at your most vulnerable that you need to treat yourself with the most compassion.

The core of mindfulness practice is mindful meditation (as described in Chapter 3). It would be worthwhile to review the material there and start to introduce some mindfulness practices into your life, if you have not already done so. When you are in the present, you avoid the trap of rumination or ANTs. Working on the areas of gratitude, letting go, simply observing your feelings and thoughts, mindful breathing and mindful walking – all these will help. And you can nurture your positive core beliefs through mindful loving kindness.

There is increasing evidence for the effectiveness of mindfulness in the treatment of depression and, importantly, in the prevention of relapses. When I worked with George, we did mindfulness work to help him engage with the present. He let go of the burden of shame and opened up. His relationship with Patricia grew stronger. She told him how much he was loved and cared for by her and their three children. He was reminded of the time before he became a successful businessman, when he and his wife and children enjoyed simple things. By re-engaging with simple family activities, being more compassionate towards himself, exercising, taking control of what he could control and using his free time more effectively, George lifted his depression and shifted his negative thinking.

Mindfulness isn't just a collection of techniques: it's about a relationship you have with yourself and others. It is such a powerful tool that I wish it could be taught in primary and secondary schools. It's a real life skill, and, like any skill, the more practice you put in, the better you will become.

12

Taking action to conquer depression

By now you have learned some ways of dealing with depression by working on your thinking and by using mindfulness techniques. It's time for action – exercise and behavioural activation. Exercise is self-explanatory. It's amazing just how powerful a tool it is when fighting depression. Behavioural activation simply means doing things in order to shift your motivation and mood: giving yourself opportunities to undertake pleasurable activities, to be with people, to make small achievements and to engage in more encouraging thoughts. 'Today I achieved . . .'

For some people, using these two techniques alone is enough to shift their depression. Exercise and behavioural activation may seem so simple that you may wonder whether they would work in the absence of any thinking tools. Please don't be dismissive. They are powerful and can lift mild to moderate depression on their own. I have found in therapy that these tasks create a good early momentum, so that we can progress to looking at what's going on at a thinking level and doing some of the work described in the previous chapter. (If you are concerned about someone's depression, you can become a supporter or encourager and help them to complete some of the tasks.)

Sinéad is a 37-year-old administrator. She has two loving parents in good health and two older sisters with whom she gets on very well, and great nieces and nephews whom she adores. Sinéad has many close friends and is single. From the outside, she seemed to have a normal and happy life. But after a long-term relationship broke down a year ago she felt depressed. And for the past six weeks before I met her she had been thinking about suicide, though not with the intention of carrying it out.

Sinéad had never really understood what depression was and she was still not sure if she had it. She only knew that she hadn't felt happy for a long time. She did not think that anyone would notice this, as she always put on a smile and a good front. Sinéad used to go out most weekends with her friends. She was seeking a relationship and wanted to have children.

'Who would want me? They are all running . . . all that is out there are married men looking for a fling. They see my biological clock before they see me, the dating game is so hard. People must find me ugly, or boring. I am a failure. Most days, I feel sad and have no energy. I feel worthless and hopeless and often struggle to complete whatever I am meant to be doing. My mother has noticed that I came home early on a few occasions from work, but I lied to her and told her that the boss let me go early. But really I just had to get home and go to bed.

'I have reduced contact with my friends. Now I rarely meet other people or socialize other than at work. I no longer do the things I used to like, such as going to the cinema, shopping at the weekends, going for meals with the girls or events I used to love like the Galway Races. I even made up an illness to avoid a hen party in Kilkenny. Now in the evenings and at weekends I do very little except watch television. I have stopped reading the daily paper. I had planned to do an evening course, but can't be bothered.'

For the past few months, Sinéad and three of her single friends had been planning to walk the Camino in northern Spain. This had always been a dream of Sinéad's, and, although she showed enthusiasm when speaking to her friends about it, she was not looking forward to it. She didn't want to talk to anyone about how she was feeling, as she thought it sounded stupid.

It sounds simple, but I suggested to Sinéad that she start to walk three or four times a week, starting at 15 minutes for week one and bringing it up by 5 minutes each week. The recommended time was between 30 and 45 minutes four times a week. The reason for starting with such a modest goal was to give Sinéad something achievable. Where she was at the outset – thinking that she could walk for 45 minutes four times a week straight away – would have been impossible for her, setting her up for failure and giving ammunition to her inner critic. Therapy can be full of paradoxes, and a maxim I firmly believe is this one: 'The slower we go, the faster we get there.'

Exercise counteracts the exhaustion of depression. It revitalizes the body and releases 'feel good' hormones. Even better, if you can find a dog – a neighbour's or friend's – borrow the dog and head off. When Sinéad began to move, so did her depression.

I also asked Sinéad to start keeping a 'Get up and go' log (Chapter 6). She identified three tasks for the first week. Again, it was about starting with small steps and building incrementally. Her three tasks were:

1. read a daily paper;
2. go to the cinema with a friend;
3. start investigating a night class.

The following week, having got through her Week 1 tasks, Sinéad was able to add some more activities.

I promise you that scheduling like this can improve your mood, particularly if you are inclined to stay in bed for extended periods with depression. The key is not to make a lengthy 'to do' list, which only sets you up for failure and feeds your inner critic. When you are making your plan for the week, don't expect to fill every space. Far from it. Start by putting down what you are required to do (e.g., meal preparation, appointments, your bedtime), then put in other tasks, such as contacting a friend, your exercise session(s), resurrecting an old hobby or interest. As the weeks go on, you can add one or two additional activities per week.

Once you have filled in your log, try to follow your plan each day. Flexibility is a good thing, and you may not get to all your activities each day, but aim for 70%. Don't let your inner critic beat you up for uncompleted tasks.

Finally, if you are waiting for the feeling that you might like to do something, remember you will be waiting for a long time. Simply do whatever it is you have planned to do because it's in your plan. The feeling will follow. When it comes to a task that you don't feel like doing, use the 5-minute rule. That is, do the activity for 5 minutes and then if you want to stop after 5 minutes you can. Chances are once you start, you won't want to stop.

Capturing your achievements and personal qualities

With depression, you have a negative lens on the world that filters out positive achievements and positive personal qualities. So buy yourself a nice little hardback notebook and fill it in with evidence from the past and present.

Sinéad's looked like this:

- My friends confide in me; they say I am a good listener.
- People laugh at my jokes.
- My colleagues in work have invited me to their house for meals and drinks.
- I always have time for my friends.
- I stay calm in a crisis.
- My boss says she values my contribution in work and has given me complex projects because she knows I deliver.
- I have a responsible job.

Your job is to continue to add more evidence to your personal qualities journal. List items as they happen. Don't let your inner critic judge them. Put down all your achievements, no matter how small they may seem. You may wish to consider including:

- things you do skilfully;
- things you have completed and accomplished;
- things that you did even when it was hard;
- things you know a lot about – specialist knowledge or interests, e.g., travel;
- things you can do easily and quickly – e.g., get information using the internet;

- things that show you are good at something – e.g., academic achievements;
- people who acknowledge you have done a good job;
- times when you were helpful to others – e.g., volunteered, completed the 'ice bucket challenge';
- evidence that people like you – e.g., compliments you have been given;
- things that show you have been appreciated – e.g., postcards, gifts;
- or times when people have been nice to you and did you a favour.

Finally, identify the qualities you possess. Select freely from this list:

accountable	charismatic	diplomatic	faithful	immaculate
adaptable	clear	direct	fearless	independent
adventurous	collaborative	disciplined	flexible	innovative
alert	committed	dynamic	friendly	inquiring
ambitious	compassion	easy-going	generous	integrated
appropriate	connected	effective	good	intelligent
assertive	conscious	efficient	good	intentional
astute	considerate	empathetic	communicator	interested
attentive	consistent	empowering	gracious	intimate
authentic	contributor	energetic	happy	intuitive
aware	cooperative	enthusiastic	hard-working	joyful
brave	courageous	ethical	have integrity	knowledgeable
calm	creative	excited	honest	leading
candid	curious	expressive	honourable	listener
capable	dedicated	facilitating	humorous	lively
certain	determined	fair	imaginative	logical

loving	peaceful	punctual	skilful	versatile
loyal	planner	reliable	spiritual	vibrant
loyal comrade	playful	resourceful	spontaneous	warm
manages time well	poised	responsible	stable	willing
networker	polite	self-confident	strong	wise
nurturing	powerful	self-generating	successful	zealous
open-minded	practical	self-reliant	supportive	
optimistic	present	sense of humour	tactful	
organized	proactive	sensual	trusting	
patient	problem-solver	serves others	trustworthy	
	productive	sincere	truthful	

Look at your journal every day for 5 minutes. At times when you are vulnerable or low, recall your personal qualities and achievements to counteract that inner bully.

Sinéad's mood lifted steadily. She followed a couch-to-5k app, and after completing the 5k she joined a local athletics club to do some fun running. She is now aiming for her first 10k run. She worked on her negative belief that she was a failure by using her real self core belief log. She was subsequently able to disprove her inner critic, who badgered her when she was vulnerable because of her relationship status. She became an active gardener, regularly weeding out her automatic negative thoughts. She completed the final section of the Camino. She regained contact with her friends and is frequently in touch with them now. She is single still, but she did snog someone and pushed herself to join an introduction and dating agency. She remains plugged in, connected and hopeful.

Keep up the good work!

When it comes to depression, don't give up if it's taking you a while to see progress. Persist with these tools. You have been thinking like this for some time, so these thoughts will not go away quickly.

When you see some improvement, you have the comfort of knowing that you have successfully mastered a number of practical and effective techniques to tackle your low mood, sadness and depression. They are not a tablet that you hold in your hand, external to you. No, these are inside of you, and you can take them with you wherever you go.

You now know you are able to heal yourself. This is powerful knowledge. Through this healing, you have gained insights into the type of person you are and how you exist in the world. You have gained wisdom. Many people who get to the far side of the tunnel become aware of themselves in a different way. They have seen the light. They have also become aware of the trip-wires that can throw them back down to a low mood. They can avoid the journey of despair and hopelessness that leads back into depression.

A new journey beckons. You have the capacity to focus on your strengths and resources. You have the capacity to grow, develop and craft new core beliefs. You are lovable, worthy and compassionate; you are in a space where you are confident, effective and resilient. You are hopeful and optimistic. There are new relationships in your life, in that you can now trust yourself and you can trust others; there is growth in your relationships with your family and friends. You are accepting of yourself. You are not a set of symptoms; you are a person who has personal, social, spiritual and community strengths, with so much to offer. You are empowered, self-determined and confident about your future. Your self-esteem is restored, and you have a new sense of meaning and an overall purpose. You are well.

13

The pros and cons of medication and other depression treatments

In Ireland and the UK, the primary treatment for low mood and depression is anti-depressant medication. That's because when a person goes to their GP, that is often the only thing the GP has to meet the patient's expectation that the GP will 'do something'. It's like taking a sick child to the GP expecting antibiotics. If he or she says, 'Let's wait 48 hours and see how it develops', there's a sense that nothing has been done. The contract between GP and patient that the GP will 'do something' is broken. Similarly, when a person with depression goes to their GP, they don't really want to hear 'You need to exercise for 30 minutes each day, for three days of the week, eat a healthy diet, talk to your family and friends, and go to meetings of the depression support group Aware.' No, there is an expectation from the patient that they're going to get a pill. This is the power of the pharmaceutical industry, which has convinced us that there is a pill for everything.

I think many times GPs feel powerless because they do not have the time or training to treat depression. Medication is the only thing they can offer. So this combination of the patient's expectation and the GP's need to meet that expectation results in a prescription. This has led to an explosion in anti-depressant medication use.

GPs and psychiatrists can choose from many dozens of medications. There are different types of anti-depressant drug, and each type works on the brain in a different way. And if that wasn't complicated enough, medications are often known by two names: their pharmaceutical or generic name and the brand name used by the drugs company. I have used the pharmaceutical name followed by the brand name in brackets. Types of anti-depressant medication include:

- selective serotonin reuptake inhibitors (SSRIs) – these common medicines include citalopram (Celexa), escitalopram (Lexapro), paroxetine (Paxil), fluoxetine (Prozac), and sertraline (Lustral);
- other serotonergic anti-depressants – these include vortioxetine (Brintellix) and vilazodone (Viibryd);
- serotonin and norepinephrine reuptake inhibitors (SNRIs) – this class of medicines includes duloxetine (Cymbalta) and venlafaxine (Effexor);
- tricyclic anti-depressants – amitriptyline (Elavil), clomipramine hydrochloride (Anafranil);
- monoamine oxidase inhibitors (MAOIs) – phenelzine (Nardil).

For depression that's hard to treat, doctors sometimes pair an anti-depressant with another prescription medicine, such as aripiprazole (Abilify), lithium (Lithobid, Eskalith), risperidone (Risperdal), quetiapine (Seroquel) or olanzapine (Zyprexa).

Medications work on the basis that depression is caused by a chemical imbalance. The biological perspective proposes that low levels of the brain chemical serotonin lead to depression; and that anti-depressant medication restores the serotonin levels to normal.

There is a massive debate about this way of understanding

depression, and many vested interests come into play. Nevertheless, most experts now agree that depression is much more than faulty brain chemistry. New research is highlighting other biological contributors to depression, including elevated stress hormones, immune system suppression, abnormal activity in certain parts of the brain, nutritional deficiencies and inflammation. In addition, social and psychological factors such as poor diet, low self-esteem, life events, lack of exercise and loneliness, to name but a few, play an enormous role.

What's important is that medication is sometimes essential in the treatment of depression, particularly severe depression.

All medications have side-effects. You need to be fully aware of the medication you are on and any of its possible side-effects. You need to be conscious of the risks of taking anti-depressant medication with alcohol, prescription painkillers or sleeping pills. Some questions to ask yourself and your GP:

- How will this medication help my depression?
- What are the drug's common side-effects?
- How long will I have to take the anti-depressant medication?
- Will withdrawing from the medication be difficult?
- Will my depression return when I stop taking the medication?
- Do I have the time and energy to pursue other evidence-based treatments such as cognitive behavioural therapy?
- What self-help strategies may help me to get my depression under control?
- Should I combine medication with therapy?

The pros and cons of medication

When it comes to prescribing medication, doctors do a cost/benefit analysis. For some groups there are higher risks, and with these the prescribing doctor may err on the side of therapy, as opposed to medication, or consider an appropriate alternative medication.

- Those over sixty-five on SSRIs may be at an increased risk of fractures and bone loss.
- Pregnant women or breastfeeding mums. In general, GPs are cautious when it comes to medication for this group of women. Mums themselves are even more cautious and reluctant to go on medication if they are pregnant or breastfeeding. Many times they independently opt for psychotherapy.
- Teens and young adults. There are concerns about an increased risk of suicide in this group.
- Bipolar. Anti-depressants can actually make bipolar worse or trigger a manic episode.

If you are on medication or thinking about going on it, you need to do as much research as you can. Pharmacists have a wealth of knowledge and are very underused. Regard your local pharmacist as a resource and ask them loads of questions.

Once on medication, it's important that you follow the instructions for taking it. Don't skip or start altering your doses. Keep an eye on possible side-effects. Contact your GP immediately if your depression worsens and you experience an increase in suicidal thoughts.

It's okay to seek a second opinion. Professional and competent clinicians see this as a benefit, not as an insult. If you have been on medication for a while, you may want to seek the opinion of a specialist, i.e., a psychiatrist who is more likely to be familiar with the latest research in mental health drug treatments.

Sometimes medication can help people's thinking to be more flexible and more open to the techniques of cognitive behavioural therapy. Medication can play a positive role in obsessive compulsive disorder (OCD). And medication is critical in the treatment of psychosis.

For some people medication is like a life-jacket that keeps them afloat in stormy waters. Therapy tries to figure out how you fell out of the boat in the first place; and it gives you some strong swimming skills, so that you can return to the boat, clamber back inside and stay there. In psychology we learn that it's important for someone to have developed a healthy replacement for any life-jacket (defence) before advising them to remove it.

The medication conversation is very common in therapy rooms. I have my suspicions that it is more common in therapy rooms than it is in the surgery rooms of the prescribing doctors. This is partly because of practical reasons – little time is allocated specifically for talking – and it's partly because the therapeutic relationship is more exploratory in nature.

Counsellors or psychologists don't prescribe medication. It's not part of our training. It's not part of our philosophy. Fundamentally, whether you are on, going on, coming off or off medication is a choice that you make. However, my colleagues and I work in the real world, and these are real-life dilemmas that people raise with us. The advice I give here is generic, based on my experiences. This is no substitute for an individualized mental health assessment that takes into account your unique story, desires, beliefs. Ideally, conversations about your medication need to include your opinion, your prescribing doctor's opinion and, if you wish, your treating therapist's opinion.

Now, let's look at the kinds of questions we are asked. The conversations usually fall into four scenarios.

Scenario 1. I am on medication for my depression/anxiety and I'm planning to come off it. What do you think? Before you come off your medication, you need to discuss this prospect with your prescribing doctor. You may think you can go it alone, or you are concerned about side-effects, or it doesn't fit in with your belief system, or it's just not working for you. The most important thing to keep in mind is that you need to develop and strengthen many alternative strategies for tackling your depression or anxiety, e.g., not drinking, exercising, yoga, nutrition, CBT and mindfulness. Should you be on medication for bipolar, however, it is critically important that you stay on it.

Scenario 2. I have been prescribed medication for my depression/ anxiety, but I don't want to take it. Many people are reluctant to commence medication. This relates to beliefs and assumptions that they hold about themselves as a person. Many times these beliefs and assumptions are rigid and unhelpful. For example, many people have the view that if they succumb to medication, they are weak. They see medication as 'the end of the line' – a false assumption based on the idea that 'once you start medication you are on it for life'. Some common phrases I hear are 'I can't believe it's come to the point where I have to take medication; I thought I was a strong person' or 'What if this doesn't work for me, what's left for me then?' I don't buy these false assumptions. I don't believe that being on medication makes you 'weak'. No. This is really down to judgement. Let's say I have completed an assessment and the depression or anxiety is first episode, mild or moderate, related to a single life circumstance, is in the absence of previous mental health history, and the individual is happy to hold off and engage in a number of weeks of therapy. In such a case it's likely that I will advise the individual to hold off for a number of weeks after discussion with the prescribing doctor. Often prescribing doctors are pleased to know that the individual has engaged with a professional therapist and are happy with this course of action. (If the questioner has been diagnosed with bipolar and prescribed medication, I advise them to take that medication immediately and to return to their prescribing doctor.)

Scenario 3. I have been given this prescription for depression/anxiety. It is in my handbag. Do you think I should start on them? This is similar to Scenario 2, except that there the person did not want to take the medication; here they are asking if they should start. So, in considering the question of anti-depressant or anti-anxiety medication, we might begin with a comprehensive assessment. Is the depression/anxiety within the severe range? Have you had experience of medication before and, if so, what were the side-effects like? Have you tried therapy before? If so, what type was it? Was it passive counselling in the talk-and-listen format or dynamic active psychotherapy that gave you lifelong skills? What strategies have you tried to manage your depression/anxiety? If you decide to go on anti-depressants, will you also be committing to therapy?

If I am comfortable with my assessment and my client is comfortable not starting medication, and it's discussed with the prescribing doctor, then I am happy to advise holding off. The reason why I do this is so that any 'gains' can be attributed solely to therapy and not confused with the benefits obtained from medication. It also is more beneficial for a client, in that this will avoid both side-effects and the symptoms of withdrawal that can occur after medication has been stopped. This is also the reason why I advise people attending me not to see other therapists or practitioners, such as reiki healers, hypnotherapists, spiritualists, etc. It is critically important that the person put their 'gains' down to the work they are doing themselves and not to some external placebo.

Scenario 4. I was prescribed medication for my depression / anxiety, and I have come off it. What do you think? Don't stop taking your medication as soon as you feel better without first discussing it with your prescribing doctor. This can cause unpleasant withdrawal symptoms, such as agitation, crying spells, fatigue, depression, anxiety, etc. Stopping abruptly is not advised. If you are considering coming off your medication, your prescribing doctor will reduce your dosage in stages, allowing a number of weeks between each reduction. Tapering off anti-depressant medication may take a number of months, and you will need to be patient. Ideally try to choose a time when there are fewer stressful life events happening and a lot of stability in your home, work and relationships.

You are best advised to figure out how you fell out of the boat and to develop strong swimming strokes. Nevertheless, once you are off medication, you will be able to get on with your therapy. The role of medication is always something that can be reassessed in the future.

Other interventionist treatments

Electroconvulsive therapy (ECT). This can be used as a treatment for prolonged and severe depression. It is not fully understood how ECT works, and it is controversial. It involves passing an electrical current through the brain to cause a brief, controlled seizure. During the procedure a person receives anaesthesia and a muscle relaxant. People can have eight to ten sessions over a period of three to four weeks. Memory loss is a common side-effect.

I am conflicted about this intervention. I have seen it used successfully in severe depression. Yet I have wondered whether ECT would have been needed, had more proactive psychological interventions been used in the early phases of the depression.

In a small number of research trials, *deep brain stimulation (DBS)*, which involves the implantation of a device that sends electrical impulses to specific parts of the brain, has been used in tackling severe clinical depression. It's early days yet for this treatment; nevertheless, it could become an option in the future.

Some non-medication options for dealing with depression

Some people have the idea that the only way to manage their depression is the medical approach. There is nothing wrong with this, if it is what you believe. People with very fixed medical views sometimes see psychological intervention as a secondary treatment, rather than as an equivalent or even an enhanced intervention. People with such fixed beliefs may struggle when doing psychological-based work. But over time some individuals find their beliefs becoming more flexible and they end up doing really well.

Very often people who have difficulty with psychological approaches think that these therapies do not have the backing of science. However, many talking therapies – as they're called colloquially – have been extensively researched and analysed, and have a proven track record. In the UK the National Institute for Health and Care Excellence (NICE) provides independent, evidence-based guidelines for the health service on the most effective ways to treat disease and ill-health. It endorses many talking therapies, on the basis that they are well-researched, successful treatments for mental health issues.

I have already explored cognitive behavioural therapy and mindfulness at some length (and will continue to do so throughout the book, as they offer powerful techniques for dealing with a wide spectrum of mental health challenges). Mindfulness-based cognitive therapy has been endorsed by NICE as an effective treatment for people with a history of recurrent depression. Combining traditional cognitive behavioural therapy methods with the psychological strategies of mindfulness and meditation, it aims to prevent relapse.

Dynamic interpersonal therapy (DIT). This is a form of short-term psychodynamic psychotherapy developed for the treatment of depression. It focuses on the disruption in relationships that people experience while depressed. This, in turn, can cause the many distortions in thinking and feeling that are typical in depression. DIT aims to help the individual understand the connection between depressive symptoms and what is happening in their relationships, by identifying and focusing on unconscious and repetitive patterns of relating.

I think when it comes to transforming depression into hope we must use all the tools in our armoury. With many health issues, it seems to me that doctors try out treatment approaches sequentially; if one approach doesn't work, they move on to the next one. That's not the way to treat depression. Because depression is so insidious – it can creep up on you, grab you and potentially choke the life out of you – the treatment needs to be incredibly proactive, utilizing multiple approaches simultaneously. This is the view that I maintain as sensitively as possible in my practice.

I would like to throw a few other things into the mix. Often these are called adjunct therapies or treatments. Adjunct therapy is the combination of a second or third approach with a primary treatment to increase the effectiveness and speed of response. I often use multiple approaches in treating depression, though I introduce them gradually: the last thing a person with depression wants is another overwhelming list. Too often, however, the medication route is the only one considered, and these further options are paid lip service or ignored.

Dialectical behaviour therapy (DBT)/acceptance and commitment therapy (ACT). Both dialectical behaviour therapy and acceptance and commitment therapy are known as third-generation therapies. They are offshoots of CBT and grounded in high-quality research. These newer forms of CBT put more emphasis on reacting to our thoughts in new ways, placing them into context, rather than challenging the content of the negative thoughts.

ACT encourages the individual to just notice and accept

their thoughts. With this shift of focus, the person becomes an 'observer' of their thoughts, memories, feelings and sensations. Thus they become distinct or detached from their internal experiences. This distancing can stop the individual from being overwhelmed by these inner experiences and help them to make better choices.

DBT has its roots in the treatment of individuals who are experiencing borderline personality disorder. It is a form of CBT that has proved to be of help with severe and persistent emotional and behavioural difficulties, including substance misuse, suicidal behaviour, self-injury, eating disorders, personality presentations and depression. DBT is about acceptance and about change. It is practical, and includes skills training in mindfulness, emotional regulation, distress tolerance and interpersonal effectiveness.

Bibliotherapy. This is the use of self-help books for therapeutic purposes. The effectiveness of self-help books has been well established in clinical trials and is recommended by NICE as a useful starting point in treating mild and moderate depression as well as other presentations.

Computerized cognitive behavioural therapy programmes. I often recommend free online CBT therapy programmes such as the MoodGYM (www.moodgym.anu.edu.au) to assist individuals in addressing depression. They can play an important role in tackling mild depression or can be used in conjunction with other approaches for transforming moderate depression.

Exercise. There is increasing evidence to support the role of exercise in overcoming mild to moderate depression. Exercise such as walking, jogging, cycling, dancing or swimming all help to release endorphins. These are our bodies' 'feel good' hormones. Regular exercise has been shown to reduce stress, boost self-esteem and improve sleep, all of which positively impact on depression. I recommend that clients walk three to four times a week for 30 minutes. For some, the time obviously must be built up gradually. A good exercise habit is very important in maintaining health after depression has gone; and letting exercise lapse is a very good early-warning sign for recurrence.

Nutrition. I have worked on the popular RTÉ One show *Operation Transformation* for the last five years. *Operation Transformation* takes a group of five or six overweight individuals – 'leaders' – and, through healthy food planning, exercise and positive thinking, helps them to reshape their lives. Having worked on the show, and read widely on how nutrition and mood are related, I am convinced that there is indeed a strong link between the two. The overconsumption of processed foods that are high in fats, salt and sugar – such as prepared meals, cheeseburgers, French fries and doughnuts – saps people's vitality.

My psychology background does not allow me to make specific recommendations about nutritional supplements, but it's something I would like to explore more in the future. It's a bit of a conflict for me, as I don't want to introduce tablets into treatment, even nutritional supplements. It's my goal to reduce the amount of tablets people consume. When nutritional supplements are introduced, any lift in mood is associated with the tablet rather than with the therapy. Therefore people don't benefit from a sense of having internalized something that will help them in the future. The bottom line is that if you are experiencing depression and low mood, it's important that you eat a varied and healthy diet.

Support groups. Aware (www.aware.ie) and GROW (www. grow.ie) are two groups that provide information and support for people experiencing depression. Such groups can play an important role in helping those with depression.

Talking and relationships. Another way of thinking about social support is to view it as a 'relationship'. The relationships we make safeguard us from isolation. As human beings we all have a need to belong. The social support we receive from family, friends or groups is a vital and effective part of recovery from depression. Talk to friends and family members you can trust. The old saying that 'a problem shared is a problem halved' has stood the test of time. Social support limits the damage that can be caused by isolation and can positively affect how a depressed person looks on the world.

A word on alcohol and drugs: *don't*. Alcohol is a depressant. Using drugs and alcohol is the equivalent of throwing petrol on your emotional fires. While they might offer some temporary comfort, the relief doesn't last. Drinking and drug-taking stop you from dealing with your issues. They are a way of zoning out and numbing yourself.

Stopping drinking and drug-taking, even for a short period, can have an incredibly positive effect on low mood. Many people, in many situations, have come to see me with mild to moderate depression. I ask some individuals to commit to periods of abstinence from alcohol or drugs, including over-the-counter drugs such as codeine. Others do it without my having to ask. After a short period of intervention – say, six sessions over three months – individuals report a remarkable improvement. The key to this improvement is the absence of alcohol – increased energy, a better sleeping pattern, and so on. I cannot overstate how much staying away from alcohol and drugs can help in the fight against depression.

Reach higher – you deserve it

As you can see, there are various options available to you or to your family member who is depressed. Exploring the choices will help you to decide what intervention mix is most likely to work best for your particular situation and needs.

Medication alone is not enough. Medication may reduce the symptoms of depression and anxiety, but it doesn't address what's keeping the problem going. Not only have countless studies shown that therapy works just as well as medication in the treatment of depression and anxiety, but, significantly, it's also better at preventing relapse once treatment ends.

Medication is something external to you. But imagine being able to carry all the tools needed to take on your depression or anxiety inside of you. Tools that aren't made of chemicals and that have no side-effects, that empower you, give you confidence and that fundamentally say, 'I trust you to be able to manage your life.' This can be you. I truly believe this. Therapy will help you to get to the root of your depression or anxiety and allow you to move to a place of well-being. Therapy will help bolster your ability to cope with the ups and downs of everyday life. It will speed you towards your dreams. It will help you to develop a relationship with yourself, with others and with the world. It will support you in becoming your real self.

14

The right to live

I am going to stand up for the right to live. I believe that each individual with mental health difficulties has the ability to overcome these problems and lead a full life in which they are their real self. Philosophical debates about the right to choose death by suicide are not dissimilar to discussions about how many angels can dance on the head of a pin. They are academic, and do not relate to the real world of individuals who have led fulfilling lives after suicide attempts, or of families bereaved by suicide. I choose to fight on the side of families whose lives are devastated and say there is a better way.

A person contemplating suicide may not ask for help, as often they feel alone and isolated. Sometimes they think that nobody understands them or can help them. But that doesn't mean that help isn't wanted. Most people who die by suicide don't want to die; they just want to stop hurting. If you are worried about someone, what you need is a tool kit to help you to understand and prevent suicide by recognizing the warning signs and taking them seriously.

Obviously, as clinicians, we are deeply concerned about the issue of suicide among our clients, and it may help if I explain our thinking on the subject. We seek to distinguish between suicidal thoughts (ideation) and suicidal intent.

Suicidal ideation is when a person has active thoughts

about suicide but no plans to follow through on them. This is a common symptom of depression. In the therapy situation we make a contract with the individual in which they promise not to act on such thoughts in the course of the therapy. I find that people who experience depression are conscientious and genuine, and they have always honoured this promise to me. There may be fears on the client's part that a counsellor or therapist may overreact and initiate hospitalization, or that they may be judged by the clinician. This is where the relationship with the therapist is important: when that is one of trust, they come to understand that the clinician's response will be appropriate. Suicidal ideation is managed by therapists from session to session, and with successful therapy it disappears as the depression lifts.

Suicidal intent is when someone is having thoughts of how and where they will kill themselves and moving towards suicide. This can be an emergency situation and requires immediate intervention: the person should be taken to A&E or to a place of safety for a comprehensive assessment and the commencement of appropriate treatment.

Other key warning signs that we monitor in the therapy situation include:

- early-morning awakening – waking up 1–2 hours early and not being able to get back to sleep – is a red flag of the biological side of depression;
- withdrawing from friends, family and life in general;
- giving away possessions;
- sudden improvement in mood after being down or withdrawn;
- 'feeling trapped' – as if there is no way out;
- dramatic mood changes;

- an increase in alcohol or drug use;
- hopelessness about the future, seeing no reason for living or feeling they have no purpose in life.

If you are reading this and experiencing any of these symptoms, seek assistance from your GP immediately.

Asking about suicidal ideation and suicidal intent does not increase the likelihood of someone thinking about suicide or killing themselves. It may be the first discussion of this kind for the client, because they have been asked about suicide directly, but it's a frequent conversation for the psychologist. I do not, however, take such conversations lightly, as I am trying to distinguish between ideation and intent. At times we must ask the hard questions that other people don't, and subsequently hear details of pain, trauma and hurt. The experience of most clinicians, however, is that most clients report a sense of relief when a caring, non-judgemental clinician attempts to understand their pain and distress.

The truth about suicide

Having explained how the professionals look at suicide, let me dispel some common myths about it that I've come across in everyday life.

Myth. Talking about suicide is a bad idea, as it may give someone the idea to kill themselves.

Fact. You do not give a suicidal person the idea of killing themselves by talking about suicide. The opposite is true. By asking directly about suicide, you allow the individual to tell you how they feel. People who have felt suicidal often recount that it was a huge relief to be able to talk about what they were going through. Talking about suicide can save a life.

Myth. People who talk about suicide are not serious and never go through with it.

Fact. 80% of people who die by suicide have talked about it. Sometimes it can be in very subtle ways, such as 'Life's not worth living' or 'I have no future'. Some might have been more direct and said that they wanted to die. It is critically important to take anyone talking about suicide seriously.

Myth. People who threaten suicide are just attention-seeking and should not be taken seriously.

Fact. It bears repeating that people who threaten suicide always need to be taken seriously. A person who is suicidal is in pain and often reaches out for help because they do not know what to do and have lost hope. We all need loving care and attention: who does not need some attention in their life? It may well be that they want attention in the sense of calling out for help. Giving them this attention may save their life.

Myth. A person who has made a serious suicide attempt is unlikely to make another.

Fact. People who have tried to kill themselves are more likely to die by suicide than other people.

Myth. You need to be clinically depressed to attempt suicide.

Fact. Not necessarily. Not all people who die by suicide had mental health problems at the time of their death. Suicidal thoughts can follow serious life events such as losing a job, debt, death of a loved one, breakdown of a relationship, etc. Nevertheless, depression is often a feature in financial suicides.

Myth. People who attempt suicide are crazy.

Fact. No. Most people who die by suicide are not psychotic or insane. They are in great pain. They may be upset, grief-stricken, depressed or despairing. Extreme distress from emotional pain is not necessarily a sign of mental illness.

Myth. If a person is serious about killing themselves, there is nothing you can do. Suicide cannot be prevented. People who are suicidal want to die.

Fact. Suicide can be prevented. Most people who are suicidal do not want to die; they just want to stop their pain. Many times feeling actively suicidal is temporary, even if the person is in great distress. This is why getting the right kind of support at the right time is so important.

It can be helpful to think about suicide by envisaging the image of a light at the end of a U-shaped tunnel. You know that the light is there, but unfortunately the person experiencing great pain – possibly suffering from depression – cannot see this light. Tragically, when the person is in the dark end of the tunnel, they can kill themselves, because they see no light. Essentially the person thinks that it will be best for everyone if they kill themselves. It's faulty problem-solving. The lens that the person wears is so dark it obliterates all hope. It is a desperate attempt to escape a suffering that has become unbearable.

This permanent solution to a temporary problem is catastrophic, particularly for the surviving family members. The challenge is to provide an intervention that enables the person to turn the corner so that they can see the light. It's about raising hope. I have seen many individuals survive serious suicide attempts who were in the darkest part of the tunnel. We worked together for a period of time, and every so often I see them now in my day-to-day life, getting on with 'ordinary' lives – marrying, having children, working and staying in the light. If you're contemplating suicide, please believe that you can turn the corner, that there is light at the end of the tunnel and that you can live a fulfilling, contented and authentic life.

It's just that you can't see the light at the moment

Stay, turn the corner and see the light of hope

Don't check out here

There is always light at the end of the tunnel

What to watch out for when you think someone is suicidal

Most individuals considering suicide give warning signals about their intentions. The best way to prevent suicide is to recognize these signs and to know how to respond. If you believe that a friend or family member is suicidal, you can play an important role in suicide prevention.

If you are concerned about someone, take note of the following.

The situation. What's happening in the person's life? Have they experienced any major life events recently?

- loss – of a loved one, friend, child, job, relationship, pet, livelihood;
- physical illness – cancer or newly diagnosed chronic health problem, such as arthritis, MS, motor neuron disease, anything causing chronic pain;
- change in circumstances – separation, divorce, retirement, redundancy, children leaving home;
- mental health difficulty or trauma;
- suicide of a family member, friend or indeed a public figure;
- financial and legal problems;
- disappointment – being overlooked for promotion, failed exam.

Emotional well-being. How does the person feel about their life? For some people, major life events can be difficult and devastating. Be conscious of:

- how a person feels about what happened;
- what meaning it has for them;
- whether they feel the pain is temporary and that they can cope with it or whether they feel they can't cope with it;
- any feelings such as desperation, depression, hopelessness, pain, anger, sadness, shame, loneliness, isolation.

Physical well-being. Have there been physical changes? Have you noticed:

- a lack of self-care – showering, shaving, personal grooming;
- excessively sleeping or can't sleep properly;
- reduced appetite or excessive eating;
- agitation or pacing;
- difficulty in concentrating;
- little interest in sex.

Behaviour. What are they doing? Many times people at risk of suicide exhibit clues in their behaviour. These may include:

- speaking or joking about suicide – they talk of escape, of finding a way out, of having no future;
- looking for ways to kill themselves – seeking access to pills, weapons or other means;
- talking or writing about death or dying – preoccupation with death, regrets about previous suicide attempts;
- expressing feelings of self-hatred, having a belief that they are a burden – 'everybody would be better off without me';
- withdrawing from friends, family or society; losing interest in previously enjoyed activities;
- getting affairs in order, making a will or giving away possessions;
- increase in self-destructive behaviour – alcohol, drug use, reckless driving, law-breaking and fighting;
- saying goodbye – unusual or unexpected calls or visits to family and friends;
- having a sudden sense of calm and happiness after being extremely depressed – this can be a warning sign that the person has made a decision to die by suicide.

Warning signs for suicidal teens

There are some additional suicide warning signs for teenagers:

- changes in eating and sleeping habits;
- bullying experiences – unsupportive friends or school environments, avoidance of school;
- running away, out-of-character violent or rebellious behaviour;
- drug or alcohol use;
- recent traumatic event;
- exclusion from peer group;
- exposure to other teen suicides;
- persistent boredom, decline in quality of schoolwork because of difficulty in concentrating;
- not engaging in family activities and not enjoying rewards or praise;
- frequent illnesses – physical symptoms associated with emotional upset, including stomach ache, headaches and fatigue;
- pressures to fit in – struggles with self-esteem, self-doubt;
- concerns about sexual orientation and acceptance by others.

This last point is a concern for young gay teenagers. I recently met James, a former client, who is in his mid-teens. He had suffered from depression but is now doing very well. I told him about this book and invited him to put down his thoughts, so that others with similar struggles might read them. Here is his story.

'When I was young, I was always a bubbly well-mannered child who tried to be as helpful to all of my friends and teachers as I could. This lasted all through primary school. Once I got into secondary school, I changed. I became quiet and withdrawn from my friends. I began to talk to only a few people who I trusted a lot, but never really told them what I was thinking. I had all these thoughts that were whizzing through my head: "Why am I here?", "I hate myself", "I am weird", etc. I felt so confused and sad. I soon began to feel depressed and sad, but I chose not to tell anyone. No one. One day, while texting my friend Sophie, she texted, "You okay you seem sad all of a sudden." I replied, "I'm okay don't worry." Sophie persisted and I began to pour out my mind and heart to her and she sat there and helped me through every second, even when I was telling her that all I wanted to do was die.

'Soon after I told her, I felt a lot happier. Sophie helped me a lot. I was close to ending my own life, but she held me back. Sadly the friendship crumbled and I fell to pieces when I was left all alone again.

'I fell in and out of depression but I told one other person and they did the right thing and went to an adult and told them all about me and my thoughts. At the time I believed it was the worst thing they could've done; my parents and school were keeping watch on me. I was referred to local services, but there was a massive waiting list. I still didn't like talking to anyone; I kept it in; I didn't want to disappoint or hurt. My GP insisted on my visiting a psychologist. I soon felt a lot happier in myself and my mood levels increased. But I still didn't like talking to anyone.

'Months later I began to accept that I was gay and told a

few of my friends. The few I came out to helped me understand that it was okay to be gay. Soon I realized that one of the reasons I was having suicidal thoughts was that I wasn't okay with my sexuality and believed that being gay was wrong. That I would be cast out of society for being gay. My friends showed me that it was okay to be yourself. Soon I began to develop feelings for someone who was never going to like me the way I liked him. It broke my heart to know it would never happen, so I began to fill my mind with self-destructive thoughts again. I thought about ending my life, but I realized how stupid it would be to do that. I had a life to live.

'I now think how stupid I was to ever think of ending my own life, as I now see the true love and affection my family and friends feel towards me. I owe my life to the people who stood by me at my lowest points and I thank them wholeheartedly. One of the main pieces of advice I took away with me is what I now live my life by; that saying is "Thoughts are thoughts; they are not facts." I don't need to act on my thoughts now. I am okay with who I am. I am my real self. You can like me or not, but I like me.'

This is a remarkable insight into the adolescent mind. For example, you can see that at first James found it easier to talk by text. In face-to-face talk with friends, parents, teachers and health care workers, there was no disclosure of the inner conflict that he was experiencing.

James came out to his peers. The reality is that your teenager will more than likely share his thoughts with another teenager and not with an adult. James's parents were very enlightened, accepting and supportive, despite James's initial false assumptions. His story shows the struggles, the ups and downs, and the immediacy of teenage emotions. It shows that it's very difficult to put an 'old head on young shoulders'. It also shows that when you are true to yourself and true to others, you are your real self. And when you are your real self, you are very far away from the darkness of suicide.

Suicide and older people

While we consider suicide mainly to be a phenomenon among young males, it is in fact a key concern in those over sixty-five. Depression in the elderly is often under-diagnosed and left untreated. Warning signs of suicide for persons aged sixty-five and older include:

- recent death of a loved one;
- major life changes, such as retirement;
- physical illness, disability, chronic illness or chronic pain;
- loss of independence;
- isolation and loneliness;
- stockpiling medications;
- loss of sense of purpose;
- saying goodbye;
- rush to revise or complete a will.

What to do if you think someone is suicidal

Now that you have some background in the warning signs of suicide, what other key suicide prevention skills do you need if you are concerned that a person may be considering taking their own life?

First, I have created a 'Bill of Rights' for you as a life saver. Learn your rights: this will give you confidence and ensure

that you don't become ensnared by promises you don't need
to keep.

The Life Saver's Bill of Rights

1. I have the right to ask if you are safe.
2. I have the right to show I care.
3. If I am concerned that you may be thinking of
   killing yourself, I am going to ask the question
   'Have you active plans for killing yourself?'
4. I have the right to try to protect you without
   harming myself.
5. I have the right to contact other people and
   share information relating to your safety with them,
   even though you have asked for confidentiality.
   Your life is more important than your
   confidentiality.
6. I have the right not to be sworn to secrecy. If I do
   so swear, the oath must be considered temporary. I
   will contact others, as your life is more important
   than your secrecy.
7. If I am a teenager, I have the right to pass this
   knowledge to a responsible adult – teacher, school
   counsellor or parent.
8. I have the right not to carry this burden of
   information on my own.
9. If you get angry because of breaches of
   confidentiality, I respect your right to be angry,
   while knowing that I did the right thing.
10. I have the right to believe that I did the best I could
    with the knowledge I had at a particular moment in
    time. I know that I am not in full possession of the

facts, because it is impossible to know someone else fully.

11. While I understand that I have these rights, I also understand that you too have rights.

Step 1. Do something now – approach the person

If you are concerned that someone you know is considering suicide, act immediately. Often we are reluctant to get involved in other people's business. There are many reasons, including fear and embarrassment. Sometimes we think that we may be seen as interfering. But if somebody fell into a river and you had a lifebuoy in your hand, would you hold on to it or would you throw it? Of course you wouldn't think twice about throwing it.

If you are trying to save somebody's life, then you have permission to approach the person. After all, if the outcome is that someone's life has been saved, what does it matter if you feel a little embarrassed or fearful? Your heart and intentions are in the right place.

Don't assume that they will get better without help or that they will seek help on their own. It's understandable that your natural reaction may be to panic, or to ignore the situation in the hope that it will go away.

Be direct. You may wish to start a conversation by saying 'I've been feeling concerned about you lately' or 'I've noticed some differences in you recently and I am concerned because you don't seem to be yourself'. You may wish to ask: 'Did something happen to make you start to feel this way?' or 'How best can I support you right now?'

Step 2. Be supportive

Be yourself. Let the person know you care and that they are not alone. There are no particular right words. You may wish to say, 'You are not alone in this', 'I'm here with you', 'I may not be able to fully understand how you feel, but I care about you and want to help you', 'You may not believe it right now, but the way you're feeling will change', 'I understand you can't see the light at the end of the tunnel, but there is light there, hold on, let's get the right help and you will get there', 'I am here to help you'.

Allow the suicidal person to unload their despair and to ventilate anger if necessary. Try to be sympathetic, patient and calm. Offer hope. Let them know that their life is important to you. Don't argue with the person. Avoid saying things such as 'Look on the bright side' or 'Your suicide will hurt your family'. Don't lecture them on the value of life. Don't promise confidentiality. Don't allow yourself to be sworn to secrecy. A life is at stake and you have the right to protect that life by breaking confidentiality and secrecy. Don't blame yourself. You can't fix someone's depression. Your loved one's happiness or depression is not your responsibility. Don't feel like you have to provide an immediate solution. Just listen.

Step 3. Be direct – ask the hard questions and check out their safety

You need to ask a very hard question. Unless you do, you will not know if the person has an active suicide plan. Remember: asking the question does not put the idea into their head but rather will encourage them to talk about their feelings. You are saving someone's life. Take a deep breath and say:

'Have you an active plan to kill yourself?' If the answer is yes, you will want to explore more. 'Do you have what you need to carry out your plan?' 'Do you know when you plan to kill yourself?' This information will tell you how immediate the situation is and what you need to do. If you are really concerned about imminent danger, don't leave the person alone and make sure you seek help. Remove any means of suicide available, including weapons, medication, alcohol or even access to a car. Be conscious of your own safety. Never be afraid to call the ambulance service or the gardaí on 999. They, like you, are life savers. If it's late at night or at the weekend, and you can get them to accompany you, go immediately to your nearest A&E.

Step 4. Decide the next step – persuade the person to get help

More often than not, the person is relieved after they have opened up and discussed their despair. Now that you have this information, you can discuss together what the next steps should be. You may need the help of others to persuade the person to get professional help. This may include their partner, parents or close friends. Only by sharing this information can you make sure that the person gets the help and support they need. You may wish to call a crisis line for advice, such as: the Samaritans Freephone 116 123; your general practitioner or out-of-hours GP service; Pieta House 01 6235606; the Aware Support Line 1890 303 302 (Monday to Sunday, 10 a.m. to 10 p.m.); or the Console suicide helpline 1800 247 247 (24 hours, 365 days a year) or text HELP to 51444.

If the risk is an immediate, encourage the person to get help from a range of professional and support people: GP, counsellor, psychologist, mental health services, school counsellor, Pieta House, support groups such as Aware or GROW Ireland, or Mind in the UK.

In some situations the person may refuse to get help. This may be very difficult for you. While you can do your best to find the help they need, you cannot force them to accept it. You do not need to shoulder this responsibility alone. Let other relevant people be aware of the situation.

Offer to accompany the person to the appointment. After the appointment, check that they have conveyed their thoughts of suicide and ask what help they were offered. Help them follow through with the recommendations.

Step 5. Make a contract and help to develop a safety plan

In the event that thoughts of suicide return, the person needs to have a safety plan in place. Ask them to make a commitment to you that they will not kill themselves, at least not for an agreed amount of time, until they have looked at the options that life holds.

Ask the person to reach out and to connect with an agreed resource place or person. If that person is not available, ask them to reach out and tell someone else. If that person is not available, ask them to ring a suicide crisis line, such as the Samaritans Freephone 116 123. If there is an immediate risk, ask them to ring 999 and explain the situation, so that they can be taken to a place of safety.

Here is a sample safety contract and plan.

SAFETY CONTRACT AND PLAN

When I feel unsafe and I am thinking about dying by suicide, I promise to contact:

1. In the first instance I will contact: ....
2. If they are unavailable, I will contact: ....
3. If they are unavailable, I will contact: ....
4. If they are unavailable, I will contact: ....
5. If none of these is available, I will contact the Samaritans on Freephone 116 123 or Console 1800 247 247 or text HELP to 51444.
6. In addition I will contact my GP: ....
7. Or the GP out-of-hours service on: ....
8. If I am in immediate danger, I will contact the ambulance service or the gardaí on 999, and I will ask the person to bring me to a place of safety – the local A&E department at .... which has access to 24-hour mental health services.

Signed: ....

I commit to be there for you, support you and say Choose Life.

Signed: ....

1. .... supporter
2. .... supporter
3. .... supporter
4. .... supporter

Step 6. Look after yourself

It's an incredibly difficult time for you if you are supporting somebody who is considering suicide. It is emotionally draining, particularly if your support has been offered over a long period of time. As clinicians, we receive supervision, because it can be extremely difficult to listen to a person's thoughts about suicide, and talking about it can relieve some of the weight. Therefore, it's important for you to talk to somebody else. Don't do it all on your own. Find other people to support the person you were worried about. I know this is hard, but try not to let the concerns about the other person dominate your life; otherwise you are at risk of becoming swamped by them.

Asking someone about their suicidal thinking is a very brave act. You can look back and say, 'I did my best.' You have indeed. It is more than likely that you have saved a life.

Step 7. Stay involved

Your involvement and that of family and friends is very important. Suicidal thoughts don't easily disappear. You may need to advocate for the person. Sometimes you need to shout to be heard in order to access services. Check to see that a safety plan has been written out.

If you are suicidal

If you are reading this and contemplating suicide, there is an internal debate going on within you: one voice is tempting you with a solution to your pain and another voice is asking you to live. I believe that there is a better life for you, if you have the right tools to obtain it. Please reach out. Complete a safety contract and plan, which can help you through the fog of faulty decision-making. Reach out and contact your family, friend, GP, crisis lines, therapist, psychologist, mental health service or support group. Do what you need to do to keep safe, right now.

Through these pages I want to support the voice that is asking you to live. Your life is worth living. You have a lot to offer. With the right help and support, you will move to a place of hope; to a place where you will grow, be nurtured and nurture others; to a place where you will be loved and you will love others. It may not seem like that now. But you can move towards a life in which you will live with compassion towards yourself and others. You have so much to give. You have so much more to grow. Give yourself time and space to live authentically.

We increasingly need to have the conversation about preventing suicide. This is made more difficult by the stigma attached to mental health issues. Public attitudes need to change: awareness and understanding need to increase. There are times in life when it's okay not to be okay.

Many great organizations exist to tackle the epidemic of suicide in Irish society. Three times more people die by suicide than through road traffic accidents. Brave people have stepped forward to start this conversation. Among them are Paul Kelly of Console (www.console.ie); Joan Freeman of Pieta House (www.pieta.ie); Jim Breen of Cycle Against Suicide (www.cycleagainstsuicide.com); 3Ts: Turn the Tide of Suicide (www.3ts.ie); and family members bereaved by suicide up and down the country. The National Office for

Suicide Prevention (NOSP) (www.nosp.ie) has details of excellent training courses – Applied Suicide Intervention Skills Training (ASIST) and safeTALK – that are available to members of the public. In addition, NOSP has an office in every region with suicide resource officers who will be able to give you further information. For resources in the UK check out the website of TASC, the Alliance of Suicide Prevention Charities (www.tasc-uk.org).

While I applaud these individuals and organizations for shining a light of hope in order to dispel the stigma of suicide, I believe we need to have a broader national conversation about living well – a conversation that moves beyond mental health to the development of mental and emotional fitness as a proactive strategy to protect ourselves and our youth. A conversation that teases out what type of relationships we value and that leads to a debate about what we think is important as a society. Are our lives about the level of economic activity – i.e., human doing – or are they about human being? Avenues of discussion need to be opened on how we achieve health and happiness for ourselves, our children and our society. When we focus on our well-being, we are transforming, self-aware, insightful and becoming our real selves.

CHALLENGE THREE

Anxiety and panic attacks

15

The 'straitjacket' of anxiety

Worrying is not a useful pastime – it only helps us if it motivates us to do something about the problem. Unfortunately, most worry just creates doubts about our abilities and increases our fears. We get absorbed into catastrophic thinking, worst-case scenarios and 'what ifs'. This just exhausts our emotional energy and heightens our anxiety. Worrying can create fear, panic attacks and anxiety. All of these drain joy, life and energy, and cause incredible distress. The good news is that there are very effective tools to banish panic and anxiety from your life. Remember: the more clearly you can define the problem, the easier it is to target your treatment tools. I often liken anxiety to a virtual 'straitjacket'. This anxiety straitjacket restricts your breathing, talking, walking, engaging, connecting, working, relating, communicating and, ultimately, living. (Of course sometimes panic attacks are a feature of other mental health difficulties, including social anxiety, obsessive compulsive disorder or post-traumatic stress disorder. The information about coping with panic attacks in this chapter, however, applies across the board.)

It's worth noting that for many people depression and anxiety can happen together. I imagine it like a train with two coaches. It's critical that there is a careful assessment to determine whether anxiety/panic is the primary or secondary issue, as the treatment needs to be highly targeted.

Essentially, I am trying to figure out what is driving the train. For some people, the exhaustion from carrying around anxiety leads to their mood dropping to depression. For others, the primary issue is depression, and their anxiety/panic is secondary to this low mood. More often than not, when you target the primary issue the other one falls away.

When someone comes into my therapy room and panic attacks are the primary issue, I am confident that within two to three months their lives will be changed dramatically. As the weekly sessions progress, I enjoy the revelations, freedoms and small but significant things that are recounted as the straitjacket is removed. The power of panic to restrict is reduced, and the individual regains control. Let's examine the common types of anxiety problems.

Understanding panic attacks

Often people find themselves in the midst of an intense, terrifying panic attack with no warning. The terror generated is such that the person is fooled into thinking they are dying, going crazy, about to faint or to have a heart attack. The symptoms are so overpowering and alarming that the person is convinced that they are in extreme danger. Other symptoms associated with the adrenaline response to panic – the 'fight/flight/freeze' response – include breathlessness, dizziness, sweating, trembling, choking sensation, fast heart rate, nausea and feelings of dread. Indeed, some people find it hard to believe that a panic attack can be such an overwhelming experience. Many have the above symptoms, while others can have very unusual experiences. Once having had a panic attack, the victim often develops 'fear of fear' – they worry about having other attacks in the future, so the whole cycle becomes a vicious circle. (A full list of panic attack symptoms is available here: www.anxietycentre.com/anxiety-symptoms.shtml.)

It's important to know your enemy in order to defeat it. Panic attacks affect the way we think, how we behave and how our body reacts. Take Linda, who was driving on the motorway and had to pull over.

> 'The feeling came on me all of a sudden. I thought I was going to lose control, pass out or even die, there was sweat rolling down my back, my body was shaking and cold, it was like an electric-shock feeling with a shooting pain and pressure in my neck and head, it's like my heart was pumping out of my chest, my legs were like jelly. I had never felt anything like this, I was so scared, I pulled over and dialled 999. An ambulance came and they took me to hospital. I was so relieved when I saw their blue lights because I knew I was going to be safe. All in all it lasted a number of hours. I got to the hospital and the doctors scanned my brain and did all the usual tests. They said everything was okay. How could that be, given what I experienced? Now I worry all the time about this happening again – what would happen if I suddenly snapped again? What if I lost control again? In A&E they said that this was a panic attack. I find that hard to believe, given how powerful this experience was.'

You can have a sudden rush of intense fear, a strong feeling of losing control and a sense that something awful is about to happen. Common thoughts during panic include: 'I'm losing my mind', 'I'm having a heart attack', 'I'm going mad', 'I'm going to die', 'I'm going to do something stupid', 'I'm going to faint'. During panic, *the brain cannot distinguish between what is real and what it is thinking.* So if you think you're going to die or you're having a heart attack, your brain protects you by sending out more adrenaline and stress hormones. This in turn leads to more of the 'fight/flight/freeze' response. A vicious circle is thus created.

Many people who experience panic try to manage it by avoiding places that might induce it, such as a large supermarket or an airport. They might only drive if there is another person with them in the car, or only sit near the exit or aisle of a cinema. Sometimes these safety behaviours are done in a discreet way, so only the person with panic attacks knows it's happening.

What causes the attacks?

The exact causes are unclear, but there does seem to be a connection with stressful life events, including bereavement, illness, redundancy, getting married, having a child. Many people have told me how their panic attack happened out of the blue. However, when you analyse life events in the year preceding the attack, you often find factors such as bereavement or illnesses such as cancer in other family members. There is also some evidence for a genetic predisposition; if a family member has suffered from panic attacks, you are at increased risk, particularly at stressful times.

Physical and psychological causes of panic disorder can work together in a negative cycle. For example, if a person with panic experiences a racing heartbeat caused by drinking too much coffee or exercising, they might misinterpret this as a symptom of a panic attack and, because of their anxiety, actually trigger one.

Recurring panic attacks can take an incredible emotional toll. The memory of the fear can significantly impact on self-confidence and disrupt many parts of life. The bottom line is that skewed thoughts and a misinterpretation of bodily cues cause panic attacks. The good news is that if someone can think their way into a panic attack, they can think their way out of it.

When worry is constant

We all worry from time to time – it's part of life. However, generalized anxiety disorder (GAD) is worry on a whole other level. With GAD the worry is intrusive, persisting to such an extent that quality of life is seriously affected. With GAD the level of anxiety is less intense than that of a panic attack, but it hangs around much longer, making normal life difficult and relaxation impossible. Symptoms include constant worries running through someone's head, a constant feeling of dread, exhaustion, concentration difficulties, sleep disturbance, an inability to relax and a constant habit of putting things off because of a feeling of being overwhelmed. GAD is one of the most common anxiety disorders.

A panic attack can be imagined as a bomb of adrenaline exploding inside, causing you to believe that you were going to die or go mad. Now scale that back and imagine continual low- to medium-grade anxiety, as well as pervasive worrying, nervousness and tension. This chronic worry, most often unfounded, revolves around health, family, work or money.

Ruby described her GAD.

'I have always been a worrier. I know that my mum was one too. I seem to worry about everything: my children, even though they are adults now, my brother and sisters, my work, my home, everything. I work as a nurse, and each day as I go into work I worry whether I'll be able to cope, if my manager is going to say something to me, and yet I've been a qualified nurse for more than twenty years. I feel tense all the time and unable to wind down. Recently it has got worse. It was a combination of having a health problem associated with breast cancer, which will require further investigation, and my husband being made redundant from work. My GP has had me on Prozac for the last four years. It takes the edge off my worry but leaves me feeling emotionally numb. What brought me to your door was having to put my twelve-year-old dog to sleep – the last straw.

'Between worrying about everything and my mood dropping, my life has become a misery. I worry about the smallest things. What are we having for dinner tonight? What time should I put the meat on? What time should I put on the potatoes? I hope my sons eat out today and that I don't have to cook for them later on – hadn't I better ring and check? I wonder, what did Mrs Duffy think of the dress I wore to the wedding last week?

'Sleep is such a difficulty. Even when I fall asleep I can still wake up in the middle of the night just worrying. How are we going to survive with Tom out of work? Will I have to increase my hours? My heart races. I get so tense. It's just exhausting me, it's draining me. My concentration is shot. I cannot watch telly or even read a newspaper. I am giving myself an ulcer.'

As you can see from Ruby's story, with GAD there is persistent, excessive, unrealistic and chronic worry about everyday things, such as family, work, finances, education and home life. This worrying goes on every day, and for some people it lasts all day long. The sufferer predicts the worst outcome and catastrophizes about every situation. This worry cycle is pervasive and affects concentration.

GAD triggers our stress response. Since chronic worry is ever-present every day, these increased levels of stress hormones gradually become toxic. Symptoms include general tension, muscle tension, fatigue, restlessness, disturbed sleep, irritability, being on edge, gastrointestinal issues (IBS, diarrhoea), trembling, sweating and light-headedness.

GAD is characterized by checking and reassurance-seeking behaviours. Initially the instinctive response from the person being checked is to provide reassurance. That, however, provides only a temporary relief to the GAD sufferer, whose anxiety is then strengthened. As you can imagine, this excessive checking can become very annoying for the person being checked. Take for example Josephine, who checks in on her daughter Joanne. Before Joanne, who is twenty-eight, goes out, Josephine wants to know when she will return. During the evening Josephine checks in with Joanne by ringing her four times. Joanne comes on some old friends and decides to stay out longer. By now she's sick of her mother's calls and ignores her. Josephine goes to bed and tries to read, awaiting Joanne's return, dreading the worst. Other examples of checking and getting reassurance include persistent visits to the GP for a never-ending list of concerns. GAD is draining for the individual and both irritating and draining for their family members.

What causes GAD?

The exact cause of GAD is unknown; however, it appears biological factors, elements in the family background and stressful life experiences can all play a role. The disorder emerges slowly, starting in adolescence and evolving over time through to middle age. Symptoms can wax and wane, depending on different levels of stress and the life events encountered. Some people with a mild form of GAD are able to manage well enough to hold down a job. Others experience severe anxiety constantly, finding even the simplest tasks overwhelming. With GAD the individual's quality of life is eroded. The chronic worry reduces a person's ability to cope with the normal ups and downs of everyday existence. The good news is that with the tools of CBT (Chapters 4–6) this chronic worry can be weeded out and quality of life restored.

Some other common anxiety disorders

Anxieties come in many guises. Too often they can be lumped together, resulting in poor treatments and even poorer outcomes. Here are some of the more common varieties.

Phobias. An intense fear of a specific object or situation. Common examples are fear of dogs, snakes, lifts, heights or flying. Treatment for specific phobias is relatively quick and straightforward, and there are excellent outcomes with the technique of graded exposure (explained in the next chapter).

Agoraphobia. This is the most common type of phobia and affects 5% to 10% of people within their lifetime. A person with agoraphobia fears places and situations where they think that escape may be difficult or help will not be available. It is often linked to certain places such as the supermarket, shops, lifts or the church. Many times to overcome this fear the person engages in common safety behaviours, such as arranging to go out with other people. The reason for this is to address the question: 'What if something happened to me?' The answer is: 'If something happened, somebody would be there to assist.'

Obsessive compulsive disorder (OCD). This is a particularly distressing anxiety condition, and typically has a four-step pattern.

- *Step 1. Obsession.* Unwanted, unpleasant intrusive thoughts or images. The mind is overwhelmed by a constant obsessive fear or concern, such as needing to have clean hands all the time.
- *Step 2. Anxiety.* The obsession (intrusive thought) that has overwhelmed the person provokes a feeling of intense anxiety and distress.
- *Step 3. Compulsion.* A pattern of compulsive behaviour is adopted to reduce the anxiety and distress, such as checking all the windows and doors are locked at least three times before leaving the house.
- *Step 4. Temporary relief.* The compulsive behaviour brings temporary relief from anxiety but the obsession and anxiety soon return, causing the cycle to begin again.

Health anxiety. This anxiety, also called hypochondria, causes the sufferer to be significantly concerned with the idea that they are, or will become, seriously ill. People who experience health anxiety are 'super scanners' and interpret harmless physical symptoms as indicators of disease or medical conditions. So a chest tightness must be a heart attack, a headache must be a brain tumour, or slight forgetfulness must be Alzheimer's disease. Sufferers often spend a lot of time (and money) visiting doctors and specialists needlessly.

Social anxiety. The person fears being scrutinized, judged or evaluated negatively by others in social situations. Sufferers often fear they may do things that will cause embarrassment or lead to ridicule. The person engages in mind-reading – making false assumptions about how other people will think about them. These assumptions are negative and include being seen as embarrassing, shameful, stupid or ugly. As a result the person with social anxiety fears rejection, criticism, humiliation or embarrassment. People can experience blushing, shaking and sweating. Social anxiety leads to avoidance and safety behaviours. See Chapters 22 and 23 for a more in-depth analysis of this disorder.

Post-traumatic stress disorder (PTSD). When a person goes through an event where they think they or a family member might die or be seriously injured, this can have a profound impact. Cognitive symptoms include flashbacks, nightmares and loss of concentration. Behavioural symptoms include being overly alert or jumpy, having difficulty falling asleep, and feeling irritable and angry. Many people engage in avoidant behaviours such as not allowing themselves to get upset when they think about the trauma, staying away from reminders of the trauma, actively trying to push the trauma out of their memory and actively not talking about it. Most often these are common reactions to an abnormal event.

The buffer zone

I would like to close this chapter by introducing you to the concept of the buffer zone. The larger your buffer zone, the more ability you have to tackle the ups and downs of everyday life. Imagine a scale from 0% to 100%, where 0 is calm and 100 is a full-on anxiety or panic attack.

Strong buffer zone

Many of us carry stress levels that are somewhere around 30%. As you've read in Chapter 7, we all need a certain amount of stress to get us up and going. This gives a capacity, or buffer zone, of 70%. This strong buffer zone allows us to cope better when faced with new challenges or life events. Imagine facing a life challenge such as illness or bereavement with a strong buffer zone, in comparison with a limited buffer zone.

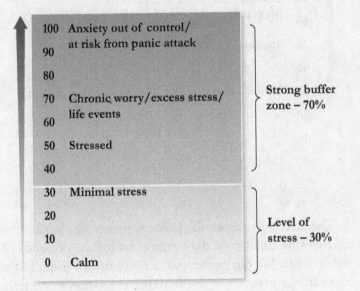

Limited buffer zone

By contrast, a person experiencing excessive stress, depression or chronic worry, such as in GAD, is more likely to be running a stress level of around 80%. This significantly reduces the capacity of their buffer zone. When your buffer zone gets squeezed like this, it doesn't take much to tip you over the edge. Essentially, you are at risk of developing out-of-control anxiety or a full-on panic attack.

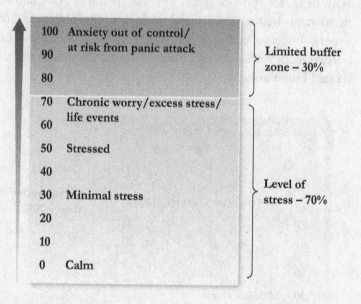

The goal is to reduce the baseline percentage in order to create more capacity in the buffer zone for the demands of modern life. We can proactively achieve this by using all the tools in our armoury – the thinking and behavioural techniques of CBT, tackling our core beliefs, breathing and mindfulness.

But before going down the therapy or self-help route, it's a good idea to have a full health check to exclude any underlying issues such as thyroid problems or heart issues.

Two treatment options are available for the panic and

anxiety syndromes outlined in this chapter: medication and CBT. CBT is the most effective form of treatment for panic attacks. Typically, treatment with a counsellor or therapist consists of approximately six to ten sessions, and the outcome is usually excellent.

This is a real message of hope – a message that means worry, fear, panic attacks and anxiety can be consigned to the past and the freedom to be your real self can be envisaged for the future. Let's go into treatment.

16

Transforming anxiety and becoming free

Let's consider some truths about panic attacks and anxiety. No one has ever gone 'crazy' from these. It can't happen. It's impossible to pass out or faint. Why? Because with adrenaline flowing through your system, your heart rate and blood pressure rise. People faint because there is a sudden drop in blood pressure. During panic, people focus on the heart rate; but during a heart attack they are focusing on crushing central chest pain. Some people having a panic attack believe that they will stop breathing and suffocate. This is impossible. Some believe that they will 'lose control of themselves' and that they may do something foolish in public or that other people may notice. This just doesn't happen. Why? Because anyone thinking they could 'lose control' actually is in control. With a panic attack, you have awareness and you are in touch with reality. And even when you are having a full-blown attack, the likelihood of another person noticing is almost nil, unless you tell them.

Anxiety and panic attacks are sustained by a lens on the world that selects threats in the present and in the future. Your 'here and now' automatic negative thoughts (ANTs) (Chapter 5) are fear, insecurity and threat-based ideas; catastrophizing thoughts play a very important role. In chronic worry or GAD, the persistence and pervasiveness of worry ANTs maintain the ongoing state of anxiety. Your thoughts and feelings of panic seem so real that the brain is tricked into thinking that you are in danger, when, in fact, you are not. You are in an anxiety trap. *Your thinking creates your reality.*

The solutions to worry, anxiety and panic attacks

Remember the buffer zone that I introduced in the last chapter? The bigger your buffer zone, the greater your capacity to deal with stress and anxiety. Your challenge is to stretch out the boundaries of this zone, so that you can overcome the trials and tribulations that life throws at you. Ways to stretch this zone include physical exercise, mindfulness practice, meditation, walking, having a bath, talking about your difficulties, getting support, or doing yoga or tai chi.

Proactive CBT has been shown by multiple research studies to be the most effective treatment for worry, anxiety and panic attacks. While the past is acknowledged, the focus is on making the present better, so that the future is anxiety and panic free.

The feelings associated with anxiety – fear, terror, stress, dread, vulnerability – are all horrible and significantly impact on your well-being. It's difficult to imagine a life where these emotions dominate for long periods. In order to transform these negative emotions, we need to use strategies from the other CBT hats – body, behaviour and thoughts. By thinking differently and acting differently, you will be well on the way to taking these feelings out of your life.

Body tools to combat panic and anxiety

When in 'fight/flight/freeze' mode, as happens during an acute anxiety/panic attack, you are generating massive amounts of stress hormones, including adrenaline. This, in turn, increases your breathing rate, heart rate and blood pressure. In a panic attack there is a complex interaction between rapid breathing and your blood gas levels, and as a result of this you hyperventilate (short shallow breaths) even more. Indeed, 'I can't catch my breath' is the most common panic symptom, and it seems that the more you try to do so, the harder it is to breathe. You know that you need to 'take a deep breath' but you seem to have forgotten how. But there is a first-aid tool that you can call upon immediately in this situation, which will control the adrenaline flow and restore your blood gases to normal levels.

Abdominal breathing. I have talked about abdominal breathing before. When it comes to anxiety, controlled abdominal breathing, or 'belly breathing', is a tool that really works. You simply breathe in for 5 seconds, hold for 5 seconds, then breathe out for 5 seconds. Repeat until your anxiety/panic tapers off. It is important to hold the breath for 5 seconds – this is the equivalent of the brown paper bag technique, in which a person breathes into a brown paper bag and then breathes in the released carbon dioxide, restoring blood gas levels and reducing hyperventilation.

If you want this skill to work in a crisis, you need to practise it regularly. Try focusing on a square shape in your environment, such as a window. Now, focusing on just one corner of that square, breathe into your abdomen with your belly rising for 5 seconds. Hold for 5 seconds. As you breathe out for 5 seconds, move your eyes along the edge of the square. Now you are in the next corner. Repeat until you have completed the square.

Complete this 'square breathing' ten times. You can take this imaginary square with you anywhere. At night-time, when you are in bed, you can try abdominal breathing for 15 to 20 minutes. What you will find is that after a while you will understand the difference between your body being tense and being relaxed as a result of this abdominal breathing. Soon you will be able to tune into this difference. And when it comes to a panic situation, you will be able to apply this square breathing and arrive at the relaxed state more quickly because you know what it feels like.

Physical exercise. There is significant evidence to show that physical exercise helps to manage anxiety. For those with panic attacks, however, engaging in physical activity is a big no-no, because the physical sensations of exercise are similar to those of a panic attack. It's important to change your viewpoint on this, as physical exercise is hugely beneficial.

Skip the c's. You would be surprised by the extent to which coffee influences anxiety and panic attacks. Analyse how much tea or coffee you drink each day. If you are experiencing anxiety, you need to cut out the c's – caffeine, Coke and cigarettes. They all set your heart racing, which is exactly the opposite of calming you down!

Thought tools to combat panic and anxiety

Catastrophizing is the most common kind of thinking associated with panic and anxiety. Let's say you notice that your heart has skipped a beat; you automatically think 'Oh my God, I'm having a heart attack!' Essentially, you are taking something happening in the moment or in a given situation and predicting the worst possible outcome.

Catastrophizing the future relates more to GAD. When you look ahead, you anticipate all the things that will go wrong. An example of a typical ANT is 'I can't do that, it will go wrong, there is no way I could achieve that.' Many times when we believe that something will go wrong, the belief ends up becoming a self-fulfilling prophecy. Such beliefs about ourselves limit our ability to thrive and impact on our relationships, work and our real selves.

Other common thinking errors present in anxiety are overgeneralizing, predicting the future, all or nothing thinking, and discounting the positive. These are the equivalent to having a faulty software code. Your task now is to become aware and change your ANTs.

Capture the ANTs and then squash them. When you're having a feeling rooted in worry, anxiety or panic, ask yourself: 'What is going through my head right now? What thoughts am I having?' Once you have captured the 'hot' thought, take your ANTs to court and use the relevant questions to squash your ANTs. Let's go back to Linda, who had a panic attack on the motorway in the previous chapter. She was concerned that she would have further attacks. She had a belief that the doctors had missed something and that it might not have been a panic attack. Linda's hot thoughts were: 'This could happen again, I could die, it was so powerful, the doctors might have missed something important.' You can see how such catastrophizing would lead to more anxiety, distress and even panic if left unchecked. Use these powerful questions (introduced in Chapter 5):

- What type of crooked thinking am I engaged in?
- If my best friend told me they'd had this thought, what advice would I give them?
- Am I wearing 'fear glasses' or 'dark glasses'?
- The words in my mind: are they fact or opinion?

- Doctors have spent a lot of time training in medicine – why am I doubting their opinion?
- What are the pros and cons of this thought?
- What is the most helpful thing that I can do in this situation?
- Do I need to stop to take a deep breath?
- What is the realistic and balanced thought?
- Is this threat a real one or is it unlikely to happen?
- Am I exaggerating the threat?
- Am I misreading things?
- I feel bad, but that doesn't mean things really are so bad. Where's my focus of attention?

Linda arrived at a resolution when she replaced these fear-based ANTs with more realistic and balanced thoughts: 'This is a fear thought. I was examined thoroughly in the hospital, and when I went to my GP I got further proof that I did not have a heart problem. Since the event on the motorway, I have done a lot of exercise, and if my heart were struggling, I would have known.'

The hot-air balloon tool. This is a good tool for tackling the chronic 'what if' thinking associated with GAD. Imagine asking yourself these questions from the elevated perspective of a hot-air balloon:

- What does the situation look like, now that I'm seeing it from a distance?
- What is the wisest path for me?
- If I were a coach, what advice would I give to my friend if they were in the same situation?
- What would a wise person do here?
- Is there anything I can do about my behaviour now?
- Can I engage in mindful practice?

Attach your worry thought to a cloud and watch it float away. Imagine that jet planes are flying above you. Each one is carrying your thoughts away. The baggage on the plane is the baggage in your life. Imagine. Visualize.

Positive self-talk. Your next tool is a set of things to say to yourself before, during and after situations that make you anxious or panicky.

Before.
- Stress and anxiety are normal.
- Everybody experiences anxiety and panic at times.
- I am at risk of blowing things out of proportion/ catastrophizing.
- There is no real risk or danger.
- I think my way into panic attacks; therefore I can think my way out of them.
- I am able to handle this – anxiety comes, but it also goes.
- I have a plan to handle this.
- If I feel myself getting panicky, I'll know what to do.
- Anxiety and panic are not dangerous.
- Anxiety and panic will pass naturally, given time – they don't last forever.
- I won't engage in the escape, avoidance or safety behaviours, as these only strengthen my fears.
- By facing my fears, I am reducing them.

During.
- I need to do my square breathing.
- Stay calm, relax, and breathe easy.
- Slowing my breathing down is the best thing I can do at the moment.
- Abdominal breathing will control my adrenaline flow.

- I have never fainted, choked, gone crazy or had a heart attack.
- People can't tell if you are having a panic attack.

After.
- I managed that well. I can do this. I'm getting better at this.
- I felt anxious, but I used my tools.
- I tolerated the symptoms of anxiety and panic without their getting out of control.
- I stayed in the situation, and my panic has eased.
- I am in control.

Turn down your 'super-scanner' radar. The idea of super-scanning refers to the way that, as an anxious person, you are hyper-vigilant as to what is happening in your body. Your attention is self-focused for any signs of physical change that may suggest a panic attack is on its way. This self-imposed 'super-scanner' reminds you that you are not safe, and because of this reinforces or strengthens your fear. You can counteract your super-scanner by noting 'There is my super-scanner again; it's over-interpreting normal body symptoms.' Alternatively, you can imagine there is a volume switch on your super-scanner. Now turn down the volume switch. Switch your attentional focus to something external: the radio, music, a phone call, a walk, people going about their business, writing, playing with your child.

Mindfulness. In the past year Tracy has buried her mum and is grieving again as her sister enters the late stages of cancer. She is experiencing the pain of anticipatory grief (Chapter 10). As a result, Tracy is experiencing a lot of anxiety. She struggles to sleep at night and says, 'How is it that I can't stop the thoughts coming through? I have a list of jobs in my head: make sandwiches, go shopping, make dinner, read an article I am interested in, and so the list goes on.' Tracy is a perfectionist. When she doesn't achieve what she set out to do, her ever-present inner critic comes to chastise.

Over time, Tracy has been coached in the practice of mindfulness with a focus on compassion. Tracy has worked hard to observe her emotions and thoughts. She struggles to take her ANTs to court, so, rather than squashing them, she simply observes them passing by without engaging in them. She knows that she is not her emotions or her thoughts. She is an observer. As an observer, she reduces the strength and intensity of painful emotions. She opens up to her worry and anxiety with compassion, kindness and acceptance. She scans her body and notices where her anxiety resides. She breathes into that part of her body. She sits with the experience, neither fighting it nor running away.

You too can try this mindful approach (Chapter 3) when you feel worried or anxious. Understand that you are an observer of your thoughts and feelings. You are separate from your thoughts and feelings. Carry your story lightly. The breath is the cornerstone of mindfulness practice. Breathe. Bring your attention to your breath. Notice your in-breath and your out-breath. See how each breath is unique and supports your health and well-being.

Mindfulness meditation takes practice, but it's worth it. There is a growing wealth of research evidence to show its value in tackling worry and generalized anxiety and thus promoting overall well-being.

Core beliefs — real self core belief log. There is a strong connection between the pattern of your thinking and your core beliefs. Often these core beliefs are linked to experiences in your early childhood. For some people who experience worry and anxiety, their early childhood may have been characterized by a dominant emotion of fear. This meant that they learned certain lessons about how to negotiate the world. 'Tread softly as the world's a dangerous place' was the 'rule' that was learned or passed down. Other rules may also have been laid down:

- To be good enough/accepted your efforts must be perfect. *I must be perfect.*
- Unknown people, places or things are dangerous. *I am scared.*
- The world is unsafe. *I am unsafe.*

Core beliefs of danger, perfectionism, safety and fear affect your ability to be your real self. These beliefs were laid down in your childhood; you can now bring mature adult reasoning and wisdom to them. You can change them. They may have helped you when you were a child; they are not helpful now. They limit your horizons.

A powerful behavioural tool to combat panic and anxiety – graded exposure therapy

You have acquired some tools, using your body and thoughts, to help with anxiety and panic. Now it's time for the action phase. For the individual experiencing these difficulties, this is the scariest but most powerful way to gain control of your anxiety and panic.

Before we consider how to tackle anxiety from the behavioural aspect, we first need to look at the actions that strengthen the 'anxiety-muscle'; they relate to avoidance, escape and safety. People use avoidance and escape in places where they think a panic attack could be triggered – such as supermarkets, the cinema, buses, cars or restaurants. Avoiding these places prevents you from realizing that you can cope in them better than you might think. It is more difficult to face situations that have been avoided for a long time. The problem with avoidance is that it is like oil: it starts to spread, and soon you are avoiding more and more, until your life is severely constrained.

Many times people use safety behaviours, for example only going places with someone else, so they can be rescued if they panic. Again, safety behaviours give you a short-term hit of reassurance, but this just serves to strengthen the anxiety-muscle. Safety behaviours are unhelpful in the longer term because they reinforce the idea that you can cope only when you put these defences into place. Before long, you cannot leave the house without using a safety behaviour.

Behaviours associated with worry, perfectionism and generalized anxiety include reassurance seeking and checking behaviour. No doubt you know someone who has beaten a path to their GP seeking reassurance about worries or another person who continually checks on their sons, daughters, wife, husband and partner by phoning, texting, etc. All of these behaviours strengthen your worry and anxiety.

The quickest solution is to STOP these behaviours. Some people will accept this advice and do it straight away; others will need to use established behavioural tools that are grounded in research. The most important tool is *graded exposure therapy*, where you face your fears step by step using the CBT tool of drawing up your unique ladder of freedom and success with the least anxiety-provoking item at the bottom and the most anxiety-provoking at the top (Chapter 6). Now, the prospect of facing situations that previously caused you severe anxiety can be terrifying. The difference is you are going into these situations with new thinking, as well as breathing and behavioural tools that *will* reduce your anxiety and stop your panic attacks.

The idea of graded exposure therapy is to go into a place or situation that you fear, so that you are deliberately made to feel the symptoms of panic. Be sure to stay in the feared situation until the anxiety dissipates. To tackle the anxiety trap, spend time with your fear, exposing yourself to the thoughts, situations and feelings that make it up. As these sensations subside, power will transfer from the anxiety to you. Graded exposure is gradual (step by step), prolonged (30 minutes to an hour per day), and it's done regularly (one to three times a day). Here is the deal: your anxiety may well be high when you enter the situation, and will increase even more when you rise to face it, but it will soon fall if you remain in the situation for long enough. Each time you do this your anxiety will climb less and fall faster.

When doing graded exposure, start by listing all the things that make you anxious, or that you try to avoid or escape, or that you will confront only when using a safety behaviour such as having someone with you. After making your list, rate the level of anxiety for each one, from 0% to 100%, where 100 is the most anxious you have ever felt and 0 is the most relaxed you have ever felt.

Now put these items on your ladder of freedom and success. Here is Linda's ladder, which she used to regain control over her panic about driving. For approximately six months after her panic attack, she stopped driving. She joined a colleague on the train to work instead. Effectively, she was avoiding driving, and travelling with a colleague was a hidden safety behaviour, as the colleague did not realize she was there for Linda's safety!

To return to driving to work alone on the M7 motorway as she had done before panic attack
To drive alone on the M7 motorway at the site of the panic attack day and night
To drive with a friend on the M7 motorway at the site of the panic attack day and night
To drive on the dual-carriageway alone
To drive on the dual-carriageway with a friend
To drive alone on a busy town road during the day
To drive with a friend on a busy town road during the day
To drive alone on a town road at night
To drive with a friend on a town road at night
To drive alone on a quiet road
To drive with a friend on a quiet road
To drive with Dr Eddie on a quiet road
To travel on the train alone
To travel on the train in one carriage, while her friend stays in another

Linda confronted the first item in her hierarchy – to travel on the train in one carriage, while her friend stayed in another. Her task was to stay in the situation until her anxiety reduced by at least half. For example, when her panic went to 90 during an exposure task, she was to remain in the situation until it reduced to 40 or less. Linda brought to her tasks her square breathing and positive self-talk, tuned down her super-scanner, squashed her ANTS and faced her fear knowing that this would give her freedom. Linda has now been panic-free for three years.

Sometimes people need a lot of help at the start of exposure therapy. I have sat in cars, trains and planes, walked through shopping centres, coffee shops, streets, crowds and isolated country areas, all to coach people in facing their fears. I like doing this, as it brings the therapy out of the therapy room and into the real world. When a person comes to me for therapy, I truly believe they can achieve this change, and it's my job to make it happen. So if someone is willing to take on their fears, I will go all the way with them. There is nothing better than seeing a person liberated.

An exciting and liberating part of the treatment for panic attacks occurs around the fifth session, when I induce a panic attack in the client in the treatment room. What? That sounds just nuts. Up to this point, we have worked very hard on abdominal breathing and calming strategies, so why would I do this and why would a client want to go through it? Yes, I induce a panic attack by asking the individual to hyperventilate. Off we go: they deliberately breathe rapidly and change their blood gases, until they are experiencing the symptoms of panic – heat, increased heart rate, sweating, and so on.

If the client thinks they are going to faint, I get them to stand up in order to disprove their belief that they are going to do so (it's impossible to faint with increased heart rate and blood pressure). We use a scale of 0 to 100 to establish how close in severity the symptoms are to previous attacks. When we are up at the 90 to 100 level, the client begins the first-aid square breathing.

When I first introduce the concept of inducing an attack, there is natural resistance, as you might imagine. You, the reader, have the advantage of hearing about this strategy, but the individual attending doesn't know that this will be happening. The key is support and encouragement.

Don't be put off or think: 'I couldn't do that.' You could if supported. All clients who come to me with panic attacks do this exercise. When they return the following week, they all report incredible shifts both in their current fears and in their fear of future panic attacks. The hard work has been done and the back of the fear has been broken. They are on the pathway to freedom.

Too many people go to therapy for panic attacks and talk about it. Treating panic is an active treatment. You need support to be pushed gently into regaining control of your fears. That's why I induce panic attacks. However, this approach is less successful for people on anti-anxiety medications, which are designed to dampen down the symptoms of anxiety, the very symptoms I want to awaken in order to show a client that they can control them.

This is a pivotal session. Individuals report being liberated and having a sense that they have the procedures in place to control their future panic symptoms. Once this freedom has been achieved, they move on to tackling all their fears and the bigger dreams of becoming their real self.

What comes after freedom?

Mindfulness and CBT are proven therapies for anxiety and panic attacks. If your real self is blocked by worry, fear or anxiety, catch hold of these tools and go for it. A life in which you are free from the straitjacket of fear is waiting for you. If you want your life to change, you need to choose between avoidance and facing your fears. Remember the ones who succeed are the ones who think that they can. You deserve this. Believe this. It takes courage to do this; I salute your courage. Persistence is the key. There is no magic wand; you need to do it step by step.

With this new-found freedom you can divert your energies into the positivity of being authentic, satisfied and real. You will be able to take on challenges you never dreamed of. Think and write down your bucket list – things you would like to do before you die. Now that fear is not holding you back, what are you waiting for? What's on your list? What should you do first? Do it. Today is the best day for starting your journey to the place where you are free from fear, to the place where you are your real self.

CHALLENGE FOUR

Anger

17

When anger is your enemy

We all experience anger. It is a normal human emotion. It can run the gamut from mild irritation to intense fury and rage. Anger is not all bad: it can focus attention, propel us into action to find solutions to difficulties, and help us to tackle injustices. Anger can empower us and give us strength and determination. However, for many, when anger gets out of control it can harm our health and our relationships with ourselves and others – at home, in school, at work and in our communities. If your anger is toxic, it is your enemy, and you need to look at what fuels it. Let's take Fergus as an example. He was always fiery and hot-headed, but when he started secondary school things escalated.

'When I got angry I would completely lose the plot. I would scream, shout, throw things, hit things, lash out and couldn't calm myself down. Sometimes this led to fights at school. I am sure it was scary to others, particularly my parents. I find that I get mad over the tiniest thing, and just blow up. I have broken two mobile phones in the past six months from throwing them so much. I have made holes in walls, ruined furniture, and almost killed myself during incidents of road rage. It's like I get an overload of adrenaline in my system when I'm mad, and I literally cannot control my actions. I get so scared that one day I'm going to hit someone I really care about (or, for that matter, hit anyone at all) or lose someone I love because I always scream at them even when I'm not mad at them specifically.'

Here is a classic example of someone whose angry style is that of an 'exploder'. This is very common in men. Fergus described his father as being hot-tempered as well. For some people, their anger is associated with hereditary factors as well as having had poor role models who were unable to manage their anger. Anger is also a feature of low mood and depression, especially the sort of anger that seems to start very suddenly. Careful assessment can determine whether the problem is anger only, depression only, or both.

Paula is thirty-five and lives with her older sister Anne-Marie (forty-three). There is a simmering tension between the two sisters. Silence is punctuated by frequent skirmishes. Paula said: 'She always picks me up on what I do or don't do; nothing is good enough. I have been putting up with her sniping crap for years. I would love to tell her to fuck off. She just criticizes all the time, I just take it and boil up inside. I am bitter towards her.'

When I investigated further, Paula revealed a history of irritable bowel syndrome and stomach ulcers. She was an 'imploder': her anger mounted and mounted within her, and she never let it out. This had consequences on her physical health. Effectively, Paula was not being 'real', because she suppressed her anger. Over time, this continual suppression is toxic and she was at risk of expressing her pent-up anger explosively.

When is anger a problem?

Anger becomes a problem when it creates trouble for you with other people, in your work, with your health, with day-to-day living or when you cross the line and break the law. Anger is also a problem when the people around you are frightened, hurt or feel they cannot talk to you or disagree with you in case you become angry.

Let's look at when anger becomes a problem.

1. When it happens too often. Some people get angry at the slightest little thing. The challenge for you is to be able to tell the difference between those times when it is appropriate to be angry and those times when your anger is harmful to you or others. If you find that you are getting angry several times each day, the likelihood is you are struggling with excessive and inappropriate anger emotions.

2. When it is too extreme. Anger has different levels of intensity, from low to medium to high. High-intensity anger is very rarely useful. If your anger is high-intensity, it will become toxic to your health, and you are at risk of acting impulsively without thinking. During periods of high-intensity anger, wisdom flies out the window!

3. When it leads to aggression, i.e., when you intend to hurt somebody either physically or verbally.

4. When it lasts too long. When someone is angry for too long a time, they may be replaying the injustice and upset they have experienced over and over again. Prolonged periods of suppressed and expressed anger result in prolonged stress responses, which in turn cause harm to our bodies, emotions, minds and relationships.

Patterns in anger

Physical sensations

When angry, our bodies go into a stressed state, the 'fight/flight/freeze' response. This awakens the adrenaline hormone, causing the following sensations:

- increased heart rate;
- muscle tension (fists, jaw, shoulders);
- increased blood pressure;
- rapid breathing;
- butterflies in the stomach;
- pupil dilation;
- feeling hot;
- sweating.

Can you identify which physical sensations *you* experience when angry?

Behavioural patterns

Intensive angry behaviours last a long time and are triggered very easily, leading to difficulties and breakdowns in family life. When they become totally out of control, we are at real risk of the law needing to intercede. Common behaviours associated with anger include:

- swearing;
- storming out;
- arguing;
- saying hurtful things;

- lashing out;
- throwing things;
- physical violence;
- shouting;
- pacing;
- clenching fists;
- self-harm;
- calculated silence;
- internal fury.

Emotions

There are a lot of emotions associated with anger, and having them consistently is incredibly damaging for you and for those around you. Emotions associated with anger include:

- stress;
- tension;
- irritability;
- rage;
- fury;
- irritation;
- outrage;
- annoyance;
- hatred;
- impatience;
- smouldering;
- feeling incensed;
- feeling cross;
- feeling threatened;
- fuming;
- feeling offended.

Thinking patterns

Particular thinking patterns can occur when we believe we are being treated unfairly or disrespected, or when we think that others have gone against what we believe to be the right way to do things. Angry thoughts feed and fuel our anger. They make us feel worse. When angry, our thinking becomes very inflexible. Remember our thoughts are thoughts, not facts. Do any of the following thoughts sound familiar?

- This is unfair.
- It should not be like this.
- I am not going to stand for this.
- I'm being insulted.
- Why can't he do it the way it should be done?
- They are making a fool of me.
- They just can't see what I want.
- They let me down so much.
- Why don't they care?
- Why can't they see that . . .?
- He is stupid.
- I hate her.

Mapping your anger

Now that we've identified the different patterns in anger, have a go at mapping your own anger, using the following questionnaire.

1. Anger body cue – when angry, what physical symptoms do I get? Add any more that are not on the list.

Body cue	Please tick
Increased heart rate	☐
Increased breathing	☐
Clenched jaw	☐
Clenched fists	☐
Sleep problems	☐
Headaches	☐
....	
....	
....	
....	

2. Anger behaviour cue – what are my angry behaviours?
....
....
....

3. Anger emotions cue – what am I feeling when I am angry?
....
....
....

4. Anger thinking cue – what thoughts are going through my mind when I am angry?
....
....
....
....

Anger myth-busting

There are many myths around anger that need to be dispelled, as too much anger is *never* a good thing.

Myth. It's okay to have a blowout – it's healthy to vent anger.

Fact. Some people say: 'It's better out than in, express it, blow it.' This is a dangerous myth, and some people have used it to justify hurting others. 'Letting it rip' escalates anger into aggression. It effectively keeps anger going. It is harmful to you, as it increases your heart rate and blood pressure. Worst of all, it can be harmful to others. It does not lead to a solution to the problem that has caused the anger.

Myth. Anger gets me the things I want, including respect.

Fact. Leadership and honesty gain you respect; not the exertion of power. Think about it: you may get what you want, but at what cost?

Myth. Anger just comes on me – it's something I can't control.

Fact. The situation can't be controlled. But you *can* control your response. This is key. Your response does not need to be verbally or physically abusive.

Myth. Controlling anger is about learning to suppress your anger.

Fact. Suppressing anger is generally ineffective and eventually it will re-emerge. Remember anger is a normal emotion. The challenge is to express it in a way that is win-win, rather than win-lose, using the skills of assertiveness.

Anger's four ugly relations

Imagine that every day your dominant emotions were hostility, jealousy, bitterness and aggression – as well as anger. These are anger's four ugly relations.

- *Hostility* is when the individual has a distorted worldview in which other people are threatening and the world is unjust.
- *Jealousy* is a feeling generated by core beliefs of low self-esteem and insecurity. Often there is a fear or suspicion of unfaithfulness or rivalry towards another. In its extreme form, morbid jealousy, a person has a delusional belief that their partner is being unfaithful.
- *Bitterness* is associated with persistent and pervasive slow-burning hostile thoughts and resentment towards somebody, something or life itself.
- *Aggression* is the behaviour that can cause physical, emotional or psychological damage to others. Verbal communication and nonverbal communication – including punching, hitting and silence – used to threaten, hurt or demean are all part of aggressive behaviour.

With anger, it is important to look at what life-scripts or core beliefs are being activated. If your life-script or core belief is to play out anger, this will lead to toxicity for yourself and others. You may be interpreting information as being unfair or threatening, when it is in fact neutral. How can you change the life-script? First, recognize that you're an angry person. Then set about changing your beliefs to calm and controlled ones, until you have the ability to see the big picture. In the next two chapters we will look at ways of dealing with anger. You can become someone whose judgement and behaviour are no longer dictated by unhelpful and damaging beliefs.

18

Managing anger

Anger management is about understanding your anger and why it happens. It is about learning and practising better ways of expressing it, and knowing how to prevent it from occurring in the first place. Specifically, anger management is about knowing the triggers and early-warning signs of anger, and learning techniques to calm down and manage the situation before it gets out of control. Often you cannot get rid of, or avoid, the things or the people that anger you, but you *can* learn to control your reactions. Let's start figuring out how to manage your anger.

Think of anger as a stick of dynamite. You have the fuse, dynamite and a match to light the fuse. The match triggers your emotional reaction of anger. This 'match' can be as simple as spilling a cup of coffee on your shirt while on the way to work. Some people have short fuses and others have long fuses. What sort of fuse do you think you have? The length of your fuse can be influenced by genetics, role models, alcohol and other drugs, mood or even a head injury. Next, we have the dynamite part. Some people are imploders – they explode inwards, suppressing their anger. Others are exploders. Many are a mixture of both, depending on the situation.

Your challenge is to figure out the triggers and warning signs of your anger. For me, hunger or tiredness can be a big trigger. Can you think of some of yours? Is it when you're driving? At work? At home? With particular people? With alcohol? Awareness of your triggers and insight into what causes them can allow you to manage them appropriately, thereby 'heading anger off at the pass'.

Certain life events can lengthen or shorten your fuse. These may include bereavement, stress, redundancy, loss of a relationship or a serious illness. If you have experienced these, you may be quicker to anger than previously, as your fuse has been shortened. The link between alcohol or drugs and anger is well established.

A word on head injuries. If you have a family member who is struggling with anger, it may be because they have had a head injury that has caused frontal lobe damage. This can be a significant factor in shortening their fuse. (Information is available from www.headway.org.uk or www.headway.ie.)

Paddy and Eileen have been happily married for twenty-four years. They have two lovely children and live in their dream home in the countryside. Paddy is a manager in a construction company, and Eileen works in the civil service. In the last few years, Paddy's work has become increasingly stressful, and, although he would never have considered himself short-fused, he has found himself having to leave meetings to calm down for fear of saying something he shouldn't. His doctor has warned him about his elevated blood pressure.

Eileen is very sympathetic and often suggests nights out or weekends away together, so they can unwind and de-stress. One Saturday night they were out in the local pub when Eileen bumped into an old friend, Alan. They embraced each other with a warm hug and spent the next while talking and laughing. The longer they talked, the angrier Paddy became. He believed they were flirting and mocking him. He stormed over and punched Alan in the stomach. He then dragged Eileen outside. As he waved his fist in her face, Eileen was in shock; she had never seen Paddy act like this before. He stomped off and eventually arrived home, drunk, at three in the morning.

For a week there was complete silence; then Eileen and Paddy had a strained conversation about that night. Eileen made it clear that she was very hurt but also concerned about him, and she said he had to see someone about his anger. Paddy got a referral from his GP and came to see me.

It was clear that Paddy had been imploding in work for some time and bottling up his feelings, until finally he exploded on that night out. Paddy needed to understand the reason for his explosion: not to excuse it but to ensure that it did not happen again.

The difficulties at work threatened Paddy's livelihood, role and identity. Though he had always been someone with a fairly long fuse, the combination of the work situation with high blood pressure problems and the recent death of his father, to whom he was close, had shortened it considerably. And the fact that he was drinking that night was also a key factor. So what to everyone else was a normal friendly inter-action was interpreted by Paddy as someone hitting on his wife.

Though the events at Paddy's work and in the pub seem separate, and Paddy himself would not have connected them, they shared underlying themes – a sense of threat and insecurity – relating to the loss of his company and the loss of his wife.

The challenge for Paddy was to learn how to express his anger appropriately and to prevent its building up. Paddy needed to be assertive, not aggressive. Assertiveness is just being real. It's expressing your needs and point of view in real-time, rather than suppressing your anger and imploding or exploding. Paddy needed to understand his triggers. He needed to develop better problem-solving skills in managing people at work. He needed to use thinking, breathing, behavioural and relationship-building tools. He needed to grieve for his father, to look after his health and to have honest conversations with his wife.

This was a real wake-up call for Paddy. He had particularly high levels of stress and was very close to depression but was not there yet. Within a four-month period, Paddy was dealing with his stress and anger differently. He worked a lot on his thinking skills and on being assertive. His biggest issue was the continual suppression of his anger. He became more aware of his 'internal angry self-talk', and when this occurred he expressed it. He acknowledged his grief for his father and got better at managing in work. He apologized to Alan, and this apology was accepted. He was rebuilding his relationship with Eileen.

Tools for managing anger

You need a set of tools to tackle anger in its different phases – before, during and after. Like any skilled worker, you become better at using your tools the more you practise with them.

Body tools

Tune in and notice when your body is telling you that it's angry, e.g., heart pounding, gritting your teeth, tense jaw, tightening of your fists, flushed face.

When you recognize these warning signs, engage in some calming tools before your anger gets out of control. Proactive calming tools include physical exercise, yoga, progressive muscle relaxation, mindfulness practice, reading a book, having a bath or visiting a friend. Controlled abdominal breathing is an in-the-moment calming tool: breathe in for 5 seconds; hold for 5 seconds; breathe out for 5 seconds; repeat the cycle ten times. You can also try mindfulness breathing: bring your attention to the present moment, to the present breath, and notice what is going on, without judgement and with compassion.

Thinking tools

Strengthening your thinking tools is one of the most powerful strategies in your armoury for managing anger. When you're angry, your thinking becomes exaggerated and irrational, particularly when associated with relationships. Your automatic negative thoughts, or ANTs (Chapter 5), are full of the crooked thinking errors associated with anger, including catastrophizing, predicting the future, taking things personally, mind-reading, all or nothing thinking and 'should' thinking. (To understand the last of these, think of the last time you were angry with a loved one, your boss or a co-worker. No doubt you thought they 'should' have done this, that or the other. When it comes to anger, 'should' thinking is pervasive. It is also inflexible.) First, try to identify the distortion and then take these ANTs to court. Ask questions. What evidence supports these thoughts? Is there another way that I can think about this? Have I got unrealistic expectations of somebody else? Will this matter in six months' or one year's time? What choices have I got here? Are there consequences to my behaviour? Is there a recurring theme, such as jealousy? What harm has been done? Is there a place where we can meet in the middle?

By doing this, you can replace these kinds of thoughts with more useful, rational ones, and this will have an effect on the way you feel. For example, instead of telling yourself 'I can't stand it, it's awful and everything's ruined', tell yourself 'It's frustrating, and it's understandable that I'm upset about it, but it's not the end of the world and getting angry is not going to fix it.'

Can you remember the last time you were angry? What was the situation? Now try to think what thoughts were going through your head at the time. Using the thoughts record tool, look at the situation again. The more you practise with your thought tools, the sooner you will be able to bring them into real-time situations.

Self-talk tools

You need a list of things to say to yourself before, during and after situations that may make you angry. Your challenge is to focus on what you can control in the situation, rather than what you think other people 'should' be doing. Read the examples of self-thought below.

Before the situation. 'I'll be able to handle this. It could be rough, but I have a plan', 'If I feel myself getting angry, I'll know what to do'.

During the situation. 'Stay calm, relax, and breathe easy', 'Stay calm, I'm okay, s/he's not attacking me personally', 'I can look and act calm'.

After the situation. 'I managed that well. I can do this. I'm getting better at this', 'I felt angry, but I didn't lose my cool'.

Hop into the hot-air balloon. Now that you are up in the sky, what is the big picture? What's going on in this situation? What is the wisest path for me? Can I engage in some mindful practice? Can I attach my angry thoughts to some passing clouds and let them go?

Problem-solving tools

Problems usually leave us worrying or ruminating. What can be helpful is a structured way of working through them. This lengthens your fuse and lessens the likelihood that you will become angry.

Step 1. Identify the problems. Your first task is to identify the problems and to list them. Let's take Valerie, who is married to Peter. Peter attends mental health services for depression. The family have significant financial stress, and Valerie owes her mother €5,000. They have three children. Valerie is particularly stressed and easily angered – mostly towards the children. Valerie lists her problems as follows:

- anger towards children;
- financial issues;
- Peter's illness.

Addressing one problem at a time, Valerie decides to develop an action plan for her financial stress.

Step 2. Figure out possible solutions. Try to keep the blinkers off and write down anything and everything. By ranking the solutions in order of possible effectiveness, you will arrive at the best one. Have you solved similar difficulties before? What would your family or friends suggest? How would you like to see yourself tackling the problem?

Step 3. Look at the pros and cons and select a solution. Select the best solution from your list by reviewing the pros and cons of each idea.

Step 4. Break down the solution into a step-by-step approach. Often, complex problems require that multiple actions be taken. Therefore it can be useful to break these actions into smaller steps. Valerie decided the following steps with Peter:

- Valerie will go to the GP and get nicotine patches in order to give up smoking.
- Valerie and Peter will review their household income and expenditure to see if there is any scope for economizing.
- Valerie will renegotiate the repayment agreement with her mother.
- Peter will go to the jobs club and prepare a CV.
- Peter will practise some interviews.
- Peter will look for some part-time work.
- Valerie and Peter will go to the Money Advice and Budgeting Service (MABS) (www.mabs.ie).

Step 5. Try out the solution and then review it. Valerie and Peter started step by step in tackling their debt. They reviewed the situation after three months and noted some movement on the debt. They have done well in terms of staying off cigarettes. While Peter has been unsuccessful in getting some work, Valerie has picked up a part-time job. This has the added benefit of getting her out of the home and earning income, while Peter takes on more of the home-based tasks.

If you can move towards a solution for your difficulties and problems, there is less likelihood of your stress building up and leading to anger.

Behaviour tools

The most effective strategy, particularly if you are at the explosion point, is *to walk away* and come back to talk later. This is not avoidance if you address the issues appropriately later on. Far and away the most important *behaviour* when it comes to anger is assertiveness. Because this is such a crucial area and can play a part all along the road to your real self, I have addressed it in a separate chapter.

19

The joy of assertiveness

Sarah works as a public servant. She has two married sisters and lives at home with her elderly father, Matthew. All her family live locally. Even though Matthew is elderly, he is reasonably mobile, alert and of sound mind, though 'stuck in his ways'. The family have a routine that is very inflexible. And the bulk of Matthew's support needs are met by Sarah – cooking, washing and support while bathing. As if that wasn't enough, Sarah finds herself taken for granted in work.

'I am finding it very difficult to say no. My supervisor keeps putting more and more on my table; she does not ask the others because they are able to say they cannot do any more. Invariably it falls on me. I have no family but this year in particular I was looking for some time off in August. I was persuaded to change my request. I have been with them for over fifteen years, but it was hinted at that other workers who had families needed this time off more than me. I was persuaded to take my holidays another time.

'I want to move out of the house. My sisters take me for granted in terms of looking after Daddy. I want to live a life of my own. I have looked at a house I would like to buy. I was in a relationship with someone for over four years. It finished just a few months ago – I don't know why.'

What prompted Sarah to come to therapy was the low mood associated with the loss of a relationship. Inside, Sarah was smothering. She was internally fuming with her work colleagues and with her family. Her spirit was being crushed. In nearly all aspects of her life – home, family, work and romance – there were things that she needed to say but she did not speak. With Sarah, it was a matter of focusing on transforming conversations in these different areas using the skills of assertiveness.

Do you, like Sarah, struggle to express your thoughts, feelings and desires with your spouse, partner or friends? If your answer to this question is 'yes, many times', you will need to transform your conversations using the skills of assertiveness. Some people are very fortunate enough to have had good role models in assertiveness and subsequently have strong assertiveness skills. For many, that's not the case. In some families, when someone has something to say, they often fail to speak up (conflict avoidance); at other times the person overreacts and speaks in an aggressive way. Indeed, if you don't know how to be assertive, you may experience a raft of negative consequences, such as:

Dissatisfaction. This type of question flows through your mind when you're dissatisfied with your lack of assertiveness: 'How could I be such a fool?', 'Why did I let someone walk all over me?', 'Why am I such a pushover?'

Resentment. This emotion is born from the anger you feel towards those who have manipulated you.

Depression. This arises when you turn your anger in on yourself. You experience a sense of helplessness and hopelessness, with no control over your life.

Temper/violence. If you can't express anger appropriately, it builds up until it blows.

Anxiety, leading to avoidance. Avoiding situations or people causes your life to shrink; there are fewer opportunities for friendships, relationships, work or fun.

Poor relationships of all kinds. It's destructive for any relationship when a partner can't mention their needs and wants.

Physical complaints. There are many stress-related illnesses, including ulcers, headaches and high blood pressure. Assertiveness, when it becomes a habit, is a great stress buster.

Parenting problems. It's a kid's job to test the limits that their parents set for them. If parents aren't assertive and firm, their kids will learn that 'no' means 'maybe' and 'maybe' means 'yes'. This lack of clarity has been shown to generate anxiety in these children's adult lives.

What is assertiveness?

Are you the type of person who would never express your point of view to a person in authority, such as a teacher, priest, doctor, nurse, shop assistant, boss, even though you needed to? Did you learn this from your parents? This trait is a sign of a lack of assertiveness, something that is learned from one generation to the next. Assertiveness is the ability to honestly express your opinions, feelings, attitudes and rights, without undue fear and in a way that doesn't infringe on the rights of others. The good news is that you can learn how to be assertive. Learning this skill will enable you to protect yourself against harm, as well as making you feel empowered and confident. Using assertiveness skills regularly is the key to becoming adept at it. When you are assertive, you are closer to being your real self.

Communication patterns

Let's take a look at the three main patterns of communication, through the lens of a specific situation. Liam and Ciara want to go to the cinema. Liam would like to see a violent thriller and Ciara would like to see a romantic movie.

Pattern 1. Passive (you win/I lose)

Liam: 'I think we would both enjoy the thriller.'

Ciara: 'Okay.'

Here Ciara does not express her wishes. There is no negotiation. Inside, she is annoyed at herself and calls herself a doormat, wondering why he always gets his way and why she can't open her mouth.

Pattern 2. Aggressive (I win/you lose)

Liam: 'I don't care what you want to watch. I'm going to the thriller.'

Here the person is acting as a bully, exerting power and control.

Pattern 3. Assertive (I win/you win)

Liam: 'I would like to go to the thriller.'

Ciara: 'I don't fancy that; I would prefer to go to the romantic movie.'

Liam: 'Okay, let's see if there's something that we can both agree on.'

Ciara: 'How about the comedy?'

Liam: 'I'm good with that!'

Ciara: 'Great!'

In this situation both parties agree to compromise.

The passive zone	The assertive zone	The aggressive zone
You win/I lose	I win/you win	I win/you lose
Having trouble saying no, even when you really want to.	Being real, saying what you feel.	When you have something to say but you lose your temper.

Assertiveness and managing anger

As you can see, when a person is assertive, it's a win-win. The biggest problem with explosive anger is that you might win in the short term but at what cost in the long term? Expressing your angry feelings in an assertive manner, rather than in an aggressive way, is the healthiest method of expressing anger. To do this, you have to learn how to make clear what your needs are and how they are to be met, without hurting others. Being assertive doesn't mean being pushy or demanding; it means being respectful to yourself and to others.

Unexpressed anger can create other problems. It can lead to passive-aggressive behaviour (getting back at people indirectly, without telling them why, rather than confronting them head on). People who are constantly putting others down, criticizing everything and making cynical comments haven't learned how to constructively express their anger. Unsurprisingly, they aren't likely to have many successful relationships.

Muriel sticks out in my memory. I have thought about her many times over the years. To be honest, I have worked with many 'Muriels' who had the same difficulties.

Muriel is in her mid-fifties and lives in the family home

with her younger sister Christine. Christine has a fifteen-year-old girl, Sandy. Both sisters work part time. Muriel took the brave step of coming to the therapy room, even though she didn't know why she was there; her nurse had suggested that she come. Muriel had been having daily dressings for a leg ulcer for the past five years. It was red, angry and raw. 'You know, Eddie, I shouldn't be here at all. Christine should be here: she's the problem. She's an annoying bitch. She's no good and she deliberately provokes me. She hasn't a clue about parenting Sandy. In fact, I have a better relationship with Sandy than she does.'

Muriel and Christine have not spoken in five years. The silence is entrenched. Both women come in from work and cook separate meals each night. They generally sit down in two different rooms, until *Coronation Street* comes on TV. They watch *Corrie* together in silence, and then go their separate ways in the house. Muriel could not recall what had caused the initial rift.

It took a bit of work to convince Muriel that her internalized anger was associated with her ulcer (something her nurse had worked out). In the first instance, the sessions were about asking Muriel what sort of relationship she wanted with Christine. When we figured that out, it was a matter of focusing on being assertive – expressing her needs, desires and wants in a healthy way. Somebody had to take the first step and it had to be Muriel – after all, Christine was not in the room. Eventually, after the seventh session, Christine started to attend.

Within a twelve-week period, Muriel's ulcer had healed. Both Muriel and Christine committed to a different way of relating to each other, so their relationship would thrive, as it had when they were younger. Rather than avoid situations, they were able to express themselves healthily. They regretted the years of silence. They became more compassionate to each other.

What helped Christine and Muriel on their way the most? It was the 'Assertiveness Bill of Rights'.

The Assertiveness Bill of Rights

When I am building the skill of assertiveness, I always start with the Assertiveness Bill of Rights. Knowing your rights is the first step to allowing yourself to become assertive. Imagine you are feeling stressed about making a request at home or in work. The short-term, easier path is to avoid the situation and the request. However, reminding yourself of the Assertiveness Bill of Rights will support you in making the request. You may not get the answer you want, but by asking you have avoided avoidance, which would only serve to erode your real self.

Learn these rights and use them as a building block in the development of your assertiveness. They highlight the freedom you have to be yourself without disrespecting others.

1. I have the right to have and express my own feelings, thoughts and opinions and to have them taken seriously by others.
2. I have the right to ask for what I want.
3. I have the right to say no without feeling guilty.
4. I have the right to be treated with respect and not to be taken for granted.
5. I have the right to offer no reasons or excuses to justify my behaviour.
6. I have the right to set my own priorities.
7. I have the right to make mistakes.

8. I have the right to change my mind.
9. I have the right to make my own decisions and deal with the consequences.
10. I have the right to say, 'I don't understand' or 'I don't know'.
11. I have the right to choose not to assert myself.
12. While I have these rights, others have these rights too!

Top assertiveness tips

Armed with the Bill of Rights, you need only add in my top assertive tips and you're ready to go!

Use assertive body language. Face the other person, stand or sit up straight, look them in the eye. If you find this difficult, look at the tip of their nose (this gives the impression that you're looking them in the eye – try it out). Keep your voice calm, soft and firm. Hold your hands together so you don't use dismissive gestures.

Use 'I' statements. Keep the focus on the problem you're having, not on accusing or blaming the other person. So instead of saying, 'You're always interrupting me', say, 'I'd like to talk without interruption.'

State the problem using facts, not judgements. This is a description of your difficulty/dissatisfaction, and explains why you need something to change. Instead of saying, 'Why did you deliberately let the car run low on petrol, so that I was forced to fill it up?', say, 'The car is low on petrol – could you fill it?'

Empathy/validation. Try to say something that shows your understanding of the other person's feelings. This shows them that you're not trying to pick a fight and, more importantly, it takes the wind out of their sails.

Express ownership of your thoughts, feelings and opinions. Say, 'I get angry when she breaks her promises', instead of 'She makes me angry.'

Make clear, direct, requests. Don't invite the person to say no. Say, 'Will you please . . .?', instead of 'Would you mind . . .?' or 'Why don't you . . .?'

The scratched record. This is a very powerful technique for making requests. Just like the old scratched record, you keep repeating your request. Don't get pulled into arguing or trying to explain yourself. The scratched record helps you to avoid getting caught up in clever manoeuvres by the other person. Imagine you're making a request for time off, but your boss likes to be in control. Using the scratched record, you say to your boss, 'I need the first week of July off.' Then, no matter what the boss says, you keep repeating, 'I hear what you are saying . . . I need the first week of July off' or 'I take on board your point, but I need the first week of July off'. Trust me, it works!

Fogging. This is a way to deflect negative, manipulative criticism. You agree with some of the facts, but retain the right to choose your own behaviour. Imagine that you've arrived late in to work on a one-off occasion. Your boss (who doesn't like you) says, 'You're obviously your own boss. You let the whole team down; you treat this place like it has no rules. You just come and go as you please.' You say, 'I'm sorry I was late today, but today was the only day I was late.' By agreeing with a part of what the bully says, you have taken the wind out of their sails.

Content-to-process shift. This means that you stop talking about the problem at hand and bring up, instead, how the other person is behaving right now. Use it when someone's not listening or trying to use humour or a distraction to avoid the issue. For example, 'I find it frustrating that you're not concentrating on this issue. I feel like you're not taking on board my point of view.'

Defusing. Let someone cool down before discussing a problem. If they try to stay with it, in spite of their anger, you always have the right to walk away.

Summarize what the other person is saying. This helps to ensure that you do in fact understand the other person. 'So what you're trying to tell me is . . .'

All-purpose assertive phrases for your back pocket. Have a number of all-purpose assertive phrases to hand. Memorize them, practise them and say them gently but firmly when you get stuck or tongue-tied:

- No, thank you.
- I'm just not comfortable with that.
- I'll think about it.
- I could use some help.
- I don't appreciate it when you _____. Please stop now.
- I don't like____. I'd prefer _____.

Don't expect to get it all right straight away. Practise in front of the mirror. Be compassionate with yourself if you struggle from time to time. Keep trying.

Selective assertiveness and choosing not to be assertive

It's natural for you to find it easier to be assertive in some situations than in others. It can be a lot easier to express your view with a stranger than with your loved one – someone close to you may try to manipulate you if you express your true feelings. If assertiveness is about being your real self, the more significant the relationship is to you the more assertive you need to be. When you are assertive, you will find that you are able to maintain healthy boundaries in your relationships; they will automatically fall into place. The upside of this is that others will see you as someone who respects themselves, a valuable person.

Should you always be assertive? Not at all! In some situations, you may need to be protective, aggressive or wisely non-assertive. This is okay if the situation demands that you protect yourself and your family. Nevertheless, if this sort of situation occurs regularly in your life, you will need to review how you are relating to those exerting power and control over you and squashing your ability to be your real self. Fundamentally, you want relationships that are open, honest and kind.

It can be scary to start being assertive. Try to use the ladder of freedom and success tool (Chapter 6) to get practice and gain confidence, putting on the bottom rung the person whom it would be easiest to be assertive towards and going up the ladder to the person who you imagine will give you the hardest time.

Sarah's story revisited

Remember Sarah from the beginning of the chapter? Gradually Sarah started to build up her assertiveness skills. She started by making requests at work using the scratched record technique. She found she was less angry at work and seemed not to be taken for granted as much as before. She followed this up with requests to her sisters for more support in caring for their father, because she intended to take evening courses. In Sarah's own words:

'I asked Seán why he had finished with me. He said that he didn't think I was confident or that there was energy in the relationship. He said he felt that he had to plan everything and that I made no plans, that I complained a lot about my sisters but did nothing about them, that I had dreams but was not following them through. He described how he came from a family where there was a healthy "cut and thrust" and that in our relationship I was very passive and I agreed with everything.'

Sarah's life is very different now:

'I finally bought my own dream home. Work is not an issue at all. I am well able to say no to my supervisors. Recently I called a family meeting and now we all equally share care of Dad. In addition we have privately purchased some home help to assist him in bathing. Unfortunately the relationship with Seán is no more; he moved on. I can't blame him – that old me was not much fun. The biggest change in my life is that I decided to adopt my own child . . . foreign adoption is a torturous process, but I got there . . . Sophie is amazing; she is the joy of my life.'

Everyone's journey to assertiveness is different. Allow assertiveness to become a habit. The more you practise, the more confident you will become. Your self-respect will grow. Your opinions and voice will be heard. You will become your real self.

CHALLENGE FIVE

Self-esteem

20

Being weighed down by low self-esteem

Self-esteem is your opinion of yourself. Your self-esteem affects how you feel, think and act, and it is closely linked to self-confidence. Though we don't like to think we judge people, the reality is that we judge ourselves all the time. It's how we measure our worth. That's what self-esteem is: our internal evaluation of our worth. Of course, it's not a problem if you have a healthy amount of positive self-esteem. But low self-esteem is a serious issue and causes depression, frustration, guilt, anxiety and shame. I am convinced that many people are having treatment for depression when the underlying core issue is low self-esteem. Target the low self-esteem and the depression lifts. Focus on building your self-esteem, and you will become your real self.

We all see ourselves in the light of the attitudes, comments and reactions expressed by others – parents, teachers and friends – in our younger years. Recovering from the negative messages we absorbed in those years can take a lot of effort. For some people it seems like an impossible task.

Dubliner Monica is thirty-eight. Monica never felt beautiful because from the age of five she was told by her family that she needed to change. She remembers being told regularly that she was too heavy. 'I guess the problem that I have always struggled with is my weight. I have been overweight for as long as I can remember. From a young age my mum had me on a diet.' Monica never felt at ease with her friends when growing up because she didn't have the 'cool' clothes, the nice smile or the perfect body.

Monica has felt badly about herself for as long as she can remember and her only joy is studying, at which she excels. 'Thank God for at least that,' she says.

To this day Monica has a feeling of being sad every day, constantly comparing herself with everyone else: their faces, their bodies, the way they walk and how they look. The hardest thing for her to do is to look into someone's eyes when she's having a conversation with them. She feels herself to be 'so ugly compared to everyone else'. She feels constantly depressed and sad but thinks she has become very good at hiding it.

> 'I have been taking it out on my partner. I wonder why he wants to stay with me. I'm afraid that he will meet someone who is much better than me. Of course I love him but I wouldn't blame him for looking at me and thinking: how did I end up with her? Despite what he says, I think he only says nice things because he has to.'

She says that she is suffering every day while smiling at people, 'Being the nicest person, but crying inside. I don't know peace and joy.'

> 'Everyone thinks that I am wonderful because I am a hard worker and very bright. But I don't feel that I am great. I would love to find the way to feel that, but I probably never will. In work, if I make a mistake, I dwell on it much too much and then I make other mistakes. I'm not taken seriously because I can't speak with authority in my voice and I

always talk myself down. I just have no confidence in my own ability.

'I look odd and I hate being overweight. I don't like buying clothes. I just never look right in anything that's fashionable or smart.

'Sometimes I think I wish I could just hide away from the world so that no one could see me. And I know it's all my own fault. Deep down I know I have done this to myself – I made me hate my body and hate myself, no one else.'

It is Friday night, and Claire is on a night out with her two best friends, Maura and Nicola. The girls are enjoying catching up and gossiping over cocktails as the hours pass. One too many cocktails later, they start talking about their love lives. Claire moans to her friends that, as usual, she is single. They reassure her that she is pretty and lovely and that she will meet someone when she least expects it. Claire is fed up with hearing this same story and getting the same sympathetic looks. Claire has never had a boyfriend. She knows that her friends are only trying to be kind and they don't understand what it's like to be her: Maura is in a long-term relationship and Nicola can have any man she wants. Claire thinks she is ugly, unlovable and no man will ever want to marry her.

To end the conversation, Claire goes up to the bar to order a round of shots. As the night continues, the girls have fun dancing. Feeling ill, Claire leaves her friends to go to the toilet. She feels worthless and inferior when she watches all the beautiful girls looking in the mirror. She wishes she looked like them. Why should she even bother fixing her make-up? It won't make a difference; nobody would ever look twice at her. Claire goes back out to her friends on the dancefloor with a fake smile on her face. She drags Maura and Nicola up to the bar again and orders another round of shots. In her experience the best way to escape her thoughts is through a blur of drunkenness.

It is heart-breaking that good women like Monica and Claire are so harsh with themselves. It shows how beliefs arising from low self-esteem are toxic. They are like vines that grow and grow until all you can see are the vines and not the original tree. They end up smothering the real you.

How self-esteem is created

We all have some level of self-esteem. Your self-esteem develops in childhood and during your teenage years. Events and how you are treated during those times can affect how you think of yourself as an adult. Things that lead to positive self-esteem include:

- being loved and having healthy boundaries in your early life – effectively, you were given a blueprint on how to love yourself and others;
- having regular praise;
- being listened to;
- being given attention;
- having success at school or sports;
- having opportunities to do things;
- having positive friendships.

Having low self-esteem means that you believe yourself to be of little value. Factors leading to low self-esteem often occur when you are young and vulnerable. These include:

- cold, harsh and unhealthy boundaries in your life, which meant that you were ignored, neglected or abused;
- excessive criticism;
- bullying experiences in school or at home;
- struggling academically in school or at sports;
- being different to those around you;
- when perfectionism was set as the standard, being told that anything less was a character fault – a weakness.

For some people, bad experiences in adulthood – abusive relationships, illness, health problems or traumatic events – can affect their self-esteem negatively.

How low self-esteem holds you back

When I think about self-esteem, I visualize a deep-sea fishing boat. Imagine the sea, the wind, the seabirds, and sunshine. Imagine the fishing boat going out to sea. It faces the challenges of nature. On good days it is at one with nature. On stormy days it navigates through rough waters and does its utmost to hold its course. Now imagine that the deep-sea fishing boat has a fault: it always travels with its anchor down. You can feel this anchor as it drags along the bottom and it makes the boat's efforts more difficult. In the best of conditions, it's literally a drag and it holds back the boat. But when conditions are rough, it makes it almost impossible for the boat to navigate through the choppy conditions and out to the other side. Similarly, low self-esteem is a drag on you; it complicates your ability to navigate the inevitable challenges that arise in your life; and even when everything is plain sailing, it stops you from progressing with as much purpose and direction as you might otherwise have.

Thoughts. With low self-esteem, your inner critical voice is super-strong at getting you to name-call. It sounds like this as it cracks its negative whip: 'I am worthless', 'I am unlovable', 'I am not good enough', 'I am a failure', 'I am stupid', 'I am incompetent', 'I am shameful', 'I am pathetic', 'I am ugly'.

The inner critic is a bully who knows your vulnerabilities. Other thoughts might be:

- when it comes to new tasks your first thought is to assume that you can't do it;
- you worry about what other people think about you;
- you blame yourself for things that have happened, even though they were not your fault;
- you dwell on criticisms and mistakes that you have made;
- you get frustrated at yourself and others and at times you get angry – the likelihood is you suppress this anger, or you suppress it for a long period before you blow out;
- you are very into 'comparing and despairing' – that is comparing yourself with others in terms of looks and confidence, while at the same time despairing about your own perceived shortcomings.

Body. Low self-esteem may affect your body in that you are tense and on edge, feel tired and have difficulty sleeping. You may feel panic in certain situations, e.g., when meeting new people. As a result, you are rarely fully at ease. It's almost as if you are constantly in a low-grade 'fight/flight/freeze' mode – chronically stressed. This may manifest itself in physical complaints such as irritable bowel syndrome, frequent headaches or migraine, and so on.

Behaviour. When it comes to your behaviour, your low self-esteem means that you may:

- avoid going into new situations or seeing new people;
- too often try to please others and you work too hard to be perfect at everything you do;
- hold back from doing things such as speaking out;
- be oversensitive;
- avoid sex *or* feel that you have to have sex;
- engage in emotional eating to comfort yourself *or* be very fastidious about what you eat;
- pass up opportunities, e.g., promotions;
- struggle to make decisions;
- get overly defensive when you think you're being criticized;
- be passive and shy around others *or* block out your emotions with alcohol.

You may already know that low self-esteem is a challenge for you, but you can use the questionnaire provided in the Appendix to check where you are on the scale. If you do have a problem, it's time now to release the anchor that weighs you down and let it drop to the bottom of the sea. Using the tools of CBT, you will be able to break the chain that holds this anchor. Then you will be able to set sail to a place where you will not be held back by faulty and misguided core beliefs.

21

Transforming low self-esteem into confidence

Self-esteem is like the rings inside a tree. The rings represent the core beliefs that sustain high or low self-esteem. In the same way as the rings inside a tree are affected by the conditions in which it was grown, so somebody's view of themselves says a lot about how they were raised.

Imagine a tree that grew in a walled garden. In this garden there was some, but not a lot, of the right mixture of warmth, light, water and fertilizer. But mostly the conditions were poor, harsh and inconsistent. Yet the tree developed survival strategies and it grew. The tree, being a tree, knew of no other environment in which to grow. Similarly, a child might grow up in an environment that is poor, harsh and inconsistent, and, being a child, it would know no better. That is the person with low self-esteem. All they knew was the world inside the walls of their family home, where adults were cold, distant and unreliable, and where, unconsciously, they developed strategies for survival, if not for vitality. A child in such a setting learns certain rules to appease the adults and how to avoid drawing attention to themselves.

An alternative view – one that would be explored in therapy – would be to imagine another type of garden, one where the tree has everything it needs to thrive – fertile soil, consistent care and an abundance of warmth, light, water and fertilizer. Similarly children in a positive, open environment are surrounded by lots of praise, love, warmth and encouragement, and know that if they fall down, someone will be there to pick them up.

As an adult with low self-esteem, you have to become a sort of gardener. You need to go back to your early years, nurture the tender sapling that was your young self and transform those rings inside the tree into something positive. You need to revisit the old garden with new-found wisdom and compassion and the tools to parent your inner child. There are times when you may be vulnerable. During these times your inner critic/bully – the voice you grew up with in the harsh garden – becomes more active. But now, because you know that other gardens exist, you can answer back and turn down the volume on the inner critic/bully.

Taking the battle to your inner critic/bully

The inner critic/bully never gives up. Imagine putting a volume switch on your inner critic. The volume can go from 0 to 100. How high is your inner critic turned up?

The chances are that if you ask a person with low self-esteem how loud is the volume level on their inner critic, the reply would be 'deafening'. If you ask them to rate from 0 to 100 how strongly they believe that they are unlovable and useless and so on, it would also be very high. The key message here is that the person holds these core beliefs because that's all they've ever known. A person with low self-esteem carries fundamentally negative beliefs about themselves. These beliefs have been maintained by a lens on the world that filters out information that does not support their beliefs and channels in information that does support their beliefs.

We need to get into the core beliefs of low self-esteem, for they are embedded into the pattern of your thoughts. In tackling your low self-esteem, you first need to address your automatic negative thoughts by keeping a thoughts record and taking your ANTs to court. As you'll recall from Chapter 5, essentially you look for the evidence for and against the thought. Say, some training opportunity has come up at work and a colleague has asked if you're going to go for it. You're thinking, 'Definitely not! Not a hope! Imagine having to stand up and do a presentation at the end. And I hate doing those group exercises. I'll just keep my head low and sit this out. Anyway, I know my boss thinks I'm useless at that.' Use the relevant questions from the twenty powerful questions tool in Chapter 5. For example, you might question these thoughts by asking:

- What proves that my thoughts are right?
- What type of crooked thinking am I engaged in?
- Am I mistaking thoughts for facts?
- Am I assuming I know what others are thinking?
- If my best friend knew that I'd had this thought, what would they say to me?
- Am I wearing those 'dark glasses' that filter out my strengths and channel in my weaknesses?
- How important will this situation be in one year's time?
- When I felt this way before, what did I think about or do to help me feel better?
- Are there any resources and strengths in me that I am ignoring or that I can use?
- What are the consequences of my behaviour?
- Will these behaviours bring me closer to my real self or further away?

When you use these questions, you generate new ways of thinking and counteracting the inner critic. Using the thoughts record, you will be able to come up with more realistic and balanced thoughts.

When you figure out the connection between your thinking pattern and your core beliefs, you are on the way to tackling your low self-esteem. On your metaphorical T-shirt it might say 'I am unworthy', 'I am unlovable', 'I am inferior'. The rules laid down by powerful adults or bullying experiences in your childhood mean that you learned very unhelpful lessons about how to negotiate the world.

The bottom line is negative core beliefs affect your self-esteem and your ability to be your real self. But now you can bring new thinking and wisdom to these beliefs and change them. Commit to strengthening your new real self core beliefs by using the real self core belief log. Resetting your core beliefs needs consistent application and a regular weeding out of the old beliefs.

Old core belief to be challenged: ....

New real self core belief: ....

Experiences that show that the old core belief is not COMPLETELY true ALL the time: ....

(List as many as you like here – the more the better!)

Real self core belief to be developed: ....

Task: ....

What you expect to happen: ....

What actually happened: ....

Conclusion(s): ....

Write a letter from your future self

Sit down and write a letter from yourself in three years' time to the person you are now. Write down what your life is like in three years' time. Go into a lot of detail. Talk about the things you have achieved, the people you are with, the travels you have done, the dreams that have become a reality and what living life as your real self looks, feels, sounds and tastes like. Get your future self, who is wise and compassionate, to advise your 'now' self on the journey you have taken. Get your future self to encourage your 'now' self during periods when your energy might be low or when you feel vulnerable. What would your compassionate and wise future self say to your present self?

Capture your achievements and personal qualities

In Chapters 10 and 11 on depression we talked about the 'negative lens' that stopped you seeing all of your positive personal qualities. Similarly, with low self-esteem, you have a selective lens on the world that filters out your positive achievements and positive personal qualities. It's time to get out that little hardback notebook and to write down the smallest things you like about yourself. Write down what you've done in your life that you are happy with. Write down something that took a lot of effort. Write down the times when you had to deal with stress, the times you struggled. Think about how you faced those times. What does that say about you? If you can ask people who know you well what they like about you and what your strengths are, write down this evidence too. Stick with it. When you do something that you usually avoid, reward yourself by saying, 'Well done!' Whatever you've done, be it the smallest thing – housework, shopping, completing a walk – say to yourself, 'Well done!' Keep reminding yourself when things go right. Say: 'I did a good job there.'

Essentially you are giving yourself praise, the praise you did not get as a child. This may sound strange. It is easier for you to criticize yourself. Indeed, if self-criticism were an Olympic sport, you would win a gold medal: after all, you've trained your mind to criticize yourself over and over. Now you are changing your training routine. You have a new coach: your inner nurturing/coaching voice. You are training yourself to give yourself credit. That can be hard, so look for facts, e.g.,

- People say I am a good listener.
- I am a good problem-solver.
- People laugh at my jokes.
- I have a good network of friends.
- I stay calm in a crisis.
- I deliver in my work.
- I am generous to other people who need help.
- I am good at getting information online.

Return to Chapter 5 and review the material on identifying your many achievements and positive characteristics.

To strengthen your new inner nurturing voice, you will need to look at your notebook each day for 5 minutes. In those moments when you hear your old core belief echoing in the back of your mind, recall your personal qualities and achievements to counteract that inner bully.

Many times people with low self-esteem engage in mind-reading and are overly concerned with what others think about them. As a result, you retreat and don't ask for help, as you feel you don't deserve it. To tackle this misperception, and I know this is a difficult task, ask a person you trust and whose opinion you value what they like about you and what you are good at. This is a tough ask, but it's worth doing.

When things don't go right, don't be hard on yourself. Remember to aim for 'good enough'. There is no such thing as perfection. The person who seeks perfection is more often than not a very unhappy person. Don't let the perfect be the enemy of the good enough.

If something happens, ask yourself, 'What have I learned from this situation?' 'In one year's time, will this really matter?' Try to get some perspective. If necessary, take a trip in the metaphorical hot-air balloon to gain wisdom, compassion and perspective.

Can you think of an example from your life where your old negative core belief is shaping how you are handling things? To get some perspective, try asking these questions:

- Am I being compassionate to myself?
- Has the volume switch on my inner critic gone up again?
- How would somebody outside of the situation see it?
- What are the different points of view?
- What is the wisest path to take?

Try to be compassionate in order to reduce your negative emotions. This, in turn, will give you more wisdom and confidence.

Use real self positive affirmations

If you have low self-esteem, it is helpful to develop real self positive affirmations that fit with your personality. Choose some and repeat them daily. It's okay if you don't believe them just now. But, as your self-esteem rises, your real self positive affirmations will resonate. Here are some I have taken from the fuller list in Chapter 5, plus a few I have added.

- I am lovable.
- I am worthy.
- I am authentic.
- I feel good about myself.
- My adult self is wise and compassionate.
- I'm okay with being okay.
- I take good care of myself.
- I like me the way I am.
- I have many fine qualities. I am kind, compassionate, caring, funny, considerate, thoughtful, open-minded, easy-going, hard-working, positive, motivated, creative, calm, friendly, flexible, dependable, etc.
- I am a person of value.
- I am a resilient person.
- I am a good person.
- I like myself.
- People like me.
- My life has meaning and purpose.
- I speak compassionately to myself and others.
- I am my real self.

As a child who grew up in a garden where nurturance may have been minimal, you may find it helpful to see these real self positive affirmations as fertilizer for your new core beliefs.

Stop comparing and despairing

One of the features of low self-esteem is the practice of comparing and despairing. Most people set standards. However, if you are experiencing low self-esteem, you often set the standard too high. As a result, you never quite match up to the standard where you would ideally like to be. Here is a small exercise for you to do. Write down the first words that come into your mind when you read these statements:

- What I think I am like just now . . .
- What I want to be like . . .
- What I think others think about me . . .
- What I think others would like me to be . . .

As you know, your thoughts are the engine that drives your moods, so it can be very difficult for you to read the negative thoughts that you have about yourself. You can see how such negative thoughts and reactions possess the power to influence your feelings, which, in turn, influence your actions. Now reflect on the following questions:

- How true in real life are the things you have listed?
- Do you think there is a selective filter at work?
- Do you think thoughts like these set you up to behave in certain ways?
- Are these thoughts likely to lead to success or failure?
- Many times people think in black and white terms – can

you think of a way to achieve some of the things you have listed by inhabiting not the black and white but the grey?
* What would be a more compassionate and wise way to think about yourself?
* What would someone who knows you well say about what you have written?

Mindfulness and self-esteem

Low self-esteem, like every other challenge to our emotional well-being, can be helped hugely by mindfulness techniques. In mindfulness, you are reminded to be an observer of your thoughts, images and memories. Your thoughts are not facts. As an observer, you are a skilful gardener who is wise, discerning, enlightened and knowledgeable. You can observe the rings on your tree that reflect strength-based core beliefs: 'I am lovable', 'I am worthy', 'I am real', 'I am intelligent', 'I am attractive', 'I am me'.

Mindfulness is the practice of bringing your awareness and attention into the present moment *compassionately*. Practising compassion is important if you are experiencing low self-esteem. Compassion is the antidote to your internal critic, and it strengthens your inner nurturing voice.

The core part of mindfulness practice is mindful meditation. When you are in the present, you are not caught in the trap of compare and despair. You can nurture your positive core beliefs through mindful loving kindness.

What to do to manage low self-esteem

Most of this chapter is about working on your *thinking*, because how you think is such a significant factor in maintaining or changing low self-esteem. However, there is a *doing* aspect to managing self-esteem too. In terms of behaviour, what's crucial is action, not avoidance. Sometimes it is easier to avoid seeing people or doing things, rather than having to confront failure. But remember: avoidance will always keep your problems going. If you avoid facing things, you will never find out if you could have done that thing well or coped in that situation.

So have you been avoiding doing anything recently? What did you feel would happen? If you had done what you had avoided, what were the chances of your predicted outcome actually occurring? If your predicted outcome had been correct, how would you have coped with that? In time, what would you have found out about yourself?

The reality is that, while you may have a negative view of yourself, there is also a competing view that says you are capable. Plan in advance of situations that you struggle with, rather than avoiding them. Start with small steps. Soon you will be moving in the direction of achieving bigger things. In these situations use the ready-made support of self-talk, e.g., 'I can do this', 'I will give this a go', 'In the situation I can use my breathing and thinking tools', 'I've done this before. I coped well', 'I am taking new steps in a new garden so I need to try to be curious'.

Learn to take care of yourself

When you were growing up, you may not have learned how to take good care of yourself. In fact, much of your energy may have been expended on just getting by, or on taking care of others, or on being 'well behaved'. It's now time to take good care of yourself. Treat yourself as a good parent would treat a young child, in a nurturing and encouraging way, or as one very best friend might treat another. If you work at taking good care of yourself, you will find that you feel better about yourself. Learning to look after yourself is important: it gives you the energy to tackle other things that are going on in your life. Here are some ways to take good care of yourself:

- Do the simple things right: get enough sleep, eat nutritious food, take regular exercise and practise good personal hygiene. Check out the detailed information about building up physical resilience in the parts of the book devoted to stress, depression and anxiety.
- It's important to plan some relaxing things for yourself. Make time to do the things you enjoy and stick to your decision.
- Give yourself occasional treats – a manicure, a facial, a massage.
- Try out some new things. Stretch yourself. Take up some hobbies. For example, you might want to volunteer in a community organization or work with animals. You never know: there could be a passion out there for you that you have yet to discover – singing, rambling, Men's Sheds, animal rescue, athletics, gardening, Amnesty International, blogging . . . the possibilities are endless.
- Do something that you have been putting off. Write that letter. Make a call. Pay that bill.
- Give yourself small rewards, just as a warm, connected parent would – after all you are a unique, amazing person.
- Increase the amount of time you spend with people who make you feel good about yourself, those people who treat you well.
- Reduce the amount of time you spend with toxic people.

- Learn the value of gratitude. Gratitude is the most healing of all the thoughts and emotions. Take time daily to focus on and to write down things to be thankful for.
- At bedtime, take a moment to practise being grateful for the different things that happened to you in that day, e.g., the support and encouragement of your friends and family, people who cheered you up, the times you put gratitude into action, e.g., sending letters, cards, texts or emails.
- Put your focus on what's working. Remember concentrating on your weaknesses maintains your low self-esteem. Focusing on your new-found strengths increases your self-esteem.

As you move towards more positive self-esteem, your inner nurturing voice will become dominant. You will have developed an inner coaching voice that is supportive, caring, warm, sympathetic, understanding, tender, benevolent and compassionate. Your confidence will grow and you will become more adventurous and more open to giving new things a go. Your ability to develop lasting, meaningful relationships will be stronger. The more your self-esteem grows, the more positive you will be. There will be nothing that you can't achieve. You will be plugged in, connected and enjoying the life that you deserve, the life you have created for yourself. You will be living your life with purpose. You will be reaping what you have sowed – love, joy, inspiration, wisdom, hope, humility and compassion.

CHALLENGE SIX

Shyness and social anxiety

22

The paralysing fear of being found out

We all have an in-built radar that is set internally and constantly scans our environment for threats. For a person with social anxiety, however, this scanner is focused *too much* on what's going on externally. The socially anxious person is on constant high alert as to what other people might think about them. This 'super-scanner' causes the most common thinking error associated with social anxiety: mind-reading. This is when the person believes that other people are thinking about them. And the other people's thoughts are not positive – they are negative, disapproving, judging and critical. The socially anxious person is crippled by this super-scanner, forced to adjust their behaviour (by avoiding, escaping and hiding). Their real self is crushed by fear, shame and embarrassment. This is a tragedy, because here is the reality: *most people in the world are really just concerned about themselves. Their thoughts and preoccupations are about themselves, not about you.*

Social anxiety is the persistent fear of social or performance situations in which one is exposed to unfamiliar people or to possible scrutiny by others, with such exposure provoking intense anxiety. It takes two main forms:

- *Generalized social anxiety.* This can be seen as the persistent fear of many social situations – from weddings to parties. This type of anxiety tends to continue throughout the individual's life and impacts on relationships at work and in the wider community.

- *Specific social anxiety.* In this case, the sufferer has persistent fear of performance situations. These might include giving a speech or even reading aloud.

The origins of social anxiety

Why does social anxiety develop? Have a look at the list below and see if you can identify with any of the reasons:

- Biological influence or familial conditioning – often there are family members who have a similar disposition. It is difficult, however, to determine whether a person's social anxiety is biological or learned from the family member.
- Stressful life events – these include illnesses or hospitalizations requiring separation from the family.
- Shaming experiences – situations where your personal boundaries were invaded, for example, abuse, or where you were humiliated. Counsellors and psychologists regularly have clients recount memories of a teacher mocking them in front of the class. You might think this is more common in the older generations, but I have also heard countless times from younger clients how reading in class was a key experience in the development of social anxiety.
- Abrupt changes or disruptions in family life, for example, bereavement.
- Negative family interactions, such as the impact of alcoholic parents.
- Frequent parental criticism and shaming to enforce behavioural compliance.
- Excessive parental control with little expressed warmth.

- Highly competitive, critical or hostile environments.
- Public embarrassment for poor performance.

Symptoms of social anxiety

Among the symptoms of social anxiety are those of the 'fight/flight/freeze' anxiety response. Sufferers may experience muscle tension, increased heart rate, dizziness, nausea, dry mouth and breathlessness. However, the following four symptoms have particular significance for those with social anxiety:

- blushing;
- perspiring;
- shaking;
- stammering.

This is because, unlike the 'fight/flight/freeze' symptoms, these four can be discerned by others. This is incredibly important for social anxiety sufferers, as their super-scanner is already in overdrive and they fear being judged by others. As we have learned, this judgement is always negative, and centres around the person being:

- ridiculous;
- stupid, unintelligent, thick;
- awkward;
- embarrassing;
- unacceptable.

Take Karen, who has a specific social anxiety. When it comes to socializing with friends and family and making small talk, she does okay. She works in accounts and is required to give monthly presentations to a broad group of people in her company. These presentations cause her significant stress and anxiety. She described her main concerns as follows:

> 'It's like this: two weeks before the presentation it's all I can think about. About fifteen people attend, including my managers and peers. I have prepared a talk and gone over it a thousand times. I am so concerned about blushing in front of this group that I wear special heavy-duty concealing make-up. The night before, I rehearse over and over. I walk into the room early to prepare. I am always the first in there. I am scared my mind will go blank. I am scared I will look foolish in front of others. I am scared they will think I am stupid. My heart thumps. When it's over, I am so relieved, at least for two weeks, when the cycle starts again.'

Key impacts of social anxiety

Social anxiety severely affects the everyday activities of the people who suffer from it. A number of key areas affected include:

Situations
- a dread of 'small talk';
- a dread of being the centre of attention;
- the nightmare of social situations.

Thoughts
- intense self-consciousness;
- intense levels of self-criticism.

Feelings
- anxiety, shame and embarrassment;
- feeling that you're unworthy/unlovable/not good enough;
- distress, upset and guilt;
- feeling that you're stupid, thick, unintelligent and boring.

Behaviours
- avoidant and escape behaviours – not going into the feared situation, e.g., finding excuses to avoid group social occasions, such as parties, through fear of what might go wrong;
- safety behaviours – subtle strategies to reduce social anxiety, e.g., arriving last; sitting near the exit; wearing dark clothing; avoiding eye contact; holding or fiddling with something like a pen or a cigarette; wearing extra make-up; not talking; having early drinks to quell anxious feelings.

Let's look at some examples of how people with social anxiety behave. Damien is attending a support group for social anxiety. He works for an IT company. He comes to the group after work and always arrives wearing a pair of chinos and a dark-coloured shirt. Every so often in his job Damien is required to do a presentation. He loves programming and he hates presentations. For in these presentations he becomes the centre of attention. Damien is concerned about excessive sweating, hence the dark shirts:

'I know there is sweat under my armpits – it's as if you got two glasses of water and threw them there, I'm not exaggerating – my shirts are soaking. I wear dark shirts and most times a jacket if I'm presenting. I think the others are all looking at me, hearing me stutter over my material and watching me get flustered. I wouldn't mind but I spend hours and hours rehearsing and going over the bloody presentation. And yet the sweat still flows. It even comes through my jacket. They must think: what an idiot, he can't even present a simple task. I've always struggled with this, particularly in college. I thought that by writing software I'd never have to present, but IT companies don't work like that!'

Damien is using a safety behaviour, though unfortunately it's not actually helping him. Safety behaviours strengthen your anxiety over time; they don't decrease it. Other examples of safety behaviours include arriving late to events – meetings, Mass, weddings, funerals and other gatherings – in order to sit near the back on the aisle so that a quick exit is easier.

Because social anxiety can be so intense and distressing, it's easy to understand how avoidance becomes the main strategy for coping. Unfortunately, this leads people to become more isolated. Their range of social contact gets smaller and, for a number, depression may emerge. Too often the depression becomes the focus of treatment, while the fundamental problem remains unaddressed. That's what happened to Pat.

Pat, who is sixty-eight, was referred to me with depression following a heart attack. He is married with grown-up children and grandchildren, and was not long retired after forty years working as a dispatcher for a large transportation company. He was very involved in community activities, served on numerous committees and was the chairman of the local football club. The backbone of the parish.

Pat had been on anti-depressants for thirty years. He didn't really want to be seeing a psychologist, but, like many of his generation, he didn't question the referral by his cardiologist. He had a patter and he came across as a bit of a charmer. It was a style of communication designed to keep things light and to deflect attention from himself.

While exploring Pat's story, a number of key moments emerged. He still vividly recalled being asked to read in front of the class when he was in fifth year:

'I never really liked reading out loud but this time it was different. I started with a stutter. Slowly each word came out. Then I came across a new word and I stopped, the sweat rolling down my back. There was silence at the start, there was no help, and soon there was giggling and laughing. I just wanted the ground to open up and swallow me. Each day in class a number of us were picked to read out loud. After that day, being asked to read was my worst nightmare. The day I wasn't picked was such a relief; the day I was picked was terrifying.'

In his job at the haulage company, Pat kept a low profile. Even though he believed he had it in him to progress in the company, he didn't even aim for supervisor level, because he couldn't face an interview panel or imagine himself giving feedback to workers.

While he was still in his teens, Pat discovered alcohol. When he drank, he gained confidence, his anxiety reduced, and he was able to talk to people, especially girls. Though he remained at a basic grade in work, socially he began to thrive. He joined everything – from the golf club to the Fianna Fáil cumann to the local conference of St Vincent de Paul. His method for handling himself socially was to have a few glasses of vodka before going out and then a few quick ones when he got there. It worked. He rose to the top in many of the organizations he had joined. Along the way he learned to deliver a speech when required. On such occasions the shame of being tongue-tied in that classroom seemed to be behind him. But it was never completely buried – deep down he knew he was a fraud and suspected people could see through him.

Of course, Pat was simply masking his social anxiety with alcohol, and eventually it caught up with him. He got charged with drink driving. His wife gave him an ultimatum: sober up or get out. In his late thirties Pat went into a residential pro-gramme to detox from alcohol. He got sober and stayed sober.

A number of months after coming out of his residential programme, Pat went to his GP, who referred him to a psychiatrist. He was given a diagnosis – depression – and put on medication. And he remained on anti-depressants for the next thirty years, until coming to me.

I determined that Pat's core issue was social anxiety. We figured out that he had dyslexia, which explained his early difficulties in reading. Like many, he used alcohol to mask his shyness and fear and over time developed an addiction.

Pat may have come into therapy reluctantly, but he became an enthusiastic client, and our exploration of the issue of social anxiety really made sense to him. He came to under-stand how it had affected his life and worked hard to develop the tools to manage it. He came off his anti-depressants and has stayed off them for four years.

There are so many lessons in Pat's story. First, the tragedy of misdiagnosis and the thoughtless prescribing of medica-tion. If Pat had had an early diagnosis and appropriate treatment for his social anxiety, his choices in life could have been much different. It is amazing and rather damning that someone could be on medication for so long with no serious attempt to get to the bottom of the emotional distress.

Second, we see how alcohol is so often used to deal with social anxiety. This is incredibly common. It would not surprise me if you are reading this because you have social anxiety and that you have experienced relief from the fear by using alcohol.

Third, social anxiety is a serious obstacle to progression in the work place. Most people with social anxiety have jobs much lower than their abilities. On the one hand is their real self – the person with all that ability, talent and flair. On the other is the person with fear brought on by mind-reading – believing that others are thinking negatively about them. Underneath they know they can do a better job, but fear is holding them back, as well as avoidant behaviour. They make sure to avoid:

- the terror of job interviews;
- the dread attached to a job with a lot of public contact;
- the nightmare of being promoted to a position of authority over others;
- the agony of team meetings or formal presentations.

Here's the truth, though: safety, avoidant and escape behaviours don't fix the problem; they fuel it.

Now that we have looked at the difficulties associated with social anxiety and shyness, it's time to look at how we can boot this out of your life. You do not need to live like this. You deserve to be at the centre stage of your own life – not hiding in the background.

23

Banishing shyness and social anxiety for good

Now is the time to leave behind the difficulties raised by social anxiety and to enter a place where you find your voice and confidence. You may be daunted by this, but I want to offer you some real hope. The tools outlined in this chapter are critical for the shift to take place. I've used them on many occasions with great success. I wish you success as you embark on this transformation. At the outset you might want to evaluate whether you are currently experiencing mild, moderate or severe social anxiety by completing the self-test questionnaire in the Appendix. You can also use it to track your progress as you work your way through the exercises below.

Before getting into the psychological techniques that you can use to tackle your social anxiety, I'd like to talk about drug therapy. If you go to your GP and they diagnose social anxiety, they may suggest medication. Medication can indeed play a role in relieving some of the symptoms of anxiety, but of course it comes with concerns about side-effects. To decide if anxiety medication is right for you, talk to your GP about the pros and cons of this course of action.

As I explained before, medications often have two names – the scientific, or generic, name and the brand name used by the pharmaceutical company. There are a number of medications for anxiety, including:

- benzodiazepines – alprazolam (Xanax), diazepam (Valium), lorazepam (Ativan);
- selective serotonin reuptake inhibitors (SSRIs) – fluoxetine (Prozac), sertraline (Lustral), escitalopram (Lexapro);
- tricyclic anti-depressants – amitriptyline (Elavil), clomipramine hydrochloride (Anafranil);
- beta-blockers – propranolol (Inderal), atenolol (Tenormin).

Many anti-anxiety medications work by slowing down the central nervous system. Anti-depressant medication has also been found to relieve symptoms of anxiety. Take for example SSRIs – these regulate serotonin levels in the brain to elevate mood. As I said to you in Chapter 13 on depression, you need to be armed with information, and if you are on medication you should ask your GP or pharmacist how the medication works and what are its side-effects. Ask your GP:

- How will this medication help my anxiety?
- What are the drug's common side-effects?
- How long will I have to take the anxiety medication?
- Will withdrawing from the medication be difficult?
- Will my anxiety return when I stop taking the medication?
- Do I combine both medication and therapy?

And ask yourself:

- Do I have the time, money and energy to pursue other evidence-based treatments such as cognitive behavioural therapy?
- What self-help strategies will help me to get my anxiety under control?

I believe drug therapy may play a role in reducing the symptoms of distress and anxiety associated with social anxiety. However, if the experiences of social anxiety – that is the negative feelings of embarrassment, shame, anxiety and fear – are essentially produced by cognitive-style mind-reading and the behavioural patterns of avoidance, escape and safety-seeking, I would ask you to consider this: can something that is external (i.e., a tablet) effectively change what you think and what you do?

Changing the way you think and changing the way you act will create long-term internal changes, and these will significantly impact on how you experience social anxiety. In effect, you are managing this. You are taking control. Social anxiety is not managing you any longer. CBT for social anxiety is a longer-lasting and life-changing solution to your social anxiety.

If you decide to go for medication – and you may have valid reasons for making that choice – please try to make lifestyle changes as well, and use the tools from cognitive behavioural therapy to address your anxiety at its core. Adding psychological techniques to your treatment arsenal could make a huge difference in terms of the long-term outcome.

Getting to the heart of social anxiety – and banishing it for good

The most evidence-based treatment for social anxiety is cognitive behavioural therapy (Chapters 4 to 6). As you will have seen from previous chapters, each problem – and each individual – is different, so the real self solution for social anxiety will be different from the real self solution for depression.

CBT can be provided one to one or through group therapy. If you are researching therapists, check if the one you are considering is experienced in using CBT for treating social anxiety and if they know which techniques are most effective for this disorder. As for group therapy – not surprisingly many people balk at the idea, thinking, 'You must be joking – I can't talk to one person and you want me to talk to a group of strangers!' This feeling is totally understandable, and of course the first group session will be difficult, but there are huge benefits to it, not least seeing how people's experiences can be validated by their peers. Imagine the feeling of shared understanding when you're in a room with ten people who have thoughts, emotions and behaviours that are similar to yours. Group therapy is highly structured, with particular goals for each week of the programme. Over time, people learn to open up and trust, knowing that confidentiality is assured. Experiences and learning are shared. You get 'real' feedback, because it is from fellow sufferers. There is no hiding place. So, if you are considering psychologically based intervention, please don't discount group programmes. (Details of group programmes at www.socialanxietyireland.com or www.socialanxietysupport.com.)

Breaking the cycle of social anxiety

The things we think (cognitive) and do (behaviour) keep the problem of social anxiety going. When we break this cycle and generate new, balanced and alternative thinking, combined with new behaviours, we are again on the road to defeating shyness and social anxiety. Tackling your shyness and social anxiety with the social anxiety CBT mix reduces your anxiety in groups and gives you control in social situations. The fundamental goal is to change your underlying core beliefs, such as 'I am scared, ugly and embarrassing', to other beliefs, such as 'I am brave – I try new things', 'I accept myself, I am intelligent'. It's then that you're on the road to leaving social anxiety behind. Let us illustrate the links between how we think, what we do and how we feel with an example of a social anxiety flashpoint.

Situation. Going to a friend's wedding.

Feelings. Anxiety, fear, embarrassment, self-consciousness.

Thoughts. 'Everyone will look at me, they will think I am stupid, they will think the dress I'm wearing is out of fashion and I'm the wrong body shape for it. I won't know what to say, all my old schoolfriends will be there, they will look at me, they all are so successful. I will be one of those single people at the wedding, they will think I don't have the ability to go out with somebody, I'm just a fool going – why am I putting myself through this?'

Body cues. Adrenaline response – rapid heartbeat, sweating.

Behaviour. Avoiding eye contact, sitting near the exit, planning an escape, drinking too much, not talking.

Target what's keeping the problem going

In the example above, unhelpful thinking styles and beliefs are generating the socially anxious person's feelings of worthlessness.

With shyness and social anxiety, there is an incredible amount of self-consciousness. The internal negative life-script of criticism and disapproval can be exhausting – it's like having a boxer in your head beating you up. On go the mind-reading glasses as you try to interpret every glance and gesture. You attempt to read a meaning into every word spoken in order to figure out what the other person thinks of you. This leads you to assume things – as the saying goes, this makes an 'ASS' out of 'U' and 'ME'. Assumptions create misunderstandings and cause errors in judgement.

Social anxiety sufferers are filled with automatic negative thoughts that contribute to their anxiety. CBT focuses on the problems caused by these thoughts. ANTs distort what is actually happening, increase anxiety and reduce your ability to cope. For the sufferer, they occur instantly in social situations. For example, 'I have nothing to say; people will see me as boring', 'I know I will end up looking like a fool', 'I will get all flushed, people will notice, and I'll get embarrassed', 'I will start to sweat and humiliate myself'.

Once you are aware of these ANTs, you are in a position to replace them with a more helpful, balanced way of thinking. Generating awareness and targeting ANTs requires practice and repetition, so that your new balanced thinking becomes automatic and habitual. Over time, your neural pathways and memory processes will be altered in such a way as to produce very different feelings and behaviours.

The five common thinking errors of social anxiety

Five common thinking errors are at play when the socially anxious person is at large in a social setting.

Mind-reading. Believing that you know what others are thinking and that they see you in the same negative way that you see yourself. 'She knows I've made a mess of this', 'They all thought I was stupid', 'They only asked me because they couldn't find anyone else'.

Fortune-telling. Predicting the future, and usually assuming the worst will happen, e.g., 'I can't do that presentation next week; they'll think I'm stupid and shouldn't be in this company.'

Taking things personally. Assuming that people are focusing on you in a negative way or that what's going on with other people has to do with you. 'They didn't ask me because they don't like me.'

Catastrophizing. Predicting the worst outcome. If something goes wrong, it will be a disaster. If people notice that you're nervous, it will be awful, terrible or disastrous, e.g., 'At the wedding I will look like a fool, not even able to do small talk. I know I will sweat, and it will come right through my clothes. I won't be able to cope.'

Name-calling. Calling yourself names. 'I'm such an idiot', 'I'm stupid', 'I'm bad'.

Once we have captured the negative thoughts, we can analyse and challenge them by using these two tools (see Chapter 5 for more detail):

Thoughts record. When you take your thoughts to court and look at the pros and cons of your ANTs logically. Doing this allows you to gradually replace them with more realistic and balanced ways of looking at the social situations that cause you anxiety.

Twenty powerful challenging questions. Check out CBT (Chapter 5) for these questions.

Let's go back to the example of going to a friend's wedding. Challenge the social anxiety caused by using these two tools.

Initial feelings. Anxiety (at 100, on a scale of 0 to 100), fear (100), embarrassment (80), self-consciousness (80).

Thoughts. 'Everyone will look at me, they will think I am stupid, they will think the dress I'm wearing is out of fashion and I'm the wrong body shape for it. I won't know what to say, all my old schoolfriends will be there, they will look at me, they all are so successful. I will be one of those single people at the wedding, they will think I don't have the ability to go out with somebody, I'm just a fool going – why am I putting myself through this?' First, we must identify what thinking errors are at play, so we can capture them.

- 'Everyone will look at me' is black and white thinking.
- 'They will think I am stupid, they will think the dress I'm wearing is out of fashion and I'm the wrong body shape for it' is the thinking error of mind-reading.
- 'My old schoolfriends ... are all so successful' is overgeneralization.
- 'I don't have the ability to go out with somebody' is mind-reading/exaggeration.
- Finally, 'I'm just a fool' is name-calling.

Now that you have captured your thinking errors, let's take these thoughts to court and look at the ANTs logically.

'It's true that I am attending the wedding by myself. I am single at the moment. It's true my body shape is not at its best at the moment, but I have had a back injury and I have been unable to do exercise for more than six months.

'While it may be difficult, I know that if I avoid the wedding I will feel worse and my shyness and anxiety will get stronger. By attending and facing my fears and focusing on my breathing, I know I can hang in there. I know I can do this. There may be opportunities to meet new people.'

Apply the twenty powerful questions to your ANTs and think mindfully (Chapter 3); you'll end up coming to conclusions along these lines.

'I am engaged in thinking errors including mind-reading, black and white thinking, overgeneralization, exaggeration and name-calling. These are just thoughts; they are not facts. Yes, I am single at the moment, but I have had boyfriends in the past. In general, when I look around, I am as successful in work as my peers. I have my own house. Some of my peers live with their parents or are still in rented accommodation.

'My social anxiety lenses are on; therefore I'm engaged in fear-based thinking. If my friend had had these thoughts, I would have said, "Okay, I understand that social situations are difficult for you, but, on the other side, you get the chance to see your friends, you always have a good laugh together." And if I were looking down from a hot-air balloon, where I have more perspective, I would see that this might be an opportunity for me to meet somebody; I know that there are some single guys going.

'I am able. I am brave, I try new things. I am a resilient person. I like myself and people like me.

'Being mindful is the best thing I can do; stay in the present. This is a time to stay in the moment, be centred and compassionate towards myself.'

New feelings. Anxiety (40), fear (40), embarrassment (30), self-consciousness (30).

New body cues. Settled, calm, composed.

Core beliefs in social anxiety

As we saw in Chapter 1, core beliefs are centrally held convictions that you have about yourself and negative core beliefs prevent you from being your real self. If you believe that others think you are stupid, this will affect you and your confidence. Believe that you are as intelligent as anybody else; that, like everyone else, you possess certain strengths; that you are resourceful and intuitive; and that you have areas that you can work on strengthening. Then imagine the confidence you will have with these new beliefs.

Common negative core beliefs in social anxiety are related to the ideas you have about your talents, self-image, self-worth, self-esteem, competence and confidence – in effect, your sense of self. What is your core belief?

Changing core beliefs is a medium- to long-term strategy. You will need to complete this homework from Chapter 1: keeping a core belief log.

Old core belief to be challenged: ....

New real self core belief: ....

Experiences that show that the old core belief is not COMPLETELY true ALL the time: ....

(List as many as you like here – the more the better!)

Real self core belief to be developed: ....

Task: ....

What you expect to happen: ....

What actually happened: ....

Conclusion(s): ....

Targeting behaviours that strengthen social anxiety

Imagine your social anxiety as a muscle. The three most common behaviours associated with social anxiety – avoidance, escape and safety – make that muscle stronger. (Return to the previous chapter to remind yourself of the explanation for these behaviours.) You will struggle to be your real self as long as you engage in avoidance, escape or safety behaviours. There are two methods for tackling these:

Flooding exposure. Putting a person fully into their feared situation.

Graded exposure. Gradually exposing a person to their feared situation, using a series of steps.

The second method is by far the preferred one, as many therapists, including me, believe the first one to be too harsh. Graded exposure uses the ladder of freedom and success (Chapter 6). It is critical to a mastery of your shyness, low confidence and social anxiety.

Before starting on your ladder of freedom and success tasks, you will need to practise your abdominal breathing technique. This counteracts the adrenaline flow associated with the stress response. Breathe in for 5 seconds, hold for 5 seconds and breathe out for 5 seconds. Repeat four times.

Once you start going into situations that promote social anxiety – using your thinking, breathing, mindfulness and behavioural tools to cope – your confidence will slowly grow. Your task is to go gradually, step by step, rather than launching yourself fully into the situations.

We'll finish by taking a look at an excerpt from Thomas's ladder of freedom and success. Thomas works as a sales rep where socializing is mandatory, but he suffered badly from generalized social anxiety.

| Speak at annual conference of company |
| Have dinner at table with CEO of company |
| Give sales presentation in work to small group |
| Start Toastmasters |
| Go for meal with Siobhan |
| Do a cold-call sales |
| Go on date to cinema with Siobhan |
| Take local businessman (who I find intimidating) out for lunch and make sale |
| Ask Siobhan for date |
| Drop in to local pub when match is on and meet up with brother |
| Go to local pub with brother at quiet time |

Completing the tasks on your ladder of freedom and success is of paramount importance in your fight against social anxiety. The more you do, the faster your journey of self-discovery and change will be.

CHALLENGE SEVEN

Emotional eating

24

The high price of emotional eating

Alex has been overweight for as long as he can remember. From the time he was a child, to a teenager going to school, to a young man, he found choosing clothes, hairstyles, friends and anything else to be a problem. Alex described to me how as he was growing up his parents' attempts to 'help' were more cruel than kind.

'They were helping me, they swore. It was for my own good. "We only say it because we love you. And maybe, if it hurts enough, you'll change." A favourite phrase from my father was "One day, you'll wake up and you'll see. One day you'll want to better yourself." I knew they saw me as a monstrosity. This body was not what they had in mind when they made me.

'Years of eating what I wanted did not come without interruption. I have dieted on and off. I've been through them all – the green tea diet, commercial weight-loss programmes, very low-calorie diets, laxatives, even starvation. This was all because I didn't feel comfortable enough in my own skin. I saw myself for what I am – heavy, unmanageable and out of control.

'Even though I found a partner who loved me, someone who swore she adored every inch of me, I could never believe her. I felt unlovable. I still feel unlovable and I don't know how she sticks with me.

'I'm still fighting. I fluctuate all the time. I am up and down. My latest loss of just over a stone and my sense of "triumph" died at my cousin's wedding, when one of the family, whom I had not seen for a few years, greeted me by saying, "Gosh, Alex, you never did manage to lose the weight, did you?"'

Ireland and the UK are full of people like Alex living unhappy lives because of a constant struggle to lose weight. But why do people become obese in the first place?

From a biological point of view, obesity occurs when we eat more and exercise less over a prolonged period of time. If the amount of energy (food/calories) that we put into our bodies is greater than the energy we expend (body functions/movement/exercise), the excess is stored as fat.

Over tens of thousands of years our bodies have perfected an equation to store food in case of famine or food shortages. In developed societies, however, famine doesn't happen. The combination of plentiful food supplies with our bodies' evolutionary tendency to store food has resulted in an obesity epidemic in the Western world.

Serious as the problem of adult obesity is, we have an even bigger problem looming with childhood obesity. Today, one in three children is overweight or obese. Incredibly, if not addressed, 85% of these children will become obese adults. We are at significant risk of being one of the first generations to bury our own children because of obesity-related illnesses. And the harsh truth is that children with obese parents are twelve times more likely to be overweight than if their parents were a healthy weight.

It is both tragic and preventable. After all, children don't buy or cook their own food. But there's no doubt that the pace of life and our modern environment make it increasingly challenging for parents to feed their children well and to keep them active. Any parent will know that it's a struggle to keep your children off the screens. As my children get older and are increasingly lured into this 'screen world', the challenge for me and other parents is to promote more playtime and game-time – swimming, running, GAA, walking, cycling, soccer, rugby, reading, drawing, singing, dancing, arts and crafts.

Maintaining a healthy weight is a difficulty for many people, even the healthiest and trimmest of us. Just consider: we can get fast food 24 hours a day, seven days a week. And the portions that we eat have increased over the years. Compare the plates that you eat from now to the one you ate from in your granny's house. Our plates have grown bigger and we have too. Great conveniences like TVs, computers and mobile phones encourage us to be less active. In fact, we're so connected we can order food online and never leave home. The sad truth is that this great 'connectivity' is actually disconnecting us as individuals, as a community and as a society.

The environment is also a factor – look at the powerful food industry that entices us to overeat and to eat unhealthily. The industry spends billions every year to ensure that we overeat. In our society, people overeat not because of hunger, but because of hidden, powerful influences. Most people think they are too clever to be fooled by packaging, portion sizes, mood lighting or smells; yet time and time again psychological research shows that we are all being fooled. The challenge for us is to change our surroundings and to remove the influences that cause us to overeat.

In my work with the leaders on *Operation Transformation*, I developed a deep understanding of the significant emotional and psychological factors associated with weight gain, weight loss and obesity. Emotional eating is perhaps the biggest and the most covert way that we gain weight.

There is increasing psychological evidence to show that obesity is linked to depression, anxiety, body dissatisfaction, low self-esteem, low self-worth and, most importantly, a lower quality of life. Interestingly, recent studies have indicated that obese children rate their quality of life lower than those children with cancer. Weight gain has also been linked to poor concentration levels, reduced exam results and, worryingly, more social isolation in school.

Society is moving towards a very harsh view of people who are obese. People make assumptions and judgements based on someone's weight. This leads to increasing prejudice, intolerance and even discrimination in some situations, including work, travel, schooling, healthcare, media and retail. Obesity is linked to having fewer friends, lesser school achievements and higher unemployment.

It's really important as parents that we are loving, kind, supportive and caring to children who have an issue with their weight. And if we are struggling with overweight as adults, it is equally important to be loving, kind, supportive and caring to ourselves as we try to tackle the issue. Take Alex from the start of the chapter. He internalized his parents' negative voices. His obesity related to a vicious cycle in which his internal negative and critical voice (from his parents) triggered him to overeat as a way of comforting himself. Alex has worked hard in therapy and focused on changing the internal negative and critical voice to one that is encouraging, supportive and compassionate. This is possibly the single most important work to do when tackling obesity – booting out that internal critic.

25

Developing a healthier relationship with food

'I can't seem to control myself. I had been "good" all day, but I got held up at a meeting last night, and on my way home I bought a tub of ice cream when I was buying petrol and sneaked it into the back of the freezer. It haunted me all evening. When I was eating my dinner, all I could think about was that rum raisin ice cream. I could not wait for Aidan and the kids to go to bed so I could get it out. I wasn't even really hungry; it was just something I had to have. Like an addiction. And when I get like that, I just can't put the spoon down. Halfway through I'd really had enough, but I needed to finish it. As if that wasn't bad enough, I then hid the "evidence" – I ran down the garden in the lashing rain to put the empty tub into the big recycling bin rather than under the sink. It's pathetic. I hate myself for being like this. All the time food is at the back of my mind and I can't seem to stop myself giving in, even though I know better. To think that I used to teach step classes back in the day! Now I feel like I'm losing the battle. I'm about a stone and a half overweight but I'm gaining a couple of pounds every month. If I keep going like this, particularly at my age, I'm going to end up with a really serious weight problem.'

Paula is one of the many people who have a good idea about how to lose weight – cut out high-calorie foods, eat healthily, exercise more. She is a 48-year-old mother of two teenagers and a ten-year-old. She manages a busy city-centre hair salon. Juggling her one-hour commute – each way – to work, the non-stop pace once she gets there and the endless demands of family life leaves her feeling frazzled and constantly running on empty. Inevitably, like many of us, she uses high-energy (high sugar, high fat) food to refuel – not just her body, but her depleted supply of emotional energy as well.

To tackle her situation, there are lots of important practical steps Paula can take, once she somehow gets the time and space to do some planning. But she also needs to approach the issue in a much broader way so that she develops a new perspective on the place of food in her life. Paula herself knows there is more to her weight problem than simply eating too much and moving too little. Food is meeting needs that are not being met any other way.

To tackle overeating we also need to apply psychology. The powerful thinking, doing and mindfulness tools we have already discovered are hugely helpful in that process.

The five key steps to transforming obesity

Step 1. Preparation – failing to plan is planning to fail

We all have busy lives. What regularly causes difficulty when it comes to tackling obesity is our lack of planning. It's important to plan your food shopping and your meals. It's the same with exercise: you need to make it part of your regular routine. For example, go for a 30-minute jog during lunchtime.

Prioritization. If you want to address your weight, you need to prioritize your eating and exercise behaviours so that they are a central activity in your life. Be practical – keep a pair of comfortable walking or running shoes in your car and office, and seek to find places and times to exercise regularly.

Commitment. Only you can make this change happen, so you have to be 100% committed to it. Consider this phrase: 'If you want your life to change, your choices must change and today is the best day of your life to begin.'

Attention and belief. Where you put your focused attention is where you will get your results. You need to believe that it is possible. Ask yourself this question: on a scale of 1 to 100, where 1 means you don't believe permanent weight loss is truly possible and 100 means you truly believe that it's possible, where would you put yourself right now? Use this question to track your progress. Then ask: what do I need to do to add 10 to this score? Ring somebody for support? Become more aware? Complete my food diary?

Step 2. Action – making stuff happen

Setting goals is important because they can give us direction and purpose in all areas of our lives. Often we can beat ourselves up for not achieving all our goals. When we do this, we tend to stop everything. It's okay to be 'good enough' – we don't have to be brilliant all the time. In fact, I don't think it's possible to be brilliant all the time. Goals can bring drive and passion to our lives. They are essentially a map to help guide us through choppy waters.

When we think about goals, we need to consider SMART goals. Too often goals are loosely made, such as 'I want to lose a bit of weight'. This will more than likely lead to failure. As mentioned in Chapter 1, a SMART goal is:

- **S**pecific;
- **M**easurable;
- **A**chievable;
- **R**ealistic;
- **T**ime limited.

These SMART goals can be short, medium and long term. Here are some examples of SMART goals: 'I will lose 2 lbs. per week for the next three weeks', 'I will write in my food diary each night for a four-week period', 'I will go swimming once a week with my children'. Don't be afraid to broaden your goals to health and well-being, not just weight loss!

Measuring. The biggest lesson I learned doing a business degree was 'What gets measured, gets done.' I appreciate that for many people jumping on the scales for the first time in a long time can be a terrifying experience. It's a moment of reckoning and accountability, and many have been in denial about their real weight for years. On *Operation Transformation* we have seen many people predict their weight to be much less than it actually was when weighed. Ray thought he was 18 stone – he was 22 stone. Jessica said she was 14 stone but turned out to be 16½ stone. Being weighed is a really important part of the weight-loss journey. Knowing where we are starting from allows us to know where we are going. Each small win will spur you on to additional healthy behaviours – to exercise and to work on portion control. So weigh yourself at least once a week to track your progress.

Enjoyment. You are more likely to stick with an exercise

regime if you find it fun. Some people are very good on their own, while others prefer groups.

Step 3. Knowledge – knowledge is power

As Oprah Winfrey once said, 'When you know better, you do better.' Now that you know better, you have the opportunity to do better.

The power of vision. Picture your healthy future – your energy, body, actions, career, family, friends and life. Picture it in great detail. Allow yourself to imagine what this would be like for you. Try making a vision board, a tool that provides inspiration and shows your destination. There are many tools online to assist you in their creation. You can take a picture of your board and use it as a screensaver on your computer, tablet or smartphone.

The power of motivation. When you want success, your goals, aims, ambitions and dreams become bigger than your excuses. Motivation can be seen as the energy that you use to drive the direction, intensity and consistency of your choices. Are you making choices to eat healthier foods and do regular exercise?

To keep your motivation, or mojo, going you need to know that only *you* can make change happen. Success will come if you are persistent and courageous; when you hit obstacles, you won't throw in the towel. You can ask yourself this powerful question: 'What action can I do today to bring me closer to my goal?'

The power of choices. Do we get up early and go for a run or walk, or do we hit the snooze button and pull up the duvet? Shopping in the supermarket, do we choose full-fat milk over slim, ready-made pizza over fresh vegetables, bacon over fish, white sliced bread over wholewheat? Each of these represents a 'Choice Point' and a decision. It's the accumulation of small choices that will get you to your goal. In order to make better choices, stay fully in the moment when those choices are being made and see that they are Choice Points.

These Choice Points are incredibly important and occur many times throughout the day for ourselves and our families. Becoming aware of your Choice Points allows you to stop, take a moment and then make the choice that gets you closer to your goal. You can ask this practical question: 'This is a Choice Point – what decision do I make here? Do I make the decision that brings me closer to my goal?'

Sonia, who is thirty-six, weighed 17 stone after having her second child a number of years ago. She managed to get it back to 13¾ stone.

'I'm a "healthy" size 16 in a dress. I am too afraid to wear trousers, as I know I'm too big for them. Even though I'm totally unhappy with my weight, that still doesn't stop me reaching for crisps and bars of Dairy Milk. When I look at my friends and then compare myself with them, I feel totally discouraged. Life is busy, dropping the children off to school and then dashing into work. I don't really have time for exercise. In fact by the time I get through the evening routine of dinner, homework and laundry, I am just fit to drop. And that's what I do – I drop in front of the telly and drink wine. My husband goes out playing five-a-side football three nights a week. I am deeply unhappy with how I look, even though on the outside nobody would know. People would think I'm happy-go-lucky. But, inside, my appearance and my weight occupy all my thoughts. It's got to a stage now that I think people are looking at me and saying, "How can she go out looking like that?"'

Sonia turned this around through the power of choices. She got her husband to share the household duties equally. Then she used the freed-up time to exercise three nights a week with a friend while her husband continued to do his football. She became more mindful every time she ate or drank, taking a 10-second pause and asking the Choice Point question: 'Will this get me closer to my goal?' She stopped beating herself up so much.

Through this process Sonia became more compassionate towards herself. She gained early momentum, lost some weight and, in turn, this increased her confidence and motivation. Sonia is now a size 12. She has stopped there. She is very contented and authentic, and no longer puts herself down. She says that she is in a better place for herself and for her children.

Changing patterns. Old patterns have brought us to this point in our lives right now. Our behaviours of eating and activity are physical patterns. The challenge is to change them, so that we are working on both sides of the scale, that is, reducing the energy in and increasing the energy out. This may mean being more diligent about the quality of food we eat, the amount we exercise, how we manage stress and boredom, being more open and accepting feedback from others and saying no. For instance, night-time is when many people overeat, because they are eating emotionally and snacking mindlessly. Try to make a list of positive things you can do that do not involve food. For example, join a book club, go to a yoga class, do an adult-education class or go to a movie (no popcorn!).

Buddy up. It's easier to stick to a weight-loss plan when you have support. There is significant psychological evidence to show that having a support network is very valuable in helping you to achieve your goals. Look around you and consider people who could be in your support network. This is often the advantage held by the well-known weight-loss programmes: they feature group support, group discussions and group tasks such as keeping a food diary. So enlist your family and friends – the positive ones! If people are negative or judgemental, limit their influence.

Step 4. Overcoming obstacles – transforming emotional eating

In the world of psychology, we often say, when referring to weight issues, 'It's not what you are eating, it's what's eating you.' Emotional eating plays a significant role. Are you an emotional eater? Do you 'comfort' eat or do you eat junk food because of your feelings rather than because of physical hunger?

From an early age we learn that food brings comfort. A few years ago I took my two-year-old for his swine flu vaccine. My son was crying after his injection, and as I was comforting him he was given a chocolate button by the practice nurse. From such a young age we are shown that our hurts can be healed by food. Often during times of happiness (birthdays) and sadness (bereavement) food plays such a central role.

When it comes to emotional eating, stuffing food into our mouths can become a habit when we are dealing with the emotional distress of boredom, stress, anger, loneliness, depression, sadness, fear, anxiety, low self-esteem, or relationship and communication difficulties. In effect, our eating habit stops us from learning the valuable skills needed to end our emotional distress. This becomes a negative cycle, in which overeating results in weight gain. Often this is accompanied by even more negative emotions – self-blame, criticism, guilt and anger.

There are three key stages in the process of ending emotional eating.

1. Track your emotional eating. Keep a food-mood diary that identifies what you eat, when you eat it and what your mood was like at the time. Track your negative emotions and distinguish them from feelings of hunger. Remember: what gets measured gets done. With your food-mood diary, you will be able to identify the moods that trigger your emotional eating. Tracking creates awareness. It's only once awareness has been awoken that you can effectively intervene.

2. Break the habit of emotional eating. Once your awareness increases, you will be able to identify your patterns. Many people emotionally eat when they are low, bored, stressed, anxious, depressed, low in confidence, feeling disempowered and unfulfilled. At this point think about emotional eating as a Choice Point. This creates a pause. When you are weighing up the pros and cons of the decision, you can tell yourself, 'This food will only comfort me temporarily', 'If I eat, I will have two problems: the one that was upsetting me and feeling bad about eating'. Keep in control: remember, it's a choice. Try to do something else that's pleasurable until the urge to eat passes. You will find that afterwards you will feel empowered, in control and more skilled in tackling your emotional eating.

3. Use CBT and mindfulness to break the habit of emotional eating. For some people, distraction is not enough to break the habit. For more effective ways to manage the emotional distress that leads to overeating, try relaxation exercises, meditation or mindfulness. Alternatively, you can try to deal with the thoughts that directly lead to your mood. In earlier chapters I provided more details about how to challenge the thoughts that underlie different moods. Essentially each mood that a person has is linked to powerful thoughts. It's the same with emotional eating. When someone is 'stressed', for example, underneath is an automatic negative thought that they must challenge in order to create a new, balanced thought.

Present pattern.

Mood. Stressed and low.

Automatic thoughts. 'I just can't cope any more; there are too many demands. I'm not able to do this.'

Behaviour. Emotional eating.

Challenge the thoughts that maintain these moods. Imagine your mood as a fire and your thoughts as the fuel that you are putting on to this fire. Now imagine a new pattern: you are going to take away the fuel and douse this fire. You are taking control. Remember your thoughts are just thoughts; they are not facts.

New pattern.

Mood. Stressed and low.

Automatic thoughts. 'I just can't cope any more; there are too many demands. I'm not able to do this.'

Challenge questions. I encourage you to use some challenge questions, such as:

• If my best friend told me they'd had these thoughts, what would I say to them?
• Is there another way I can look at this situation?

- In two years' time, will I feel differently about the situation?
- Am I overlooking anything positive in the situation?
- What strengths have I used before in situations such as this?

When we use these challenge questions, often we come up with more realistic and balanced thoughts that are real. Now we are in a position to replace our automatic thoughts.

Alternative balanced thoughts. 'Okay, it's tough now, but I've been in tough situations in the past and survived. I can get through this without emotional eating. I will go for a walk instead.'

New mood. Balanced, controlled.

Behaviour. Go for a walk.

Therapy may help you to identify the underlying emotional difficulties that are causing you to overeat. I have met quite a few people for whom emotional eating is related to trauma and abuse experiences in their early life. If this is the case, contact your GP; or I would strongly encourage you to contact the excellent and free HSE National Counselling Service (Freephone 1800 234 110, 10 a.m.–4 p.m.).

Let's consider another example.

Automatic thoughts. 'I will never lose weight. I have tried so many diets and look at me now: I am worse than ever.'

Which is connected to a *feeling*: feeling miserable, sad, low and hopeless.

Which is connected to a *physical state*: being low in energy and craving chocolate.

Which is connected to a *behaviour*: staying in, comfort eating of chocolate.

Using the challenge questions as indicated above, you can replace these negative automatic thoughts.

Alternative balanced thoughts. 'Yes, it's hard, but now I have to focus on what's within my control. I need to use the tools and learning. I need to keep my food-mood diary. I need to bring in my sister, who provides me with great support. I know this urge will pass if I allow it to.'

New mood. Balanced, controlled.

Behaviour. Phone sister.

Remember CBT can help you to identify the triggers of overeating. With this new understanding you are now in control.

Situation. Overeating because of certain activities – frequent business lunches, watching TV shows, going to the movies, and so on.

Feelings. Eating in response to stress, tiredness, boredom, anger, anxiety, depression; eating as a way to self-soothe and comfort.

Thoughts. Self-defeating eating as a result of low self-esteem, self-dislike, guilt and hopelessness.

Body cues. Overeating as a result of body cues. How many times have you skipped a meal and over-compensated by eating in the supermarket while shopping? Eating in the car on the way home? Eating while preparing your meal? Going back for seconds?

By understanding the triggers of emotional eating and by using CBT techniques, you can learn new skills to deal with emotional distress. You will be able to change your thinking, which will help you to feel better and to make healthier choices. With these skills, you will find that emotional eating, stress eating, night grazing and mindless eating are no more.

Step 5. Wisdom phase – from mindless eating to mindful eating

Do any of these sound familiar?

- You eat your breakfast while standing.
- You have your lunch in the car or by the computer.
- You eat your dinner in front of the TV.
- You eat because you are upset.

If they do, you are *eating mindlessly*. Mindless eating ensures that you make unhealthy choices about how much, how fast and what foods you eat. Mindless eating means you are not in control. Martin is typical of this kind of eating. He could be described as a 'white van man'. He is also a dashboard diner. He described his day to me:

> 'I'm on such a tight schedule, I have so many deliveries that I need to make. I don't get time in the morning to have breakfast. I try to leave the house without waking the children. I always stop at the garage for breakfast. They know me there and I don't even have to order. A coffee, a muffin and a breakfast roll. Then I work my day. No time for lunch – I'm eating in the van again, this time it's breaded chicken, lettuce, coleslaw in a bread roll. With a latte, of course.'

Over time, this mindless eating pattern has led Martin to a weight of 17½ stone.

When fully engaged with eating – when eating mindfully – you are tackling the big problem of overeating. Let's examine the different forms of overeating.

The blowout. Christmas dinner is a perfect example of a

blowout – a binge-eating episode where a considerable quantity of food is consumed by all. But for some the blowout is a regular weekly ritual – the Friday-night Chinese, Indian or Italian takeaway washed down with fizzy drinks or alcohol.

Grazing. The grazer overeats by frequently taking in small amounts of food mindlessly between meal and snack times. This is often associated with emotional eating. It may be a response to boredom; or it may just be a habit born out of easy accessibility to food.

Compulsive overeating. Sugary, salty, fatty foods – these types of foods often compel a person to eat when they are not hungry; they then find they cannot stop when they have had enough. Individuals may eat alone or in secret. Multinational food conglomerates – Big Food – have spent millions researching exactly how to create the optimal combination of sugar, fat, salt and texture in their products, so that they are at best 'moreish' and, at worst, totally addictive. As the ad for the well-known crisp says, 'Once you pop, you can't stop.' Let's face it: you're never going to say that about apples or lamb chops. Don't beat yourself up about this: they have engineered the foods in labs to make them very hard for the human brain to resist. Indeed, some neuroscientists are now suggesting that over-consumption of these high-sugar-fat-salt foods rewires the brain in much the same way as heroin. The trick is to be aware of what Big Food gets up to (remember Big Food doesn't care about your well-being – only delivering profits to shareholders) and to be discerning about what you let into your shopping basket.

Food addiction. The food addict has an extreme form of compulsive overeating. They cannot control their behaviour and have cravings that they cannot master. Individuals may eat secretly, feel guilty and upset, and sometimes try to compensate by restricting or purging (such as in bulimia).

When you move from mindless to mindful eating, you gain enough control to choose a healthier journey. You will choose mindful portions. The challenge of mindful eating is to slow down – look, feel, smell, chew, concentrate on the taste of the food and the speed at which you are eating. Pay attention to the here and now. Don't do other activities such as reading, watching TV, using the computer. Before eating your next mouthful, lay down your cutlery and pause for a few seconds – become mindful. This is a skill and, like all new skills, it takes practice and persistence.

On *Operation Transformation* I often tell leaders: 'If it was easy, everybody would be doing it.' We all know that dealing with a weight problem is one of the hardest things anyone can do. After all, you can't avoid food as you can something else that you might find hard to handle. Tackling obesity and emotional eating requires planning, courage and consistency. It also takes belief. And someone beside yourself to believe in you. I believe in you. I believe that you can make this change. Plan, set your goals and you will get there. Remember the power of making better choices. Move from emotional and mindless eating to mindful eating using your new tools. Remember the power of sharing this journey. Kick out the internal critic. This new, healthier you will have more energy, zest and vitality.

. . . .

PART FOUR

Putting it all together – becoming your real self

You are now close to unleashing your true potential. When you do, you will discover that the inner journey you have taken is good for you and for those who are part of your life. Your growth will give you the confidence and the ability to put away the mask and live in an authentic way.

26

Staying on track and overcoming obstacles

Life will always throw 'curve balls' at you – events that can knock you off course. This is the nature of life. Your ability to be flexible, overcome adversity and build resilience can help you to face future challenges.

Always remember that your shift from where you were to where you are now is based on the hard work that you have done. Even if you are attending a counsellor, it's the hours outside of the therapy room that count. Effectively you have learned the skills to help yourself.

Much of what you have learned requires regular practice. The key to future well-being is to spot the signs of a mood change. Now that you are in a better place, the goal is to stay there. So you need to know your unique relapse signature – what are the early-warning signs of stress, worry, low mood, anxiety, depression, anger, bipolar, social anxiety, emotional eating or whatever your particular issue may be? What causes your problems to stick around? A sign may be that you are doing more of something, or less of something, or the frequency or intensity of negative thoughts.

Some people lapse and others relapse. Lapse is a brief return to negative feelings such as feeling down or anxious. This is fairly normal, as long as it is not long lasting. Imagine your emotions as traffic lights that inhabit zones of Green, Amber and Red. Green means 'You're safe to proceed',

Amber means 'Warning – be alert; proceed with caution' and Red means 'Stop – you must not keep going the way you are'. A lapse is when you are in the Amber Zone. You need to see a lapse for what it is: a short-term setback. Your challenge is not to let it make you give up doing the things you need to do. Keep going. You can turn this around and get back into the Green Zone.

Relapse is when you enter the Red Zone. Negative thinking and the behaviours that were previously present have crept back and you are spiralling down into bad feelings. A relapse is very upsetting, and you can easily get locked into all or nothing thinking. Remind yourself of the techniques that you used before to make you feel better. Or perhaps you need to reach out and get help and support. The key thing to remember is that you can get yourself back into the Green Zone, both by reactivating skills you already have and maybe by learning some new ones.

Lapses and relapses are normal and can be overcome. You cannot unlearn all the skills and techniques that CBT has taught you, so if you relapse you're not back at square one. You know how to handle your low mood and anxiety. Lapses are commonly preceded by increased stress. Check out Chapters 7–9 to tackle your stress management. At this point you can set out a plan of what you need to do and when you are going to do it.

Many times people are unaware of slippage. Often they recount how good or bad they feel, i.e., they are either in the Green or in the Red Zone. Identify whether you have moved into the Amber Zone, and, if so, turn your mood around fast, before you slip into the Red Zone. A good way of doing this is to develop a comprehensive relapse prevention plan.

In order to do that, you must first understand what each zone represents to you. Here's a plan completed by Niamh, who experienced depression and anxiety. First, Niamh described her Green Zone: how she is and what she does when she is well.

Green Zone	What to do to stay in the Green Zone
• real;	• eat well;
• authentic;	• stick to regular bedtime of 10.30 p.m. (no crap TV!) and don't get overtired;
• happy;	
• positive;	• enjoy activities with my partner and children;
• life going well in key areas:	• stay on top of things;
- relationship – close, warm;	• go to yoga class once a week;
- children – fun, enjoyable;	• swim once a week and get in a 30-minute walk three times a week;
- work – focused, no conflict;	
- social life – in touch with friends;	• do 15 minutes of mindfulness five days a week;
- community – involved;	• positive thinking – challenge ANTs;
• health and well-being:	• work – don't take on colleagues' responsibilities;
- healthy weight;	• try not to be critical or negative towards others;
- good appetite/no emotional eating;	
- memory/concentration good;	• stay in contact with friends;
- energy levels good;	• stay off cigarettes;
- stress – nothing annoys me, able to cope.	• stay involved in voluntary organizations;
	• just do my best and don't take on other people's responsibilities.

Niamh's Red Zone looked like this:

Red Zone	What to do to move out of the Red Zone
• depression is back;	• try to keep going – do not give in;
• anxiety, panic attacks;	• reconnect with GP;
• exhausted;	• reconnect with therapist;
• feel physically sick, sluggish;	• use scheduling day – taking things step by step;
• sleep disturbed;	• rest and relax;
• no appetite, losing weight;	• try to get back to yoga;
• everything is magnified;	• eat well;
• withdraw from friends – no phone calls;	• ask a friend to go for a walk with me;
• avoid people – avoid talking;	• try to keep in contact with friends – make at least one phone call to a friend every day;
• feelings of dread – feel something is going to happen;	• practise mindfulness – focus on the moment;
• fear – dying;	• remind myself that nothing bad is going to happen;
• no interest in anything;	• list my avoidances and climb back up the ladder of freedom and success;
• everything is an effort;	• get back to work, initially on reduced hours;
• negative and worried about past, present and future;	• be assertive;
• guilt, low self-esteem;	• try to stay positive;
• no confidence;	• maintain confidence;
• just surviving from day to day;	• do not feel guilty;
• worry something bad is going to happen to the children;	• do not blame myself;
• unable to get into work;	• do not take on responsibilities that are not mine;
• stop all community activities;	• refocus on challenging my ANTs;
• stop walking, swimming, yoga;	• review my achievements and personal qualities log daily.
• feel disconnected in relationship.	

The reality is that Niamh did not jump from the Green Zone to the Red Zone overnight. It's a gradual process. So she worked hard on identifying the signs of slippage, i.e., who she is and what she does – or doesn't do – in her Amber Zone.

Amber Zone	What to do to move out of the Amber Zone
• notice mood dropping in winter months;	• now that I am aware I can intervene earlier;
• if pressurized in work by bullying boss, I feel anxious, not able to cope, panic;	• tackle my avoidances;
• more irritable with partner and children;	• assert myself at work;
	• reset my sleeping pattern;
	• reconnect with my partner and children;
• fuse gets shorter – more anger outbursts;	• connect more with my friends;
	• stay involved in community activities – swimming club;
• I don't sign up for usual evening classes;	• go to yoga class with friend;
• reduce frequency of yoga, swimming or walking;	• don't take on responsibilities that are not mine;
	• use online shopping and meal planning;
	• use skills of mindfulness;
• more easily fatigued;	• be compassionate with myself;
	• go to GP for check-up;
• don't get to bed early enough – start watching crap TV;	• go to psychologist for top-up session;
	• tackle ANTs;
• drop activities in voluntary groups;	• take some time off for myself;
	• re-engage in relaxing activities, such as taking a nightly bath;
• have additional negative feelings, including taking on responsibilities that are not mine;	• watch a funny movie;
	• spend time in nature;
	• cut back on responsibilities.

Continued

331

Amber Zone	What to do to move out of the Amber Zone

- feel guilty – sense of duty and sense of loyalty that is out of proportion;
- concentration difficulties;
- avoid friends, phone calls;
- feel I am rushing everywhere;
- start avoiding things I would normally take on;
- increased automatic negative thoughts;
- sleep pattern changes;
- feel more negative;
- losing confidence;
- drinking more wine at home.

You can see that Niamh developed a comprehensive understanding of the characteristics, for her, of each zone and devised a check-list so she could readily identify what zone she was in. By drawing up her relapse signature profile – her Amber Zone – she understood that early intervention was the key. So when she entered the Amber Zone she was usually able to bring herself back into the Green Zone. On two occasions she went into the Red Zone. This was associated with a major life event – the death of her mother. However, in the last six years, Niamh has been in the Green Zone and is able to cope with the normal ups and downs of everyday life. She knows what she needs to do to keep herself well. Do you?

If you want to develop your Amber Zone profile, figure out which things you do more of or less of as a result of your low mood (e.g., drinking more, avoidance, anger outbursts, and so on). What pervasive thoughts are you having in the early stages of your strong moods? What are your high-risk situations? For example, if you have had a problem with dependency on alcohol, events such as weddings and Christmas can make you more vulnerable.

The best way to prevent going into the Red Zone is to keep practising your CBT and mindfulness skills. In this way you will be able to face the life events that happen to us all. Become aware of your tripwires – the things that can move you quickly from one zone to another.

As a way of sustaining your well-being, I propose that you set yourself a 'well-being review day' on the first day of the month. At this time you can review how your mood has been in the past month. You may choose to ask someone close to you who is an observer to give you some feedback on your mood. For example, if you are bipolar, the people around you may have more insight into where your mood is at than you do yourself, particularly if there are subtle signs that you are in the pre-mania phase, known as hypomania, or in the mania phase. You can read through your traffic-light scheme and identify whether there are any early-warning signs flashing in the Amber Zone or if there are any Red Zone activities that you should be concerned about. Are there any signs of avoidance because of anxiety? Are you withdrawing because you feel down, or engaging in emotional eating, or having an increased number of anger outbursts? If these are present, use what helped you previously in your toolkit.

You have worked hard to overcome the problems created by the strong emotions that sometimes swamp you in daily life. Using the tools of CBT and mindfulness, you have learned new skills to overcome the negative emotions that affect your well-being. Think of these skills as like riding a bike. It takes time to learn to ride a bike, but once you know how, you never forget. If you stop cycling for a while, you might be a bit rusty and wobble, but it won't be long before you are as skilled as you were before.

It's human nature to look for the magic bullet, the one thing that will change your life. The reality is that many small things make big things happen. Fundamentally, we are all on a journey to become our real selves. It's how you manage your journey – staying on course, navigating the occasional diversion while still facing in the right direction – that will get you through.

27

Letting your real self soar

Well done – you made it! This book is about you and your journey. You moved from fear to freedom, from low mood to hope, from anger to assertiveness, and from low self-esteem to personal worth. You transformed shyness into a voice full of assurance and confidence, and you quelled emotional eating by figuring out what was eating you.

You can be proud of the changes you have made in your life. They will profoundly affect you and those close to you. They will ripple out into all aspects of your life – physical, emotional, spiritual and social.

Your new skills, beliefs and values mean that you are wiser and more enlightened. You have turned your internal critic into a positive nurturing coaching voice. You have changed your negative core beliefs. You are no longer defined by negative labels. As somebody once said, 'Labels are for jars, not people.' You have a new set of positive beliefs that will act like a magnet and pull you towards understanding, gratitude, wisdom, wonder, sincerity and calmness.

You recognize that there are things in life that you can't control – your age, sex, family history and past. However, there are things that you can control. You know the value of flexibility, and your capacity to change will allow you to face your future with resilience. You have 'bounce-back-ability'! This adaptability means you have the strength to face the greatest challenges. You have the compassion and wisdom to know that sometimes the things you cannot change end up changing you.

You have discovered that your real self is not something external. Instead, it is an inner journey of discovery on which you shed the negative beliefs holding you back. But learning to manage negative emotions was just the start of your real self journey.

The joy of continuing to grow

When it comes to being your real self, there is always room for growth. That's the exciting part. It's not just about leaving stress, fear, worry, anger, low self-esteem, low confidence behind you; no, it's about emerging into a space where there are no limits.

If you are thriving, figure out what it is that is helping you. You may find areas that you still want to work on. After all, we are all just works in progress. So, for example, you might want to work on your self-esteem, assertiveness or confidence. After you select an area, you will need to answer these questions:

* How are you going to do it?
* When are you going to do it?
* What resources do you need to do it?
* What might get in the way of achieving this goal?
* How can I overcome this?

When you are your real self, you nurture your well-being and happiness. Life is filled with positive emotions such as satisfaction, cheer, joy, love, hope and gratitude. Now you are moving into the space where your real self soars. The positive psychology movement has identified different areas for the growth of your real self:

- wisdom;
- courage;
- humanity;
- justice;
- self-control;
- meaning.

Imagine each of these areas as an orchard with different pathways to explore. These pathways point in new directions for your ongoing real self journey. You don't need to travel each one – some will fit more comfortably with your natural style than others.

In the *Wisdom* orchard are the pathways of creativity, curiosity, open-mindedness, love of learning and perspective. Think about growing your real self wisdom by trying something new: dancing, singing, art, pottery, night courses, online courses. I often recommend that clients go on a small course. Any course. I am less interested in the course than I am in the fact that the person is out in a group. They are not sitting at home, but rather are facing their fears, conversing and mixing, and learning that their opinion matters. Each time you do this task, it gets easier. You create new opportunities. Go and explore.

You have already travelled some of the pathways of the *Courage* orchard in your real self journey. You have been brave, and faced and overcome challenges. How about trying persistence – finishing what you start? Some people are great innovators; others doers; and some finishers. What are you?

Do you start projects and struggle to finish them? If so, try persistence and complete the project. And, when you do, praise and reward yourself. Courage brings vitality and integrity into how you approach life. Take responsibility for your own feelings and actions, and not those of others. Present yourself as you are. You are wonderful. You do not need a mask or a front any more. You are real. Try new things that you have never done or that you haven't done for a long time – travel, climb a mountain, swim in the sea, cycle, call someone, ask somebody on a date.

In the *Humanity* orchard the pathways are about caring for others and having positive relationships. Life is about relationships – those we have with ourselves and those we have with others. On this pathway you become more aware of the relationships that nurture you and more aware of healthy boundaries. Other humanity pathways are kindness, care and compassion. On these pathways you can explore by volunteering and doing good deeds for others. It's amazing, but when you give, you receive more in return. Not necessarily something tangible but something that's more important than anything else – love.

The *Justice* orchard is all about being fair to others. Here the pathways are fairness, teamwork, citizenship and leadership. By making fairness a principle to live by – you don't look up to anybody and you don't look down on anybody – you become even-handed and just. You treat others the way you want to be treated yourself. You can explore citizenship and fairness by tackling social injustice with organizations like Amnesty International, the Society of St Vincent de Paul, Barnardos, Bóthar, GOAL and Greenpeace, to name but a few.

The *Self-control* orchard has pathways of humility, prudence and forgiveness. These are areas you can work on, e.g., giving people a second chance, or being more flexible with others. I can think of recent examples at the top of society where a healthy dose of humility, rather than hubris and egotism, would have prevented a lot of personal hurt and saved the taxpayer a lot of money.

We have walked around many fine orchards and looked at many fine pathways, but the orchard of finding *Meaning* beyond yourself has some of the most incredible pathways for inspiring your real self. The pathways in this orchard include hope, humour, spirituality, gratitude and an appreciation of beauty. On the hope pathway you are expecting the best in the future and you are working to achieve your goals. As adults we do not travel down the pathway of playfulness and humour enough. Explore this area. If you have children or nieces and nephews, go and play with them. Let them lead the play. Jump onto the trampoline with them. Let them jump all over you! Go to the playground. Don't watch – get involved. Have a go on the swing or the seesaw. Let your inner child out to play.

For some people spirituality plays an important part in their life. For others, this pathway has not been travelled for a while. Maybe it's time to consider it again. There are many places to explore spirituality and faith – you can go to places such as the welcoming guesthouse in Glenstal Abbey in Co. Limerick (www.glenstalabbey.ie) or the Jampa Ling Tibetan Buddhist Centre in Co. Cavan (www.jampaling.org).

Maybe you will find your piece of heaven in an appreciation of nature. Take a walk in the woods, lie down in a field, take your shoes off and walk in the sea, walk the dog.

Finally, practise gratitude. This is a pathway that brings benefits physically, spiritually and emotionally. As you lie down each day, be thankful for three good things that have happened. The more you do this, the more you change the lens you have on the world to a positive one.

The more you use the strengths that you have developed on the different pathways, the more satisfaction, joy, fulfilment and harmony you will feel. As a result of focusing on your strengths and opening yourself up to new experiences, you have become optimistic, highly motivated and involved. You make decisions that are good for you and good for others. You have stronger relationships, positive thoughts and feelings, and confidence, pride and satisfaction in your life. You have discovered the value within you and the meaning beyond you. You are true to yourself and you have become your real self.

In closing, I have one request. I would be honoured if you could share with me your journey to becoming your real self. Please email me at realself@dreddiemurphy.ie and tell me about the struggles you faced and how you overcame them. Tell me what you found helpful. Tell me what becoming your real self means to you.

APPENDIX

APPENDIX

Self-assessment
questionnaire for stress

Listed below are the body signals, feelings, thoughts and behavioural patterns associated with stress. Please tick the box if you have experienced any of these symptoms regularly in the past two weeks:

BODY SIGNALS

Headaches ☐

Tense muscles – aching neck/shoulders ☐

Butterflies in stomach ☐

Tiredness/exhaustion ☐

Light-headedness ☐

Nausea ☐

Poor concentration ☐

Difficulty getting off to sleep and staying asleep ☐

Disturbed sleep ☐

FEELINGS

Tense ☐

Irritable/agitated ☐

Overwhelmed/helpless ☐

Anxious ☐

Stressed ☐

Low mood/apathetic ☐

Low confidence ☐

Apprehensive ☐

THOUGHTS

Indecision ☐
Impaired judgement ☐
Hasty decision-making ☐
Worry:
   'I can't cope with this' ☐
   'There's no way I'll be able to manage all this' ☐
   'I'm going to end up missing something' ☐
   'I'm losing control' ☐

BEHAVIOURAL PATTERNS

Loss of appetite ☐
Drinking and/or smoking more ☐
Loss of sex drive ☐
Busy non-stop ☐
Easily irritated ☐
Difficulty in concentrating ☐
Easily distracted ☐
Procrastinating ☐

If you have ticked 6–11 boxes, you are likely to be experiencing mild stress.

If you have ticked 12–22 boxes, you are likely to be experiencing stress.

If you have ticked 23–32 boxes, you are likely to be experiencing severe stress.

Self-assessment
questionnaire for depression

Listed below are the body signals, feelings, thoughts and behavioural patterns associated with depression. Please tick the box if you have experienced any of these symptoms regularly in the past two weeks:

BODY SIGNALS

Poor concentration	YES ☐	NO ☐
Increased or decreased appetite	YES ☐	NO ☐
Low energy	YES ☐	NO ☐
No interest in sex	YES ☐	NO ☐
Difficulty getting off to sleep and staying asleep	YES ☐	NO ☐
Disturbed sleep	YES ☐	NO ☐

FEELINGS

Sad/low/flat	YES ☐	NO ☐
Hopeless	YES ☐	NO ☐
Tearful	YES ☐	NO ☐
Miserable	YES ☐	NO ☐
Irritable/angry	YES ☐	NO ☐
Lonely	YES ☐	NO ☐
Unmotivated	YES ☐	NO ☐
Lost	YES ☐	NO ☐
Overwhelmed	YES ☐	NO ☐
Anxious	YES ☐	NO ☐

THOUGHTS

Self-worth: 'I feel worthless'	YES ☐	NO ☐
Pessimistic: 'Things will never change'	YES ☐	NO ☐
Failure: 'As I look back, I see a lot of failures'	YES ☐	NO ☐
Self-critical: 'I criticize myself for my faults'	YES ☐	NO ☐
Confidence: 'I have lost confidence in myself'	YES ☐	NO ☐
Hopelessness: 'I feel hopeless'	YES ☐	NO ☐
Guilty: 'I feel guilty'	YES ☐	NO ☐

BEHAVIOURAL PATTERNS

Wanting to spend more and more time alone	YES ☐	NO ☐
Staying in bed longer than usual	YES ☐	NO ☐
No longer doing things I used to enjoy	YES ☐	NO ☐
Having more arguments	YES ☐	NO ☐
Being restless and agitated	YES ☐	NO ☐
Losing much of my interest in other people or things	YES ☐	NO ☐

RED FLAGS

If you tick yes to either of these questions, please go to see your GP immediately.

I have thoughts of killing myself but would not carry them out	YES ☐	NO ☐
I would kill myself if I had the opportunity	YES ☐	NO ☐

If you have ticked any 2 in each section (i.e., having a total of 8 or more), please go to see your GP.

Self-assessment
questionnaire for anxiety

Listed below are the body signals, feelings, thoughts and behavioural patterns associated with panic and anxiety. Please tick the box if you have experienced any of these symptoms regularly in the past two weeks:

BODY SIGNALS

Heart racing	YES ☐	NO ☐
Difficulty catching my breath – smothering/choking	YES ☐	NO ☐
Numbness or tingling	YES ☐	NO ☐
Feeling hot	YES ☐	NO ☐
Dizziness/light-headedness	YES ☐	NO ☐
Poor concentration	YES ☐	NO ☐
Hands shaking	YES ☐	NO ☐
General shakiness/unsteadiness	YES ☐	NO ☐
Visual disturbance	YES ☐	NO ☐
Indigestion – a feeling of butterflies in your stomach	YES ☐	NO ☐
Face flushed	YES ☐	NO ☐
Out-of-body sensation	YES ☐	NO ☐
Hot/cold sweats	YES ☐	NO ☐

FEELINGS

Anxious	YES ☐	NO ☐
Worried	YES ☐	NO ☐
Terrified	YES ☐	NO ☐
Nervous	YES ☐	NO ☐
Scared	YES ☐	NO ☐

THOUGHTS

'I think the worst is going to happen'	YES ☐	NO ☐
'I am terrified'	YES ☐	NO ☐
'I can't breathe'	YES ☐	NO ☐
'I'm having a heart attack'	YES ☐	NO ☐
'I think I'm going mad/crazy'	YES ☐	NO ☐
'I'm scared I'm going to die'	YES ☐	NO ☐
'I think I'm going to lose control'	YES ☐	NO ☐
'I'm going to faint'	YES ☐	NO ☐
'I'm going to do something stupid'	YES ☐	NO ☐

BEHAVIOURAL PATTERNS

Unable to relax	YES ☐	NO ☐
Avoid places, e.g., supermarket, church	YES ☐	NO ☐
Regularly get check-ups to ensure I'm physically okay	YES ☐	NO ☐
Avoid being alone	YES ☐	NO ☐
Avoid being far from home – e.g., foreign holidays	YES ☐	NO ☐
Avoid physical exercise	YES ☐	NO ☐

If you have ticked any 2 from each section (i.e., having a total of 8 or more), please go to see your GP.

Self-assessment
questionnaire for anger

Do you often get angry and lose your
    temper more than once a week?   YES ☐   NO ☐

Do you become frustrated or annoyed
    by the slightest thing?   YES ☐   NO ☐

Does your temper cause problems at home?   YES ☐   NO ☐

Does your temper cause problems at work?   YES ☐   NO ☐

When you get angry, is it very, very intense?   YES ☐   NO ☐

Does your anger last a long time?   YES ☐   NO ☐

Are you quick to anger over small things?   YES ☐   NO ☐

Have you damaged or thrown things
    because you were furious?   YES ☐   NO ☐

Do you find yourself saying hurtful things
    when someone has annoyed you?   YES ☐   NO ☐

Do you cause harm to yourself or others
    when angry?   YES ☐   NO ☐

Have you been physically aggressive towards
    someone?   YES ☐   NO ☐

Do people walk on eggshells around you
    because of your anger?   YES ☐   NO ☐

If you have ticked 6 or more, please seek help for anger management.

Self-assessment
questionnaire for low self-esteem

In both sections below please tick whichever box is correct after each
of the statements that express how you are in general:

A

IN GENERAL

'I feel a sense of pride in myself'	YES ☐	NO ☐
'I value myself and my opinions'	YES ☐	NO ☐
'I am comfortable in my own skin'	YES ☐	NO ☐
'I have a number of virtues'	YES ☐	NO ☐
'I think I am a person of worth'	YES ☐	NO ☐
'I am proud of my achievements'	YES ☐	NO ☐
'I am a competent person'	YES ☐	NO ☐
'I am as good as anybody else'	YES ☐	NO ☐

B

IN GENERAL

'I think that I am a failure'	YES ☐	NO ☐
'I think I get things wrong most of the time'	YES ☐	NO ☐
'I am disappointed with myself'	YES ☐	NO ☐
'I don't have many achievements to take pride in'	YES ☐	NO ☐
'Basically I think I'm no good at all'	YES ☐	NO ☐

'I take a negative attitude towards myself'	YES ☐	NO ☐
'I am dissatisfied with myself'	YES ☐	NO ☐
'I feel useless'	YES ☐	NO ☐

If you ticked 'no' 4 times or more in Section A and 'yes' 4 times or more in Section B, you may need to work on your self-esteem.

Self-assessment
questionnaire for social anxiety

Please tick whichever statements are true for you:

1. Are you troubled by an intense and persistent
   fear of a social situation in which other
   people might judge you?   YES ☐ NO ☐
2. Do you fear that you will be
   humiliated by your actions?   YES ☐ NO ☐
3. Do you fear that people will notice that you
   are blushing, sweating, trembling,
   or showing other signs of anxiety?   YES ☐ NO ☐
4. Are you troubled by the realization that
   your fear is excessive or unreasonable?   YES ☐ NO ☐
5. Does the feared situation always cause
   you to feel anxious?   YES ☐ NO ☐
6. Does the feared situation cause you to
   experience a panic attack, during which
   you suddenly are overcome by intense
   fear or discomfort, including many of
   the symptoms listed below?   YES ☐ NO ☐

- pounding heart;
- sweating;
- trembling or shaking;
- shortness of breath;
- choking;

- chest pain;
- nausea;
- 'jelly' legs;
- fear of losing control;
- fear of going crazy;

- fear of dying;
- numbness or tingling sensations;
- dizziness;
- feelings of unreality.

7. When you are in a group setting, do you prefer to blend into the background and not stand out from the crowd? YES ☐ NO ☐

8. Do you become anxious when you have to make 'small talk'? YES ☐ NO ☐

9. Do you become anxious when you have to speak in front of a small group of people? YES ☐ NO ☐

10. Do you dislike going to places where you might meet new people? YES ☐ NO ☐

11. If most people are already seated in a room, are you highly reluctant to enter it? YES ☐ NO ☐

12. Do you try to avoid social gatherings? YES ☐ NO ☐

13. Do you dislike being the centre of attention? YES ☐ NO ☐

14. Do social situations cause intense stress for you? YES ☐ NO ☐

If you have answered 'yes' to 6 or more questions, please seek help from your GP.

Self-assessment
questionnaire for emotional eating

To explore your emotional eating tendencies, look at the statements below and tick 'yes' or 'no':

Do you crave specific foods?   YES ☐   NO ☐

Is it difficult for you to stop eating particular
    foods such as crisps or chocolate?   YES ☐   NO ☐

Do you have problems controlling the
    amount of certain types of food that
    you eat?   YES ☐   NO ☐

When you're depressed, does your desire
    to eat increase?   YES ☐   NO ☐

Do the weighing scales have great power
    over you? Can they change your mood?   YES ☐   NO ☐

When feeling down, do you think a snack
    will lift your mood?   YES ☐   NO ☐

Do you feel that food controls you, rather
    than you controlling food?   YES ☐   NO ☐

When you are stressed at work or working
    to a deadline, do you have the urge
    to snack?   YES ☐   NO ☐

Do you eat when angry or bored?   YES ☐   NO ☐

Do you feel guilty when you eat 'forbidden'
    foods?   YES ☐   NO ☐

Do you feel less control over what you eat
    when you're tired after work at night?   YES ☐   NO ☐

When you overeat while on a diet, do you
     give up and start eating without control?   YES ☐   NO ☐

Do you eat secretly?   YES ☐   NO ☐

Do you look forward to drinking wine or
     beer as a way to relax more than five
     days a week?   YES ☐   NO ☐

Do you eat more when you are stressed
     than when you are calm?   YES ☐   NO ☐

Would you say eating makes you feel better
     when you get angry or irritated?   YES ☐   NO ☐

When shopping, do you buy chocolate,
     crisps, beer or wine to help you relax
     while watching TV?   YES ☐   NO ☐

Do you tend to eat if you are worried about
     something?   YES ☐   NO ☐

Does eating make you feel better when you
     are lonely?   YES ☐   NO ☐

When you're happy, does having your
     favourite snack/drink make you feel
     even better?   YES ☐   NO ☐

Do you hide snacks away for later on?   YES ☐   NO ☐

If you ticked 'yes' for more than 10 items, you are struggling with emotional eating. Exploring your responses to these questions will give you a general idea of your emotional eating tendencies – lack of planning, secret eating, low mood/depression, anxiety/stress, loneliness/isolation, anger, boredom and indeed happiness. When you know the specifics of your emotional eating, you will be able to develop a targeted plan to deal with your emotions without using food.

How to find the right therapist for you

Choosing a psychologist or therapist can be bewildering, and it's particularly daunting if you have never sought this kind of help before. If you feel you would benefit from working with an expert on cracking a problem that's troubling you, talking to your GP is often a good place to start; they will have experiences of other patients who have attended therapy or counselling. You can use the excellent, and free, HSE's National Counselling Service if you have experienced physical, sexual, emotional or institutional abuse as a child (details below). There are also a number of professional bodies that include 'find a therapist' features on their websites. I list some of the main ones at the end.

One of the key issues is that you need to feel comfortable with your therapist and to trust them. A strong relationship between you and the therapist is a cornerstone for therapy and change. A professional service requires surroundings that are professional, not a front room in someone's home. How boundaries are maintained by your therapist is important. There is always a power imbalance in the therapy relationship. As a result, inappropriate comments, physical contact or romantic or sexual advances are completely unethical, and the therapist should be reported to the relevant professional body. Although you are likely to be nudged out of your comfort zone occasionally during therapy, any discomfort should always relate solely to the challenge of working on your problem. There is a big difference between this sort of discomfort and the discomfort that results from the therapy going off in a direction that does not feel right to you, or from a relationship with the therapist that has become inappropriate in some respect. You will know the difference.

Here are a number of questions you might want to ask before engaging in therapy. You are interviewing the therapist as much as they are interviewing you. Well-trained psychologists or therapists welcome these questions: the better the fit between the two of you, the better the outcome for you (and the greater the job satisfaction for them!).

Are you a full member of a relevant professional body? And, if so, which one?

Sometimes therapists say they are members of a professional body and are telling the truth, but they may be affiliate or associate members, which indicates that they are in training. Ring the registering body and check the status. If they are full members, they will be bound by that body's ethical guidelines; these are available online or by getting in touch with the organization.

Where did you train? For how long? Did you complete postgraduate training?

You are trying to identify the quality and length of the training, e.g., two years versus eight years.

How long have you been in practice?

The research shows the more experienced the clinician, the better the outcome.

What are your areas of expertise?

Just like many other professionals, therapists have various interests and specialities. They all have different strengths.

How many clients have you seen with [describe your problem here]?

If the therapist says 'several', ask for some specific examples of how they worked with someone with your condition, and over what period of time.

What success in treating people have you had with [describe your problem here]?

You want to get them talking about their work in the area you are particularly interested in. Find out what their definition of success is;

you and the therapist should have the same vision for a successful outcome. Or, if you don't have a vision yourself yet, you should find that what they are saying makes sense to you and that you feel they are describing a path to a good outcome.

Are you under supervision? If so, with whom?

Experienced clinicians remain under supervision to keep their practice safe and fresh. If they say they are under supervision, it's important to verify this by getting the name of their supervisor, so you can assure yourself that this is indeed the case. This would be considered perfectly acceptable by both parties.

What is your approach to treatment?

There are many approaches to psychological treatment. Some therapists might say they're 'eclectic' or that they use multiple approaches. While this is relatively common, you can ask what they consider their primary approach to be. If your difficulties are complex, your therapist should have an extensive repertoire of treatments at his disposal in order to assess you and to develop a targeted treatment plan.

How many sessions do you think I'll need?

I am not a big fan of therapy that doesn't end or that goes on for years. It says to me that the emotional control (power) in this situation is with the therapist and not with you. Any experienced therapist will know how long they work with most of their clients and will be able to give you a ball-park figure of the number of sessions you can expect to have.

When we are working together, what is expected from me?

For example, are homework assignments given?

The practical stuff . . .

- How much do you charge per session?
- Do you have a sliding scale/reduced fees policy?
- Do you work with insurance companies?
- Do you have a cancellation policy?

During therapy, you need to feel that going to your sessions is helping you. If you are not getting relief or don't have a sense that you're making some progress, you may not be getting the best treatment available. Turning up to a session and talking about the week just gone is not enough; you're not there for a chat. Your therapy needs to be dynamic and active. After your first couple of sessions, ask yourself:

- Has the therapist carried out a detailed assessment?
- Has the therapist identified your problem? And, if so, did it make sense to you?
- Has the therapist discussed a treatment plan with you?
- Has the therapist worked with you on identifying clear goals for your treatment?
- Have you agreed a review period?

And, as you progress a little further into the therapy, you might also ask:

- Does the therapist seem 'real' or as if they are playing a role?
- Do you feel comfortable with the therapist?
- Is the therapist passive or active in the session? Which do you prefer?
- Do you feel the therapist has heard what you've said to them?
- Does it feel as if the sessions are a safe place to express your thoughts, concerns and emotions?
- Do you think you are making progress?
- Does the therapist generate hope in you?
- Do you feel better or worse after your session?

Listen to your gut. It is an important gauge as to whether this therapist is working out for you. If necessary, discontinue treatment and seek another therapist.

*

Unfortunately the area of counselling and therapy is still unregulated in Ireland, which is a dangerous and disgraceful situation. There are many umbrella bodies for therapists – too many to list – but here are some of the more reputable ones:

- The Psychological Society of Ireland (www.psychologicalsociety.ie)
- The Irish Association for Counselling and Psychotherapy (www. irish-counselling.ie)
- The Irish Association of Humanistic and Integrative Psychotherapy (www.iahip.org)
- The Irish Association for Behavioural and Cognitive Psychotherapies (www.iabcp.com/IABCP)

To access therapy or counselling in your area via the HSE National Counselling Service, call Freephone 1800 234 110, www.hse.ie.

Here are some of the key umbrella bodies for therapists and counsellors in the UK:

- British Psychological Society (www.bps.org.uk)
- British Association for Counselling and Psychotherapy (www.bacp. co.uk)
- British Association for Behavioural and Cognitive Psychotherapies (www.babcp.com)
- National Health Service – Improving Access to Psychological Therapies (www.iapt.nhs.uk)

Acknowledgements

I would like to thank Patricia Deevy and Michael McLoughlin of Penguin Ireland for their interest in my work and for taking on board my ideas for this book. I would like to thank Patricia Deevy for her excellent editorial support and copy-editor Donna Poppy for her keen eye.

I would like to thank my friends Eddie, Philly, Simon, Pearse, John, Damien, Dermot, Catherine, Mary, Joe, Ellen, Avril and Gary, and to remember my late dear departed friend John. Thanks to Maire and Andy for being there, to Philip for his encouragement, to Stephen for his ongoing wisdom, and to Anne-Marie for her continuing support.

I would like to thank my Laois and Galway families: my loving parents Billy and Joan for all their life lessons, and thanks to Jean, Noel, Sinéad, Una, Eugene and Jenny, Sean, Josephine, John, Ann-Marie and Shaun, Cailín and Teresa for the wonderful support. Thanks also to the extended Murphy, Power, Rooney and McLoughlin families in Ireland and Canada.

I would like to thank my past and present health service employers in England and Ireland. Thanks to Professor Alan Carr, Head of the School of Psychology, University College, Dublin, and Director of UCD's doctoral programme in clinical psychology. Thanks also to Philip, Niamh, Steven, Sinéad and Grainne of Vision Independent Productions and RTÉ, joint makers of *Operation Transformation*, for helping to demystify psychology, therapy and mental health issues for the nation.

Most important of all are the three people who keep me real every day – my inspiring wife Carol and my beautiful boys Oisín and Darragh.